Consolidated Human Services Boards

in North Carolina

KRISTI A. NICKODEM
AND KIRSTEN E. LELOUDIS

UNC | SCHOOL OF GOVERNMENT

Some chapters in this book appeared in slightly different form in *Local Social Services Boards in North Carolina* by Kristi A. Nickodem (UNC School of Government, 2023) and *Local Boards of Health in North Carolina* by Kirsten E. Leloudis (UNC School of Government, 2025).

Printed in the United States of America
29 28 27 26 25 1 2 3 4 5
ISBN 978-1-64238-113-9

Contents

Preface

Consolidated Human Services Boards in North Carolina is a guide for individuals who serve on the governing boards of consolidated human services agencies across the state, giving them information they need to conduct their work lawfully and effectively. It is intended for both appointed consolidated human services boards and any elected board of county commissioners that serves as the governing board for a consolidated human services agency. This book may also be a useful reference tool for human services directors, county managers, county attorneys, and others who work with local human services agencies.

This book is an installment in a three-part series that also includes *Local Social Services Boards in North Carolina* by Kristi A. Nickodem and *Local Boards of Health in North Carolina* by Kirsten E. Leloudis. More School of Government resources on social services, public health, and consolidated human services can be found at the North Carolina Human Services Hub at humanservices.sog.unc.edu. We also routinely post about health and human services topics on our local government law blog, *Coates' Canons: NC Local Government Law* (canons.sog.unc.edu).

Consolidated Human Services Boards in North Carolina builds on many years of scholarship by Aimee N. Wall, Jill D. Moore, and John Saxon, whose teaching and written resources laid the foundation for this book. We are indebted to Wall, Moore, and Saxon for their thoughtful research and analysis of numerous issues discussed here. We also appreciate the support of many School of Government faculty members and external partners who provided helpful review and feedback on various chapters.

We are immensely grateful to the health and human services employees, directors, and board members with whom we have interacted during our time at the School of Government. Your thoughtful questions have helped shape the content of this book. We have learned so much from all of you, and we are thankful for your dedication to public service across this state. We sincerely hope this book will be a valuable resource for you in the years to come.

Finally, thank you to our families for your love and support while writing this book. You mean everything to us.

Kristi A. Nickodem and Kirsten E. Leloudis
Assistant Professors of Public Law and Government
The University of North Carolina at Chapel Hill
June 2025

Commonly Used Abbreviations

BOCC	board of county commissioners
BOH	local board of health
CHS	consolidated human services
CHSA	consolidated human services agency
CPH	North Carolina Commission for Public Health
DCFW	North Carolina Division of Child and Family Well-Being
DPH	North Carolina Division of Public Health
DSS	local department of social services
LHD	local health department
NCDHHS	North Carolina Department of Health and Human Services
NCLHDA	North Carolina Local Health Department Accreditation
SSC	North Carolina Social Services Commission

Note: In some counties, the consolidated human services agency is referred to as the "health and human services" (HHS) agency, the governing board is called the "HHS board," and the director of the agency is referred to as the "HHS director." This book uses "CHSA" and "CHS" for consistency, but the terms are interchangeable.

PART 1

Consolidated Human Services Agencies and Boards

Chapter 1

An Introduction to Consolidated Human Services Agencies and Boards

This book is intended to help members of governing boards for consolidated human services agencies—including both appointed consolidated human services boards and county commissioners who serve as the governing board for a consolidated human services agency—learn more about their roles and responsibilities under North Carolina law.

Part 1 of this book covers topics that are applicable to all consolidated human services boards, including laws governing the work of consolidated human services boards, the powers and duties of a consolidated human services board, the services and programs offered by consolidated human services agencies, the role of county commissioners in human services, and the role of the consolidated human services agency director.

Part 2 covers topics related to social services, including an overview of North Carolina's social services system, a description of social services programs, the consolidated human services board's role with respect to social services, and social services funding.

Part 3 covers topics related to public health, including an overview of public health in North Carolina and the consolidated human services board's responsibilities related to public health programs, accreditation, fees, rulemaking, and adjudications.

Before diving into those topics, this chapter will introduce some basic concepts about consolidated human services agencies and their governing boards.

What Is a Consolidated Human Services Agency?

A consolidated human services agency (CHSA) is created when a board of county commissioners (BOCC) consolidates two or more county human services functions under the direct control of a human services director, who is appointed and supervised by the county manager.[1] In most (but not all) counties that have created a CHSA, the BOCC has consolidated social services and public health into a single agency.[2] Some CHSAs include other human services functions, such as transportation, aging and adult services, or veterans' services. The topic of which departments and functions may be combined into a single CHSA is discussed in Chapter 2. At the time of this book's publication, over 50 percent of North Carolina's population lives in a county served by a CHSA.

CHSAs go by different names in different counties. Some counties refer to the consolidated agency as the *Department of Human Services*, while others call it the *Department of Health and Human Services* or the *Health and Human Services Agency*. Accordingly, county officials sometimes use acronyms like DHS, DHHS, HHS, or HHSA when referring to these agencies (or their directors or boards). This book will use the term *consolidated human services agency* or *CHSA* to refer to an agency created under Chapter 153A, Section 77(b) of the North Carolina General Statutes (hereinafter G.S.).

Who Serves as the Governing Board for a Consolidated Human Services Agency?

There are two different agency governance options available to counties that have formed a CHSA: an appointed CHS board or BOCC governance.

An appointed CHS board, sometimes referred to as a health and human services (HHS) board, is appointed entirely by the BOCC. State law requires a number of different professions and community members to be represented on the CHS board, which may consist of up to twenty-five members.[3] The initial formation of an appointed CHS board, the process of appointing CHS board members, and board member qualifications are discussed in Chapters 3 and 4.

Alternatively, a BOCC may directly assume the powers, responsibilities, and duties of a CHS board.[4] By doing so, the county commissioners abolish the appointed board for the CHSA (or for a new CHSA, the appointed boards for the agencies being consolidated).[5] If the CHSA includes both social services and public health, then the BOCC assumes the authority and responsibilities of a county board of social services and a county board of health by becoming the CHSA's governing board. County commissioner governance is discussed in more detail in Chapter 8.

If the CHSA includes public health and the BOCC assumes the powers and duties of the governing board, the BOCC must appoint an advisory committee for public health.[6] The advisory committee membership must meet the requirements for a county board of health found in G.S. 130A-35. An advisory committee is, as the name suggests, advisory in nature. *It is not the same as an appointed CHS board and it cannot exercise the CHS board's statutory powers and duties.* Advisory committees are discussed in more detail in Chapter 3, including what makes them different from appointed CHS boards.

What Makes a Consolidated Human Services Agency Unique?

Though every county is required to provide certain social services programs and public health services, North Carolina law gives counties many options for how they structure the agencies that deliver these programs and services. Many counties still have separate, nonconsolidated departments for social services and health. Some counties have consolidated these two departments into a single CHSA.[7] Multicounty options, in which multiple counties join together to operate a public authority to deliver these programs and services, are also available in the form of district health departments, multicounty public health authorities,[8] and regional departments of social services.[9]

The CHSA model has some key differences from a traditional county department of social services or local health department, as described below.

Appointment and Supervision of the Director

The most significant difference between a CHSA and a nonconsolidated county department of social services or health department is that the consolidated human services director is appointed by the county manager, not by the agency's governing board.[10] Although the governing board of a CHSA does not appoint the human services director, the county manager must still receive the governing board's advice and consent before appointing someone to the role.[11] The consolidated human services director also reports directly to the county manager, unlike a traditional county social services director or health director who reports solely to their governing board. More information about the director's role and appointment is available in Chapter 6.

Staff Hiring Authority

Another important difference between these models is that the consolidated human services director may only hire CHSA staff with the approval of the county manager.[12] By contrast, a county social services director or local health director in a nonconsolidated department has the sole authority to make all hiring decisions for their respective agencies.[13]

Personnel Rules and Policies

The other key difference between a CHSA and a nonconsolidated county department of social services or local health department is that CHSA employees are no longer covered by the State Human Resources Act (SHRA) and instead become subject solely to county personnel policies. This change occurs when the CHSA is created, unless the county commissioners affirmatively elect to keep CHSA employees under the SHRA.[14] To date, the majority of North Carolina counties with a CHSA have opted to remove CHSA employees from the coverage of the SHRA. This topic is discussed in more detail in Chapter 2.

What Are the Key Differences Between Organization and Governance Models for Social Services and Public Health?

Table 1.1 shows key differences between various organization and governance options for social services, while Table 1.2 shows key differences between various organization and governance options for public health.

Table 1.1. Local Social Services Organization and Governance Options at a Glance

Organization	Governing Board	Board Members Selected by[a]	Director Appointed by	Employees
County DSS	County board of social services	Appointment (3 or 5)	Board	Subject to SHRA
County DSS	BOCC	Election	BOCC	Subject to SHRA
CHSA	Appointed CHS board	Appointment (up to 25)	County manager, with the advice and consent of the CHS board	SHRA optional
CHSA	BOCC[b]	Election	County manager, with the advice and consent of the BOCC	SHRA optional
Regional DSS	Regional board of social services	Appointment (12–18)	Board	Subject to SHRA

Note: SHRA = State Human Resources Act, BOCC = board of county commissioners, CHS = consolidated human services, CHSA = consolidated human services agency, DSS = department of social services.

[a] Numbers in parentheses represent the number of members on each appointed board.

[b] An advisory committee for public health must be appointed if the CHSA includes public health. The requirement for a health advisory committee applies only to counties that abolish their health boards after January 1, 2012. This amounts to an exception for Mecklenburg County, which abolished its health boards (a county board of health and subsequently a CHS board) before that date.

Table 1.2. Local Public Health Organization and Governance Options at a Glance

Organization	Governing Board	Board Members Selected by[a]	Director Appointed by	Employees
County health department	County board of health	Appointment (11)	Board	Subject to SHRA[b]
County health department	BOCC[c]	Election	BOCC	Subject to SHRA
CHSA	Appointed CHS board	Appointment (Up to 25)	County manager, with the advice and consent of the CHS board	SHRA optional
CHSA	BOCC[c]	Election	County manager, with the advice and consent of the BOCC	SHRA optional
District health department	District board of health	Appointment (15–18)	Board	Subject to SHRA[b]
Public health authority (single county)	Public health authority board	Appointment (7–9)[d]	Board	Not subject to SHRA[e]
Public health authority (multicounty)	Public health authority board	Appointment (7–11)[d]	Board	Not subject to SHRA[e]

Note: SHRA = State Human Resources Act, BOCC = board of county commissioners, CHS = consolidated human services, CHSA = consolidated human services agency, DSS = department of social services.

[a] Numbers in parentheses represent the number of members on each appointed board.

[b] G.S. 126-5(a)(2)(c).

[c] An advisory committee for public health must be appointed if the CHSA includes public health. The requirement for a health advisory committee applies only to counties that abolish their health boards after January 1, 2012. This amounts to an exception for Mecklenburg County, which abolished its health boards (a county board of health and subsequently a CHS board) before that date.

[d] G.S. 130A-45.1(b) allows a public health authority that intends to apply for federally qualified health center status to have a board with no fewer than nine and up to twenty-five members.

[e] G.S. 130A-45.12.

What Is the History Behind Consolidated Human Services Agencies?

North Carolina's first CHSA was created in Wake County in 1996, after an early version of the current consolidation statute was enacted by the North Carolina General Assembly in 1996 at the request of Wake County's board of commissioners.[15] The version of the statute enacted in 1996 only allowed counties with a population of more than 425,000 people to create a CHSA. The statute also allowed a CHSA to include the area mental health, developmental disabilities, and substance abuse

Table 1.3. County Human Services Agency Organization and Governance Options Under S.L. 2012-126

Structure	Organization	Governance
Option A: **separate agencies with appointed governing boards**	Human services agencies (such as a local health department and county department of social services) remain separate.	Local appointed governing boards (county board of health and county board of social services) oversee the county's local human services agencies.
Option B: **separate agencies with partial or full BOCC governance**	Human services agencies (such as a local health department and county department of social services) remain separate.	The BOCC directly assumes the powers and duties of one or more of the governing boards responsible for overseeing a county human services agency (board of health and/or board of social services).[a] If the BOCC assumes the powers and duties of the local board of health, the BOCC must appoint an advisory committee on public health.
Option C: **CHSA with appointed CHS governing board**	The BOCC creates a CHSA by combining two or more county human services functions, departments, or agencies.	The BOCC appoints a CHS board that serves as the CHSA's governing board.
Option D: **CHSA with BOCC governance**	The BOCC creates a CHSA by combining two or more county human services functions, departments, or agencies.	The BOCC becomes the CHSA's governing board by directly assuming the powers and duties of the CHS board. If the CHSA includes public health, the BOCC must appoint an advisory committee on public health.

Note: BOCC = board of county commissioners, CHS = consolidated human services, CHSA = consolidated human services agency.

[a] In some counties, the BOCC governs all human services agencies, while in others, the BOCC has only assumed governance of one agency while leaving another under the control of a local governing board.

services (MH/DD/SAS) authority that served the county and granted the CHS director the authority to act as the director of an MH/DD/SAS authority.

In 2012, the General Assembly enacted Session Law 2012-126, which provided counties with broader options regarding the organization and governance of North Carolina's social services and public health functions (described in Table 1.3). Specifically, this law

- allowed any BOCC (in a county with a county manager and regardless of population size) to combine two or more county human services functions into a single CHSA;[16] and
- allowed any BOCC to directly assume the powers and duties of a county board of health, county board of social services, or consolidated human services board.[17]

Many of North Carolina's most populous counties have opted to create CHSAs. At the time of this book's publication, thirty-four of North Carolina's one hundred counties have CHSAs, covering a significant portion of the state's population.[18]

In 2012, the General Assembly also changed existing law by prohibiting the consolidation of an area MH/DD/SAS board into a consolidated human services board.[19] Despite the fact that the law no longer allows counties to consolidate an MH/DD/SAS authority into a county CHSA, at the time of publication, the CHSA statute (G.S. 153A-77) has not been revised to fully reflect that change. Consequently, some of the powers and duties granted by statute to consolidated human services directors and boards no longer align with the current structure for CHSAs and area MH/DD/SAS authorities (now known as local management entity/managed care organizations, or LME/MCOs). For example, G.S. 153A-77(e) states that the consolidated human services director has the same powers and duties as "a director of an area mental health, developmental disabilities, and substance abuse services authority"—but because CHSAs can no longer include an area authority, consolidated human services directors cannot actually exercise these powers or duties.

Appendixes and Abbreviations

As described earlier, North Carolina law allows counties to choose between many different models for the organization and governance of their social services and public health functions. For tables comparing key differences between county boards of social services, CHS boards, and regional boards of social services, please see Appendix A. For tables comparing differences between county boards of health, CHS boards, public health authority boards, and district boards of health, please see Appendix B.

Appendix C recommends resources—including books, papers, websites, and blog posts—for readers who are interested in exploring certain topics discussed in this book in more depth.

This book uses a number of abbreviations. See page xi for an explanation of the most commonly used ones.

Notes

1. Chapter 153A, Section 77(b) of the North Carolina General Statutes (hereinafter G.S.).
2. Every CHSA in North Carolina includes social services. At the time of this book's publication, Cabarrus and Person are the only counties with CHSAs that do not include public health.
3. G.S. 153A-77(c).
4. G.S. 153A-77(a).
5. Under G.S. 153A, § 76(5)–(7), county commissioners are prohibited from abolishing and assuming the powers and duties of (*a*) an area mental health, developmental disabilities, and substance abuse services board; (*b*) a public health authority assigned the power, duties, and responsibilities to provide public health services as outlined in G.S. 130A-1.1; (*c*) a public-hospital authority authorized to provide public health services under S.L. 1997-502; or (*d*) a public hospital as defined in G.S. 159-39(a). A clause at G.S. 153A-76(6) provides an exception for Mecklenburg County with respect to the abolishment of the area mental health, developmental disabilities, and substance abuse services board, as Mecklenburg County had already abolished this board prior to January 1, 2012.
6. G.S. 153A-77(a).
7. Cabarrus County has consolidated its social services department into a CHSA but provides public health services through a public hospital authority, Cabarrus Health Alliance. Person County has consolidated its social services department into a CHSA but provides public health services through a separate county health department.
8. *See* G.S. 130A-45.02(b). At the time of this book's publication, no counties have opted to form a multicounty public health authority, though it is an option available by law.
9. As of this book's publication, no counties have opted to form a regional department of social services. However, it is an option that is available by law. See Chapter 17, Kristi A. Nickodem, *Local Boards of Social Services in North Carolina* (UNC School of Government, 2023).
10. G.S. 153A-77(e).
11. *Id.*
12. The county manager has authority to approve (or deny) the CHS director's hiring or dismissal decisions regarding CHSA staff (per G.S. 153A-77(e)), but as a practical matter, a county manager may want to authorize the CHS director to handle hiring and dismissal decisions largely or entirely independently.
13. *Compare* G.S. 153A-77(e)(1) *with* G.S. 108A-14(a)(2) and G.S. 130A-41(b)(12).
14. G.S. 153A-77(d).
15. Session Law 1995-690, which enacted G.S. 153A-77(b). On July 8, 1996, the Wake County board of county commissioners adopted ordinance O-96-18, which memorialized the decision to create a CHSA. *See* Wake County Code of Ordinances, Title III § 30.025, available at https://codelibrary.amlegal.com/codes/wakecounty/latest/wake_nc/0-0-0-215.
16. G.S. 153A-77(b)(3).
17. G.S. 153A-77(a).
18. At the time of this book's publication, the following thirty-four counties have CHSAs: Alexander, Bladen, Brunswick, Buncombe, Cabarrus, Carteret, Clay, Dare, Davie, Duplin, Edgecombe, Forsyth, Gaston, Guilford, Haywood, Jones, Lee, Mecklenburg, Montgomery, Nash, New Hanover, Onslow, Pender, Person, Polk, Richmond, Rockingham, Robeson, Stanly, Swain, Union, Wake, Wayne, Yadkin.
19. S.L. 2012-126, § 2; G.S. 153A-76. An exception allowed Mecklenburg County's board of commissioners to continue exercising these powers and duties.

Chapter 2

The Creation and Composition of a Consolidated Human Services Agency

On paper, the creation of a consolidated human services agency (CHSA) by the board of county commissioners (BOCC) is relatively straightforward and simple. In practice, the formation of this new agency creates a number of decision points for county officials regarding which county functions to include in the agency, who will serve as the governing board, how to structure leadership for the agency, and which personnel rules and policies will apply to the agency's employees. The process for creating a CHSA, along with the decisions and issues a county may encounter in this process, is discussed in this chapter.

The Procedure for Forming a New Consolidated Human Services Agency

Public Hearing

If the BOCC plans to serve as the governing board for a CHSA, it must hold a public hearing and give at least thirty days' notice of the hearing in a newspaper having general circulation in the county.[1] Following the public hearing, the BOCC may adopt a resolution "assuming and conferring upon the board of county commissioners all powers, responsibilities and duties" of the governing board for social services, the local board of health, and/or other boards appointed by the BOCC or acting under and pursuant to the authority of the BOCC.[2]

The law does not explicitly state that a public hearing is required prior to forming a CHSA with an *appointed* CHS board (as opposed to having the BOCC as the governing board). However, holding such a hearing with prior notice to the public is a best practice, given that the creation of a CHSA is a significant change for a county and is likely to draw many questions from county residents and employees.

Drafting a Resolution

The law does not explicitly require counties to create a CHSA through the use of a resolution, unless the BOCC is also assuming the powers and duties of the agency's governing board. However, it is sensible and prudent for a BOCC to adopt a resolution when forming a CHSA. Among other things, the language of the BOCC resolution forming the CHSA clarifies whether employees will be subject to the State Human Resources Act or subject solely to county personnel policies.[3] The resolution also establishes and clarifies which county departments or functions are being consolidated into the CHSA. To date, every county in North Carolina that has created a CHSA has done so through a resolution.

Order of Action

When establishing a new CHSA, the county manager has authority to appoint the CHSA's director but may do so only with the advice and consent of the CHSA's governing board.[4] Because of this requirement, there is a logical sequence that should be followed when first establishing a new CHSA.

1. The BOCC adopts a resolution creating a CHSA. The resolution should include terms regarding which county human services functions or departments will be consolidated into the agency and whether agency employees will be subject to the SHRA.
2. The BOCC appoints a consolidated human services (CHS) board (based on recommendations from the nominating committee) or directly assumes the powers and duties of the agency governing board through a resolution. This process of nominating and appointing the initial CHS board, including formation of the nominating committee, is described in Chapter 3.
3. The county manager identifies a candidate for CHS director and seeks the advice and consent of the CHSA's governing board. This process is described in Chapter 6.
4. If the CHSA's governing board consents to the appointment, the county manager appoints the CHS director to lead the CHSA.

Theoretically, these four steps could take place in the same meeting or on the same day, but the order of events is significant under the law. The CHS director cannot be appointed before the CHSA has been created and the governing board is in place because the governing board must consent to the CHS director's appointment.

The timing of the meeting is also important if the BOCC intends to serve as the agency's governing board, due to the aforementioned notice and public hearing requirements. The BOCC could hold the public hearing, create the CHSA, and assume the powers and duties of the CHSA's governing board in the same meeting, but it would have to ensure that the public had at least thirty days' notice of that meeting.

County Departments or Functions Within a Consolidated Human Services Agency

State law authorizes each BOCC to create a consolidated human services agency to "carry out the functions of any combination of commissions, boards, or agencies appointed by the board of county commissioners or acting under and pursuant to authority of the board of county commissioners."[5] The word *combination* is key—the county must be combining at least two different county "human services" functions into a single agency under the purview of a CHS director. The term *human services* is undefined in the law, which gives counties some flexibility in determining which functions to include in the new agency.

A CHSA may incorporate a county health department and/or county department of social services, but other county departments and programs may also be consolidated into the agency. For example, some CHSAs created in North Carolina have included local departments focused on veterans, animal services, aging populations, or transportation.

There are, however, some limitations. A CHSA may *not* include

- an area mental health, developmental disabilities, and substance abuse services (MH/DD/SAS) authority;[6]
- a public health authority assigned the power, duties, and responsibilities to provide public health services as outlined in Chapter 130A, Section 1.1 of the North Carolina General Statutes (hereinafter G.S.);[7]
- a hospital authority authorized to provide public health services under S.L. 1997-502;[8] or
- a public hospital as defined in G.S. 159-39(a).[9]

To date, all CHSAs formed in North Carolina have included a county department of social services.[10] Most CHSAs, but not all, have also incorporated the county health department.[11] Many CHSAs also include at least one other human services function or department.

Personnel Options for a Consolidated Human Services Agency

Employees of county departments of social services and county health departments are county employees but are subject to the State Human Resources Act (SHRA).[12] When a county creates a new CHSA, the employees of the new agency are removed from SHRA coverage and become automatically subject solely to county personnel policies, unless the BOCC *affirmatively elects* to keep them under the SHRA.[13] If the resolution creating the CHSA is silent on this issue, then by default, CHSA employees become subject to county personnel policies and are removed from SHRA coverage. If the county commissioners want to keep social services and public health employees covered under the SHRA, they must explicitly state this intention in the resolution creating the CHSA.

What Are the Federal Merit Personnel System Standards?

State law mandates that all CHSAs comply with the federal requirements for the establishment of merit personnel systems, found at 5 C.F.R. § 900.603. Certain federal grant programs require, as a condition of eligibility, that state and local agencies that receive grant funding establish merit personnel systems for personnel who are engaged in the administration of those grant-aided programs.[a] This includes many grant-aided programs administered by local social services departments and health departments in North Carolina.

The federal standards for a merit personnel system require the following:

- Recruiting, selecting, and advancing employees on the basis of their relative ability, knowledge, and skills, including open consideration of qualified applicants for initial appointment.
- Providing equitable and adequate compensation.
- Training employees, as needed, to assure high-quality performance.
- Retaining employees on the basis of the adequacy of their performance, correcting inadequate performance, and separating employees whose inadequate performance cannot be corrected.
- Assuring fair treatment of applicants and employees in all aspects of personnel administration without regard to race, color, religion, sex (including pregnancy and gender identity), national origin, age (as defined by the Age Discrimination in Employment Act of 1967, as amended), disability, genetic information (including family medical history), marital status, political affiliation, sexual orientation, status as parent, labor organization affiliation or nonaffiliation in accordance with [5 U.S.C. ch. 71], or any other non-merit-based factor, or retaliation for exercising rights with respect to the categories enumerated above, where retaliation rights are available, and with proper regard for their privacy and constitutional rights as citizens. This "fair treatment" principle includes compliance with the Federal equal employment opportunity and nondiscrimination laws.
- Assuring that employees are protected against coercion for partisan political purposes and are prohibited from using their official authority for the purpose of interfering with or affecting the result of an election or a nomination for office.[b]

[a] 5 C.F.R. § 900.601; *see generally* 5 C.F.R. app. A to subpart F of part 900, Standards for a Merit System of Personnel Administration.

[b] 5 C.F.R. § 900.603.

Though some counties in North Carolina have opted to keep social services and public health employees in their CHSAs subject to the SHRA, the majority of counties with CHSAs have chosen to remove CHSA employees from SHRA coverage instead.[14] Counties have different motivations for this decision, but a key factor for some has been the desire to create consistency across county employees. Moving CHSA employees out from under the SHRA allows a county to apply a single set of policies and procedures to the majority of its employees.[15] Another important factor has been a desire to exercise more control over employee grievance, discipline, and termination processes. For example, some counties may dislike the fact that under the SHRA, final personnel decisions made at the county-agency level can be appealed to (and overturned by) the state Office of Administrative Hearings.[16]

Some counties may choose instead to keep CHSA employees subject to the SHRA. In some counties, this decision may be made for the purpose of continuity and employee retention. Some employees who become part of a CHSA may have worked under the SHRA for years and be reluctant to suddenly move out from under its coverage. Moreover, some social services and public health employees may want to remain subject to the SHRA because they do not wish to lose certain protections and rights regarding their employment, especially their "just cause" protection with respect to discipline and termination.[17]

Regardless of whether a county opts to keep CHSA employees under the coverage of the SHRA, all CHSAs are required by state law to comply with the federal merit personnel system standards (found at 5 C.F.R. § 900.603).[18] When a county wants to remove its CHSA employees from the coverage of the SHRA, the county should first conduct a careful review of its personnel policies, procedures, and ordinances to ensure that they comply with and reflect each of the federal merit personnel standards (at least as to the CHSA's employees).

Among other things, the relevant federal merit personnel system standards mandate recruitment, selection, and retention of employees based on their ability, knowledge, skills, and performance.[19] The federal standards also require that employees be given fair and equitable treatment without regard to race, color, religion, sex, pregnancy, gender identity, national origin, age (as defined by the Age Discrimination in Employment Act), disability, genetic information, marital status, political affiliation, sexual orientation, status as a parent, or labor-organization affiliation or nonaffiliation.[20]

For more information on the decision to remove CHSA employees from SHRA coverage, please see Kristi A. Nickodem, *Personnel Decisions for North Carolina's Consolidated Human Services Agencies*, available on the UNC School of Government's website.[21]

Leadership Structure Decisions Involved in Consolidation

When a county forms a CHSA, it consolidates multiple human services functions under a single CHS director (sometimes referred to as the *human services director* or *health and human services director*). Upon being appointed, the CHS director acquires all of the powers and duties of a social services director and a local health director, if both social services and public health are consolidated into the CHSA.[22] The CHS director may, however, delegate the substantive duties of those roles to other CHSA employees. Moreover, if the CHS director does not personally satisfy the statutory qualifications for a local health director, the CHS director is *required* to appoint a qualified individual (with the county manager's approval) to serve as the local health director.[23]

Many questions about agency leadership arise when a CHSA is first created. Who will be appointed as the CHSA's director? How will that individual delegate their newly acquired powers and duties within the CHSA? What will happen to the existing county health director and social services director? There are multiple options for how the leadership of a CHSA may be structured. Issues around the appointment of the CHS director, delegation of authority, and CHSA leadership structure options are discussed in more detail in Chapter 6.

The Impacts of Consolidation on Operations

The impact on day-to-day services and operations of the departments or functions being consolidated will largely depend on how a county structures its CHSA. In some counties, staff positions have been eliminated as a result of consolidation. In others, new positions have been added. In some counties, the CHSA operates out of a single building that houses both public health and social services programs and staff. In other counties, the departments consolidated into a CHSA continue to function largely independently in separate buildings and simply have a shared governance and leadership structure.

State law does not mandate operational integration once consolidation occurs. Nonetheless, one of the potential benefits of the consolidated agency model is that it can promote more cross-departmental collaboration and a focus on holistic, integrated client service delivery. This outcome largely depends on decisions made by county leaders and requires some strategic planning. Even in a county that prioritizes operational integration between different functions and divisions within a CHSA, separate funding streams, confidentiality requirements, and structures of state-level supervision can make this local integration of different departments or programs challenging on a practical level.

Notes

1. Chapter 153A, Section 77(a) of the North Carolina General Statutes (hereinafter G.S.). The board may not, however, abolish or assume the powers and responsibilities of certain boards named in G.S. 153A-76, including an area mental health, developmental disabilities, and substance abuse services board.
2. *Id.*
3. CHSA employees will be exempt from the State Human Resources Act (SHRA) by operation of law unless the BOCC explicitly elects to keep them subject to its provisions. G.S. 153A-77(d).
4. G.S. 153A-77(e).
5. G.S. 153A-77(b)(3).
6. G.S. 153A-76(6).
7. *See* G.S. 130A-45.02, regarding creation of a public health authority. At the time of this book's publication, no North Carolina counties provide public health services through a public health authority. Hertford County operated a public health authority until dissolving it in June 2018 and joining a district health department (Albemarle Regional Health Services).
8. G.S. 153A-76(5). Cabarrus County operates the only public hospital authority providing public health services under S.L. 1997-502, sec. 12.
9. G.S. 153A-76(7).
10. A brief exception to this statement was Dare County, which formed a CHSA in 2013 that initially only included public health and transportation. Just a few months after the CHSA was created, the board of county commissioners opted to consolidate social services into the CHSA.
11. Cabarrus and Person County each operate CHSAs that include social services but not public health.
12. *See* G.S. 126-5(a)(2).
13. G.S. 153A-77(d).
14. This information is based on BOCC resolutions from counties that have created CHSAs, which are on file with the authors.
15. This would not apply to employees of area mental health, developmental disabilities, and substance abuse authorities or to local emergency management agencies that would still be subject to the SHRA under G.S. 126-5.
16. *See* G.S. 126-34.02.
17. *See* G.S. 126-35.
18. G.S. 153A-77(d).
19. 5 C.F.R. § 900.603(a), (d).
20. *Id.* § 900.603(e).
21. Kristi Nickodem, *Personnel Decisions for North Carolina's Consolidated Human Services Agencies*, Soc. Servs. L. Bull. No. 49 (UNC School of Government, Dec. 2021), https://www.sog.unc.edu/sites/default/files/reports/SSLB%2049.pdf.
22. G.S. 153A-77(e). These powers and duties are primarily found in G.S. § 108A-14 (social services director) and G.S. 130A-41 (local health director), though some powers and duties are scattered throughout other portions of the North Carolina General Statutes as well. If a county chooses not to include its department of social services or health department in the CHSA, then the CHS director does not acquire the powers and duties of the director of the nonconsolidated department.
23. *See* G.S. 153A-77(e)(9). The experience and education requirements for a local health director are found in G.S. 130A-40(a).

Chapter 3

The Initial Formation and Composition of the Consolidated Human Services Board

As discussed earlier, a county that chooses to consolidate has two options for who will serve as the governing board of its consolidated human services agency (CHSA). The board of county commissioners (BOCC) may serve as the governing board for the agency, or it may appoint a consolidated human services (CHS) board. In some counties, this appointed board is called a *health and human services board*. The requirements and responsibilities when the BOCC serves as the governing board of a CHSA are discussed in Chapter 8.

This chapter discusses how the commissioners appoint the initial members of an appointed CHS board, basic membership qualifications for serving on an appointed CHS board, and the difference between an appointed CHS board and an advisory committee on public health.

Initial Formation of the Board

When forming the initial governing board for a CHSA, the BOCC must first create a nominating committee consisting of members of the current (preconsolidation) board of health and social services board, as well as the board responsible for managing mental health, developmental disabilities, and substance abuse services (MH/DD/SAS) in the county.[1] The nominating committee recommends members for the new CHS board, and the BOCC must make appointments based upon those recommendations.

The nominating committee should present the BOCC with a slate of candidates for the CHS board who are county residents and fulfill the required categories of membership described later in this chapter. After the initial board is appointed by the BOCC, the BOCC fills future vacancies on the CHS board based upon nominees presented by the members of the current CHS board.

The statutory requirements for the initial nominating committee, found in Chapter 153A, Section 77(c) of the North Carolina General Statutes (hereinafter G.S.), raise some questions.

1. **Why is the area authority (also referred to as the local management entity or "LME") board represented on the nominating committee?**[2]
   As explained in Chapter 1, the original version of the consolidation statute (G.S. 153A-77) authorized the inclusion of the area MH/DD/SAS authority in a CHSA. In that context, it was logical that the area authority board would be represented on the nominating committee, along with the boards of health and social services. Counties may no longer consolidate an area authority into a CHSA, but the nominating committee requirements in the statute were never altered to reflect that change.

2. **Should the nominating committee consist of *all* the members of all three boards (public health, social services, and area authority)?**
   G.S. 153A-77(c) states that the initial board shall be appointed "upon the recommendation of a nominating committee comprised of members of the preconsolidation board of health, social services board, and area mental health, developmental disabilities, and substance abuse services board." Does "comprised of members" mean that all the members from each of these three boards must be included in the nominating committee, or merely that each board must be represented? The law does not answer this question. It may be challenging for the county to secure the participation of the area authority board members and align the schedules of the full membership of all three boards. It is also possible that some members of any of the three boards might be unwilling to participate in the process of nominating members for a new consolidated board.

   Given that the statute does not provide any procedure for selecting a limited number of members from each board, a county should make a good-faith attempt to recruit the participation of the full membership of all three boards for the nominating committee. The nominating committee could then consist of all members that are willing and able to participate (which may or may not be the full membership of each board).

3. **May the nominating committee nominate members of the existing (preconsolidation) county board of health or social services board to serve on the new CHS board?**
   Yes. The initial CHS board could, in theory, include members from the preconsolidation board of health and social services board, provided that those individuals otherwise meet the membership qualifications described below. Including some preconsolidation board members could help to provide continuity in board operations when the CHS board is first formed. Moreover, some counties may be unable to fulfill all the

required categories of membership for the CHS board without nominating and appointing some of the preconsolidation board of health members.

Creating a Staggered-Term Structure

In order to establish a uniform staggered-term structure for the CHS board when it is first created, the BOCC may appoint some CHS board members for less than a four-year term.[3] This will prevent all of the board's members from rolling off at the same time. The term length of each of the initial CHS board members is determined at the discretion of the BOCC, though it must always be four years or less. To maintain continuity and stability, the BOCC will likely want to ensure that at least some of the initial board members are appointed for a full four-year term.

Membership Qualifications

An appointed CHS board must be composed of no more than twenty-five members. All members of the CHS board must be residents of the county in which the CHSA is located.[4]

The composition of an appointed CHS board must reasonably reflect the population makeup of the county and must include

- four people who are consumers of human services;[5]
- eight professionals, each with qualifications in one of these categories: one psychologist, one pharmacist, one engineer, one dentist, one optometrist, one veterinarian, one social worker, and one registered nurse;[6]
- two physicians licensed to practice medicine in North Carolina, one of whom must be a psychiatrist;
- one county commissioner; and
- other persons, including "members of the general public representing various occupations."[7]

The BOCC may appoint a member of the CHS board to concurrently fill more than one category of membership (from the categories described above) if the member has the qualifications or attributes of more than one category of membership.[8] For example, if a candidate for board membership is a registered nurse *and* a "consumer of human services," that single individual could fulfill the requirements for representation in both categories on the board.

Questions frequently arise about the required categories of membership on an appointed CHS board.

1. **What happens when there are no county residents who fulfill one of the categories described above available to serve on the board?**
   The CHS board statute does not answer this question.[9] Recruitment for board service is a challenge for many counties across North Carolina, especially in light of the many professions that must be represented on the CHS board. If no county resident is available to serve in one of the professional positions, then that seat on the CHS board likely must remain temporarily vacant. The BOCC and the CHS board should, however, continue to make diligent efforts to recruit CHS board members who will fulfill all of the required categories of membership.

2. **Who is a "consumer of human services"?**
   The term *human services* is not defined under state law, which means counties have some leeway to interpret the concept. A cautious interpretation would be to treat *human services* as a service, benefit, or program that is provided by the CHSA in the county. However, the term could reasonably be interpreted more broadly. For example, a consumer of MH/DD/SAS services could be considered a consumer of human services, even though those services may not be provided directly by the county's CHSA. Some counties have also interpreted the category to include parents whose children receive "human services" as well (for example, a parent whose child has a developmental disability or a parent whose child receives services through the health department).

3. **Do the professionals on the board have to maintain their qualifications or licensure while they serve on the board?**
   State law does not squarely address whether board members must continue to maintain their professional qualifications for the duration of their terms on the CHS board. Arguably, the answer is yes, since "failure to maintain qualifications for appointment" is one of the statutory grounds for removal of a CHS board member.[10] Moreover, the apparent intent behind the required categories of membership is for the board to have relevant, current expertise in a variety of fields, so that it can provide well-informed advice to the CHS director and county leadership. An individual whose professional qualifications have lapsed or who is otherwise no longer actively engaged in the relevant profession may be less able to provide up-to-date guidance and perspective in their field.

The Role of the Director in Relation to the Board

For an appointed CHS board, the consolidated human services director acts as the board's secretary, unless this duty has been delegated to another employee.[11] The CHS director, however, is not a member of the CHS board. This means that the CHS director may not vote as a board member or vote to break a tie vote by the board. It also means that the board is not *required* to allow the CHS director to attend a closed session of the board, though it may choose to do so. More information on conducting board business in closed session is available in Chapter 10 of this book. Chapter 6 provides additional details about the role of the CHS director, including the board's role in appointment and dismissal decisions regarding the director.

Legal Status of Consolidated Human Services Board Members

Appointed CHS boards are not political subdivisions, departments, agencies, or units of state government.[12] Instead, appointed CHS boards are local government boards that are part of North Carolina's system of county government. They are subject to state statutes that apply generally to local government boards, such as North Carolina's open meetings law[13] and public records law.[14] More information about some of the legal requirements that apply to CHS boards and board members is available in Chapters 9, 10, and 11 of this book.

Members of CHS boards are appointed local government officials, meaning they are subject to the provisions of the North Carolina Constitution and state statutes governing appointed local government officials. For example, the North Carolina Constitution and state laws require public office holders, including CHS board members, to take and subscribe an oath of office (described in more detail in Chapter 4).[15]

Advisory Committees

Since the law changed in 2012 to allow more North Carolina counties to create CHSAs and have county commissioner governance of county health and social services agencies, there has been confusion over the difference between *appointed consolidated human services boards* and *advisory committees on public health*. These are two different types of public bodies with different sets of authority and responsibilities under state law.

An *appointed consolidated human services (CHS) board*—sometimes referred to as a health and human services (HHS) board—acts as the board of health and board of social services in the county (if the CHSA includes both public health and social services). Except for differences in appointment and dismissal authority over the agency director (discussed in Chapter 6), an appointed CHS board takes on the full powers and duties of both of these preconsolidation boards. This includes many substantive responsibilities, an overview of which is provided in Chapter 5.

An *advisory committee* is something entirely different. If a BOCC decides to assume the powers and duties of a board of health or a consolidated human services board (where the CHSA includes public health) instead of having an appointed board, the BOCC is required to appoint an advisory committee for public health.[16] This is true whether the BOCC is becoming the governing board for a standalone, nonconsolidated county health department or for a CHSA that includes public health. The advisory committee must include members representing all of the required categories of membership for a county board of health, which are found in G.S. 130A-35.[17]

There is no corresponding legal requirement to create a social services advisory committee when the BOCC assumes the powers and duties of a social services governing board. The BOCC could appoint a separate advisory committee for social services (or for other human services functions consolidated within the CHSA), but it is not required by law to do so.[18] Some counties with BOCC governance of public health functions have a "health advisory committee," while others have a "health and human services advisory committee" or "human services advisory committee" that focuses on multiple functions within a CHSA (in addition to public health).

How does an advisory committee differ from an appointed CHS board? By way of example, in a county with a CHSA governed by an appointed CHS board, it is the CHS board that has the authority to adopt or repeal a local public health rule (discussed in Chapter 19). In a county where the BOCC acts as the governing board for a CHSA that includes public health, it is the BOCC that has the authority to adopt or repeal a local public health rule (though it can seek advice on the rule from its health advisory committee). If the BOCC acts as the governing board for a CHSA that includes public health, then it is the BOCC—not the advisory committee—that acquires the core powers and duties of the board of health, including rulemaking.

The law provides very little details about these advisory committees.[19] G.S. 153A-77(a) is silent on how often they must meet, what responsibilities or functions they must perform, or how long individuals may serve on these committees. What is clear is that an advisory committee cannot legally function as the county board of health or the consolidated human services board. As the name suggests, the advisory committee is *advisory* in nature only—it exists to advise county commissioners (who are acting as the governing board for public health) on public health matters. And if desired, the committee may advise the county commissioners on other human services functions as well (e.g., social services).

North Carolina statutes do not grant authority to an advisory committee to carry out any of the functions or duties of a board of health or consolidated human services board. If the BOCC assumes the powers and duties of a governing board for a county health department or CHSA, then the BOCC *itself* must carry out these functions and duties. State law prohibits county commissioners from "assign[ing] elsewhere a function or duty assigned by law to a particular office, position, department, board, commission, or agency."[20]

Notes

1. Chapter 153A, Section 77(c) of the North Carolina General Statutes (hereinafter G.S.).
2. *See* G.S. 122C, §§ 3(1), 3(20b) (defining *area authority* and *local management entity*).
3. G.S. 153A-77(c).
4. *Id.*
5. At the time of this book's publication, G.S. 153A-77(c) still states that a CHS board exercising the powers and duties of an area MH/DD/SAS board (no longer an option under North Carolina law) must include *eight* persons who are public advocates, consumers of human services, or family members of the CHSA's clients, including one person with mental illness, one person with a developmental disability, one person in recovery from substance abuse, one family member of a person with mental illness, one family member of a person with a developmental disability, one family member of a person with a substance abuse problem, and two consumers of other human services. G.S. 153A, § 77(c)(1)–(1a).
6. State law does not squarely address whether board members must continue to maintain their professional qualifications for the duration of their term on the CHS board. Arguably, the answer is yes, since "failure to maintain qualifications for appointment" is one of the grounds for removal of a CHS board member listed in G.S. 153A-77(c).
7. G.S. 153A-77(c).
8. *Id.*
9. By contrast, the statute for county boards of health allows county commissioners to appoint a member of the general public when a qualified professional is unavailable to fill the seat. *See* G.S. 130A-35(c).
10. G.S. 153A-77(c).
11. G.S. 153A-77(e)(4).
12. *See* Meyer v. Walls, 347 N.C. 97 (1997).
13. G.S. 143, art. 33C.
14. G.S. 132.
15. N.C. Const. art. VI, § 7; G.S. 153A-26; G.S. 11-7.
16. The requirement for a health advisory committee applies only to counties that abolish their health boards after January 1, 2012. This creates an exception for Mecklenburg County, which abolished its health boards prior to that date.
17. This means that the advisory committee must include one physician licensed to practice medicine in North Carolina, one licensed dentist, one licensed optometrist, one licensed veterinarian, one registered nurse, one licensed pharmacist, one county commissioner, one professional engineer, and three representatives of the general public.
18. *See* G.S. 153A-77(a).
19. For more information about public health advisory committees, see Jill Moore, *What Is a County Advisory Committee on Health and Who Has to Have One?*, Coates' Canons: NC Loc. Gov't L. (blog) (June 21, 2013), https://canons.sog.unc.edu/2013/06/what-is-a-county-advisory-committee-on-health-and-who-has-to-have-one/.
20. G.S. 153A-76.

Chapter 4

Appointment, Terms, and Removal of Consolidated Human Services Board Members

This chapter discusses requirements in state law related to the appointment, terms, and removal of members of an appointed consolidated human services (CHS) board.

Appointment Authority and Procedure

Only the board of county commissioners (BOCC) has the authority to appoint members to a CHS board.[1] As described in more detail in Chapter 3, the initial CHS board must be appointed by the BOCC based on a slate of candidates recommended by a nominating committee composed of members of the preconsolidation board of health, the social services board, and the area mental health, developmental disabilities, and substance abuse services board.

When subsequent vacancies arise after the initial appointment of the CHS board, the members of the current CHS board must present a slate of nominees to the board of commissioners. The commissioners must then fill the board vacancy from this list of nominees.[2] Accordingly, though the BOCC holds sole appointment authority, the CHS board itself has an important role in determining the pool of nominees from which the commissioners may choose board members. For professional roles on the CHS board, some counties will find it challenging to even find a single qualified individual who is able and willing to serve, which may limit the number of nominees that the CHS board is able to present to the commissioners. The CHS board may find it helpful to work with the CHS director and other county leaders on strategies for recruitment of new board members.

The CHS director has no legal responsibility with respect to recruiting, nominating, or appointing members of the CHS board. However, state law does not prohibit the director from providing assistance, making recommendations, or suggesting potential nominees to the BOCC or the CHS board with respect to CHS board appointments. If the director is involved in recruiting or nominating CHS board members, that involvement should be handled in a way that does not compromise the independent judgment and discretion of the CHS board in choosing nominees or of the BOCC in making appointments.

Term Length

The regular term of an appointed CHS board member is four years.[3] As described in Chapter 3, the first terms of the board's *initial* members may be shorter in order to create a staggered board term structure. Regular appointments (or reappointments) to the CHS board should be made shortly before the expiration of an incumbent board member's term or as soon as possible thereafter.

If the BOCC fails to make an appointment to the CHS board before the end of an incumbent board member's term or a newly appointed board member has not assumed office when that term ends, the incumbent board member continues to hold office as a "holdover" member until the incumbent's successor is appointed *and* takes the oath of office.[4] A subsequent section of this chapter discusses the oath of office requirement.

The term of a county commissioner who is appointed to the CHS board is tied to that individual's term as a commissioner. Specifically, the commissioner member may only serve on the CHS board for as long as the member is a county commissioner.[5]

Vacancies on the CHS board must be filled for any unexpired portion of a term.[6] A partial term begins on the date that the new board member assumes office after being appointed and ends on the date that the term of the predecessor would have expired. In other words, the new CHS board member appointed to fill the vacancy completes the unexpired remainder of the former board member's term, rather than serving a new full four-year term.

Term Limits

State law provides that a person generally may not serve more than two consecutive four-year terms on an appointed CHS board.[7] Terms are consecutive when a subsequent term begins *immediately* after the expiration of a prior term.

Theoretically, any CHS board member could serve an additional (third) term on the board so long as the term did not *immediately* follow the first two consecutive terms. How long must a former board member wait before becoming eligible for reappointment? State law does not answer that question. A cautious approach might be to require board members who have served two consecutive terms to wait for the length of a full term (four years) before they can be reappointed to the board, but the law does not explicitly state that a full four-year break from board service is required before reappointment. A shorter break in board service may be permissible.[8]

What about members who serve partial terms on the board because they are appointed to fill a vacancy caused by the death, resignation, or removal of a board member? The language of Chapter 153A, Section 77(c) of the North Carolina General Statutes (hereinafter G.S.), which states that the two-consecutive-term limit applies only to "four-year terms," suggests that a partial term in which a member serves the unexpired remainder of a former board member's term does not count toward the two-consecutive-term limit.[9] Likewise, the fact that the two-consecutive-term limit only applies to "four-year terms" suggests that if an *initial* member of the CHS board is appointed to a shorter term for the purpose of creating a staggered board term structure, that shorter initial term does not count against the consecutive-term limit.

Qualifications for Appointment

All members of a CHS board must be residents of the county in which the consolidated human services agency is located.[10] State law does not require a prospective appointee to reside in a county for any minimum period of time before being appointed to the CHS board.

State law requires a number of different professions and categories of persons to be represented on the board, as described earlier in Chapter 3. Specifically, the board must include four persons who are consumers of human services, a psychologist, a pharmacist, an engineer, a dentist, an optometrist, a veterinarian, a social worker, a registered nurse, two physicians licensed to practice medicine in North Carolina (one of whom must be a psychiatrist), and one county commissioner. One individual serving on the board may fulfill more than one of those categories. Common questions about these required categories of representation are discussed in Chapter 3.

In addition to appointing individuals who fulfill the statutorily required categories of membership, a board of commissioners may appoint other county residents to the CHS board (up to a total of twenty-five members).

County boards of commissioners have authority to establish additional qualifications for members of the CHS board as long as those additional qualifications are not inconsistent with state law and do not waive any state-law requirements.[11]

Choosing Nominees for Board Service

Since the CHS board is responsible for presenting nominees to fill vacancies, it may want to gather and evaluate additional information about prospective appointees to help the BOCC choose from the qualified individuals interested in board service. For example, the CHS board may want to ask questions of potential appointees regarding why they are interested in serving on the board, whether they have any relevant professional or volunteer experience, and whether they have any current or past experience serving on any other state or local government boards, commissions, or committees.

Legal Disqualifications to Appointment

North Carolina law establishes only three express disqualifications that prevent the appointment of certain individuals to an appointed CHS board.[12]

First, North Carolina's laws that limit multiple office-holding disqualify a person from serving on an appointed CHS board if, at the time the appointee would assume the board seat, the appointee already holds

- two appointive public offices or
- one elective public office and one appointive public office.[13]

This prohibition does not apply to a county commissioner who is appointed to the CHS board by the BOCC (an *ex officio* appointment).[14] Ex officio appointments are discussed in more detail in Chapter 8.

Second, a person is not eligible to be reappointed to the CHS board if that person is an incumbent board member and has just served two consecutive four-year terms on the board. As described earlier in this chapter, a board member may eventually be eligible for reappointment after a meaningful waiting period following the two consecutive terms, but the length of that waiting period is not defined by state law.

Third, the North Carolina Constitution disqualifies a person from holding any public office, including the office of CHS board member, if the person has been removed from any public office by impeachment or has been found guilty of corruption or malpractice in any public office.[15]

While there are only three express disqualifications that legally prohibit a person from serving on an appointed CHS board, there are certainly other reasons that might cause the BOCC, in the exercise of its discretion and judgment, to decide that a particular person should not be appointed to the CHS board. In a county where the consolidated human services agency includes both social services and public health, the CHS board has significant responsibilities and powers, including the ability to review certain confidential social services information and to adopt local public health rules.

Although the fact that an individual has been convicted of a crime may be considered in determining whether the individual should be appointed to the CHS board, the fact that an individual has been convicted of a felony does not legally disqualify the individual from being appointed to the CHS board if the individual's citizenship rights (such as the right to vote, hold public office, and sit on a jury) have been restored.[16]

Conflicts of Interest Related to Social Services That May Limit CHS Board Service

In a county where the consolidated human services agency (CHSA) includes social services, there may be some conflicts of interest that prohibit an individual from serving on the CHS board. As a general matter, the fact that an individual or the individual's spouse, child, parent, sibling, or other close relative is receiving or has received public assistance or social services from the county's CHSA (or preconsolidation department of social services) does not legally prohibit that individual from being appointed to the CHS board or from continued service on the CHS board. To the contrary, the CHS board is required to have "consumers of human services" represented among its members, and the experience of receiving public assistance or social services may help a board member provide a valuable perspective to other board members.

However, two unique conflicts of interest related to public assistance and social services may limit an individual's ability to serve on the CHS board, as described below.

Payment for Adult Care or Nursing-Home Residents

State law expressly prohibits a county commissioner, a county social services board member, or a commissioner or board member's spouse from receiving payments under the State-County Special Assistance or Medicaid programs on behalf of persons who are residents or patients in adult care or nursing homes that are owned or operated, in whole or in part, by a commissioner, board member, or board member's spouse.[17] This prohibition also applies to members of CHS boards and their spouses when the CHS board serves as the governing board for social services. This law does not prohibit an individual who owns an adult care or nursing home (or someone whose spouse owns such a facility) from serving on the CHS board, but it does effectively cut off an important source of revenue for these individuals in a way that will likely preclude them from serving on the board.

Foster Parents for the County

Regardless of whether the governing board for a CHSA is the board of commissioners or an appointed CHS board, the members of the governing board are prohibited from (1) being licensed as foster parents through the social services department of the county in which they serve on the CHS board or (2) being supervised or considered as a placement resource by the social services department of the county in which they serve on the CHS board.[18]

The Appointment Process

Appointments to the CHS board must be approved by a majority vote of the commissioners who are present at an official meeting of the BOCC where a quorum is present. A majority of the membership of the BOCC, without regard to vacancies, constitutes a quorum.[19]

All discussions and actions by the BOCC regarding the appointment of CHS board members must take place in an open session of an official, public meeting, in accordance with North Carolina's open meetings law. Although the open meetings law allows a public body to hold a closed session to discuss or take action with respect to some matters, the board of commissioners' appointments to the CHS board may not be considered or made during a closed session.[20] Likewise, the members of the CHS board may not consider the qualifications, competence, character, or fitness of a potential nominee for appointment to the CHS board in a closed session.[21]

The open meetings law also prohibits the appointment of CHS board members by "secret ballot." Each commissioner who votes on the appointment of a CHS board member must do so by voice vote, show of hands, or signed ballot (and if signed ballots are used, each member's vote must be announced when the ballots are counted, and the minutes of the meeting must show the vote of each voting member).[22] The open meetings law is discussed in more detail in Chapter 10 of this book.

Oath of Office Following Appointment

As public officials, CHS board members are required to take an oath in which they swear or affirm that they will faithfully discharge the duties of their office and will support and maintain the constitutions and laws of the United States and North Carolina.[23] Board members must take this oath prior to exercising the powers of the office to which they have been appointed.[24] The oath may be taken at any time between the date when an individual is appointed to the board and the date when the individual assumes office as a CHS board member. Newly appointed CHS board members often take their oaths of office at the first board meeting following the beginning of their terms. However, there is no requirement in state law that the oath of office be taken at an official meeting of the CHS board.

The oath of office may be administered anywhere within the state by a judge, magistrate, clerk of superior court, state legislator, county or city clerk, mayor, chair of a BOCC, notary public, or other public official described in G.S. 11-7.1 (or that official's deputy).[25] A written copy of the oath signed by a newly appointed CHS board member must be filed with the county clerk.[26]

If a CHS board member is reappointed for a second consecutive term, the board member should take a new oath of office and file a signed copy of the oath with the county clerk. A county commissioner who is appointed to serve on a CHS board is not required to take a separate oath of office as a CHS board member.

If an official—including a CHS board member—who is required to take the oath fails to do so, there can be serious consequences. It is a misdemeanor to enter upon the duties of a public office without first taking, subscribing, and filing "the oath of office prescribed."[27] A public official who fails to take the oath of office may also incur a $500 penalty and ejectment from office.[28]

Revoking or Rescinding Appointments

State law does not allow a county board of commissioners to revoke or rescind an appointment after the board of commissioners has taken action to appoint a person to the CHS board. However, CHS board members may be removed from office following appointment, as described in the following section.[29]

Removal of Consolidated Human Services Board Members

Legal authority to remove a CHS board member from office is vested in the BOCC; the CHS board has no authority to remove one of its members on its own.[30] State law provides these specific, limited grounds for the removal of a CHS board member:

- commission of a felony or other crime involving moral turpitude,
- violation of a state law governing conflicts of interest,
- violation of a written policy adopted by the board of county commissioners,
- habitual failure to attend meetings,
- conduct that tends to bring the office into disrepute, and
- failure to maintain required qualifications for appointment.[31]

Conduct that falls within any individual category in this list would be sufficient grounds to remove a CHS board member.

State law also provides several grounds for the removal of *any* public official, which would apply to CHS board members.

1. A public official is subject to being ejected from office for failure to take the oath of office prior to assuming the duties of the office.[32]
2. A public official may be removed from office for willful failure to discharge the duties of the office.[33]
3. A public official who holds office in a manner that is contrary to article VI, section 9 of the North Carolina Constitution "forfeit[s] all rights . . . incident thereto."[34] This would include someone who violates the prohibition on multiple office-holding described earlier in this

chapter, someone who is appointed to the CHS board despite having previously been removed from any public office by impeachment, or someone who is appointed to the CHS board despite having been found guilty of corruption or malpractice in any public office.

A CHS board member may be removed from the board by the BOCC only after the member has been given written notice of the basis for removal and has had the opportunity to respond.[35] The law does not specify exactly what sort of "opportunity to respond" must be given to the board member, but for due process purposes, it may be prudent for the BOCC to conduct a hearing in which the CHS board member is given an opportunity to present testimony and evidence (if the board member desires to have such an opportunity prior to removal).[36]

Judicial Review of a Removal Decision

The removal of a CHS board member by the BOCC is a quasi-judicial action that, on the petition of the removed board member, may be reviewed by a superior court judge.[37] A CHS board member who has been removed from office also may bring a declaratory judgment action in superior court regarding the removal decision.[38]

Notes

1. Chapter 153A, Section 77(c) of the North Carolina General Statutes (hereinafter G.S.).
2. *Id.*
3. *Id.*
4. *See* N.C. Const. art. VI, § 10; G.S. 128-7; *see also* Baxter v. Danny Nicholson, Inc., 363 N.C. 829, 830 (2010) (holding that the authority of an appointed officer continues until the date on which his successor takes the oath of the office in question and thereby becomes qualified to begin performing the duties of that office).
5. G.S. 153A-77(c).
6. *Id.*
7. *Id.*
8. Nonetheless, a break between terms should not be so short as to constitute an obvious attempt to evade the law regarding consecutive term limits.
9. G.S. 153A-77(c). Compare with G.S. 108A-6, which explicitly states that appointments to fill vacancies on a social services board do not constitute a "term" for purposes of the consecutive term limit.
10. G.S. 153A-77(c).
11. G.S. 153A-25.
12. A legal disqualification is any condition that, as a matter of constitutional, statutory, or common law, absolutely and unconditionally prohibits a person from being appointed to the consolidated human services board or serving as a consolidated human services board member.
13. N.C. Const. art. VI, § 9; G.S. 128-1.1. North Carolina's law limiting multiple office-holding is discussed in detail in A. Fleming Bell, II, Ethics, Conflicts, and Offices: A Guide for Local Officials (UNC School of Government, 2d ed. 2010).
14. G.S. 128-1.2.
15. N.C. Const. art. VI, § 8.
16. *Id.* See also G.S. 13-1, regarding restoration of a felon's citizenship rights. More information about the restoration of citizenship rights is available on the UNC School of Government's microsite *Relief from a Criminal Conviction (2025 Edition)*, https://www.sog.unc.edu/resources/microsites/relief-criminal-conviction/citizenship-rights.
17. G.S. 108A, §§ 47, 55(d).
18. Title 10A, Chapter 70E, Section .1105 of the North Carolina Administrative Code.
19. G.S. 153A-43.
20. G.S. 143-318.11(a)(6).
21. G.S. 143, § 318.9–.18. The state open meetings law is discussed in more detail in Frayda S. Bluestein & David M. Lawrence, Open Meetings and Local Governments in North Carolina: Some Questions and Answers (UNC School of Government, 8th ed. 2017). The open meetings law's requirements do not apply with respect to the appointment of a county social services board member by a senior resident superior court judge.
22. G.S. 143-318.13(b).
23. N.C. Const. art. VI, § 7; G.S. 11-7.1; G.S. 128-5; G.S. 153A-26. For more information about the language of the oath of office, please see Trey Allen, *One Oath or Two? What Is THE Oath of Office?*, Coates' Canons: NC Loc. Gov't L. (blog) (Jan. 27, 2017), https://canons.sog.unc.edu/2017/01/one-oath-or-two-what-is-the-oath-of-office/.
24. The authority of a "holdover" member continues until that member's successor takes and subscribes the oath of office. *See* Baxter v. Danny Nicholson, Inc., 363 N.C. 829 (2010).

25. G.S. 11, §§ 7.1, 8.
26. G.S. 153A-26.
27. G.S. 14-229.
28. G.S. 128-5.
29. Frank v. Savage, 205 N.C. App. 183, 191 (2010) (finding that plaintiffs stated a cognizable claim that BOCC violated the law when revoking plaintiffs' appointments to the county board of social services).
30. *See* G.S. 153A-77(c); *see also* Kinsland v. Mackey, 217 N.C. 508 (1940) ("[T]he general rule is that in the absence of all constitutional or statutory provision for the removal of such public officers, the power of removal is incident to the power of appointment. . . .").
31. G.S. 153A-77(c).
32. G.S. 128-5.
33. G.S. 14-230.
34. G.S. 128-2.
35. G.S. 153A-77(c).
36. *Berger v. New Hanover Cnty. Bd. of Comm'rs*, No. 13 CVS 1942, 2013 WL 4792508, at *11 (N.C. Super. Sept. 5, 2013).
37. G.S. 1-269; *Russ v. Bd. of Educ. of Brunswick Cnty.*, 232 N.C. 128 (1950). This review may occur through a writ of recordari or certiorari.
38. G.S. 1, §§ 253–67 (declaratory judgment actions); *Frank v. Savage*, 205 N.C. App. 183, 191 (2010) (holding that appointees to county board of social services stated claim for declaratory relief that county board of commissioners acted outside its statutory authority in invalidating their appointments). A CHS board member who has been removed from office also may seek judicial review of the removal through a *quo warranto* proceeding (an action brought to determine the right of a board member's successor to hold office). *See* G.S. 1, §§ 515–32 (quo warranto actions); State *ex rel.* Pitts v. Williams, 260 N.C. 168 (1963) (quo warranto action for order declaring individual to be the duly appointed and qualified member of a county welfare board).

Chapter 5

An Overview of the Powers and Duties of a Consolidated Human Services Board

This chapter provides a broad overview of the powers and duties that are assigned to a consolidated human services (CHS) board by state law, some of which are discussed in greater detail in Parts 2 and 3 of this book. If a board of county commissioners (BOCC) decides to act as the CHS board (as opposed to appointing a CHS board), then the BOCC assumes all of the powers and responsibilities assigned to the CHS board by state law, including those described in this chapter.[1]

Differences Based on the Composition of the Consolidated Human Services Agency

One unique aspect of the consolidated human services agency (CHSA) model is that a county can choose any two or more human services functions to consolidate into the CHSA. In many counties, that includes combining social services and public health into the CHSA (and, accordingly, abolishing the appointed boards of those agencies). However, other counties may choose a different combination of human services functions—for example, combining social services and veterans' services into the CHSA, while leaving the local health department separate.

If both social services and public health are consolidated into a CHSA, then the CHS board is responsible for carrying out all the powers and duties assigned by law to the county board of social services and local board of health, except that the CHS board may not appoint or dismiss the CHS director (this power lies with the county manager).[2] However, if the county department of social services or county health department is *not* consolidated into the CHSA, then that standalone, nonconsolidated department continues to have its own separate governance structure, and its governing board retains its statutory powers and duties (rather than transferring to the CHS board). For example, if a county forms a CHSA by solely consolidating

Table 5.1. Governance Responsibilities Based on CHSA Composition

CHSA includes public health and social services	CHSA includes public health, but NOT social services	CHSA includes social services, but NOT public health
CHS board (or BOCC acting as CHS board) assumes the powers and duties of a local board of health and county board of social services.	CHS board (or BOCC acting as CHS board) assumes the powers and duties of a local board of health, but not those of a county board of social services.	CHS board (or BOCC acting as CHS board) assumes the powers and duties of a county board of social services, but not those of a local board of health.

its public health and transportation functions (but leaves its department of social services untouched), then the CHS board does not acquire the statutory powers or duties of the social services board. These distinctions are summarized in Table 5.1.

Sources of the Board's Legal Authority

A CHS board's authority, powers, and duties are based on state law. This means that the North Carolina General Assembly may enact legislation to change the powers or duties of CHS boards. CHS boards are prohibited from exercising powers that are not explicitly or implicitly granted to them by state law or that are vested by state law in another public official, board, or agency.[3]

Some of the powers and duties of CHS boards are found in the primary CHS statute, Chapter 153A, Section 77 of the North Carolina General Statutes (hereinafter G.S.). For the governing board of a CHSA that includes social services, the CHS board's social services powers and duties are primarily specified in G.S. Chapter 108A, with additional provisions found in Title 10A of the North Carolina Administrative Code. State law also expressly provides that the state Social Services Commission, the North Carolina Department of Health and Human Services (NCDHHS), or a BOCC may assign additional duties and responsibilities to county social services boards (which would include a CHS board acting as the governing board for social services).[4]

For the governing board of a CHSA that includes public health, the CHS board's public health powers and duties are primarily established by G.S. Chapter 130A, as well as by the local health department accreditation requirements found in Title 10A of the North Carolina Administrative Code.

When exercising their powers and duties, CHS boards are required to comply with applicable federal and state laws. For example, CHS board members must comply with the requirements of the state open meetings law (discussed in Chapter 10), the state public records law (discussed in Chapter 11), and the state conflicts of interest law (discussed in Chapter 9).

The Board's Powers and Duties

State law authorizes the CHS board to carry out duties and responsibilities in the following areas.

The CHS Director

Unlike a traditional board of social services or local board of health, a CHS board does not have authority to appoint or dismiss the director of the agency it governs. In the CHSA model, this authority lies with the county manager. The CHS board does, however, play a role in these decisions—it must provide "advice and consent" to the county manager's decision to appoint or dismiss the CHS director.[5] Another difference from the traditional board of social services or local board of health model is that in a county with a CHSA, the agency's director reports directly to the county manager, rather than the governing board.[6]

Chapter 6 provides more detailed information on the board's responsibilities with respect to the CHS director.

The CHS Board

An appointed CHS board is required to meet at least quarterly, or more often if a special or emergency meeting is called by the board chairperson or by any three board members.[7] If the BOCC is acting as the CHS board, it may conduct business related to the CHSA as part of its regular county commissioner meetings. The BOCC is not required to hold separate meetings in its capacity as the CHS board or solely devoted to CHS board business, though it may choose to do so.

An appointed CHS board must also elect the board's chairperson on an annual basis.[8] The CHS board may adopt rules of procedure for its board meetings and for the annual election of the board chairperson. Chapter 10 provides more detailed information on board meetings and procedures.

In the event of a vacancy on the CHS board after it is initially established, the CHS board is responsible for presenting names of nominees to the BOCC for appointment to the CHS board.[9] Chapter 4 discusses the appointment of CHS board members in more detail.

The CHSA Budget

The CHS board may assist the CHS director in planning the proposed budget for the CHSA.[10] However, the CHS board does not have authority or a duty to present or transmit the agency's proposed budget to the BOCC.[11] Chapter 7 provides more detailed information on funding for human services programs and the board's role in the budgeting process for the CHSA.

The CHSA's Programs and Services

By statute, the CHS board is responsible for the following functions:

- ***Ensuring the CHSA's compliance.*** The CHS board is responsible for ensuring the CHSA's compliance with laws related to state and federal programs.[12] State law also gives the CHS board authority to conduct "audits and reviews" of human services programs, including quality assurance activities, when required by state and federal law or periodically as the board may deem necessary.[13] However, in many circumstances, the CHS director's ability to share information about individual cases with the board may be limited by federal and state confidentiality laws. These confidentiality limitations arguably make the CHS board's power to "audit" the CHSA's programs relatively limited in scope.
- ***Recommending new programs.*** The CHS board may recommend the creation of new human services programs in the county.[14] Seeking out information regarding the programs and services offered by the county's CHSA, as well as programs and services offered by other community organizations, will help CHS board members understand potential gaps in service delivery to community members.
- ***Setting fees for services.*** The CHS board has the authority to set fees for certain services provided by the CHSA, based upon the recommendations of the CHS director.[15] Any fees set by the CHS board are subject to the same restrictions on amount and scope that would apply if the fees were set by a county board of health or a county board of social services. The CHS board cannot establish a fee for a service that the CHSA is legally required to provide free of charge. For example, state law prohibits a CHSA from charging a fee for certain public health services, such as sickle cell syndrome testing and counseling,[16] examination and treatment for tuberculosis or sexually transmitted diseases,[17] and administration of certain vaccines to children in low-income families who meet specific criteria.[18] Fee-setting for public health services is discussed in Chapter 18, while the board's role in setting fees for certain social services programs is discussed in Chapter 15.
- ***Public relations and advocacy.*** The CHS board is responsible for performing public relations and advocacy functions on behalf of the CHSA.[19] This may include advocating at the local, state, and federal level for the adoption, implementation, and funding of plans and policies to address social, economic, and public health problems facing the community. It could also include fostering community partnerships and educating the community about the services and programs offered by the CHSA.
- ***Developing dispute resolution procedures.*** The CHS board has the authority to develop dispute resolution procedures for human services contractors, clients, and public advocates, subject to applicable state and

federal dispute resolution procedures for human services programs.[20] Under a former version of the CHSA statute, a CHSA could include the functions of the area authority for mental health, developmental disabilities, and substance abuse services (MH/DD/SAS). Changes made to the law in 2012 now prohibit a BOCC from consolidating an area MH/DD/SAS board into a CHS board.[21] This language regarding dispute resolution procedures in the CHS board statute is likely intended to reflect the responsibility of area authorities to develop dispute resolution procedures[22]—a responsibility that no longer applies to CHS boards—but it was not omitted or changed when the statutes were revised in 2012.

Responsibilities Specific to Social Services

Social services boards in North Carolina—including CHS boards that function as the governing board for social services—have relatively limited authority regarding social services policy and the administration of social services programs. However, state law does give county social services boards some responsibility to

- make certain decisions regarding public assistance programs,
- review cases of suspected fraud related to some public assistance programs,
- review some social services records, and
- enter into certain types of contracts.

If a CHS board serves as the governing board for social services, it assumes these responsibilities and powers.[23] Part 2 of this book provides more detailed information on the board's powers and duties with respect to social services programs and policies.

Responsibilities Specific to Public Health

Local boards of health in North Carolina—including CHS boards that function as the governing board for public health—are responsible for:

- adopting local health rules;[24]
- hearing appeals concerning the enforcement of local health rules and the imposition of administrative penalties by a local health director;[25]
- protecting and promoting public health;[26]
- establishing fees for services to be rendered by a local health department (except where the imposition of a fee is prohibited by statute or where an employee of the local health department is performing the services as an agent of the state);[27] and
- engaging in activities as required for the local health department to achieve accreditation status.[28]

If a CHS board serves as the governing board for public health, it assumes these responsibilities and powers.[29] Part 3 of this book provides more detailed information on the board's powers and duties with respect to public health programs and services.

Contracting with an Attorney

Appointed CHS boards generally have no authority to appoint, retain, or hire an attorney to provide legal services. Two potential exceptions to this general rule are described below.

Contract Attorney

The BOCC must approve legal services contracts.[30] However, the BOCC may delegate this authority to the county manager, the county attorney, the CHS director, or another county official or board (including the CHS board).

Special County Attorneys for Social Services

State law allows the BOCC, with the approval of the county social services board (which may be the CHS board, in a county with a CHSA), to appoint an attorney to serve as the "special county attorney for social service matters" or to designate the county attorney as the special county attorney for social service matters.[31] The duties of a special county attorney for social services may include providing legal advice to the county social services director, the county social services board, and the BOCC with respect to social services matters; representing the county board of social services in appeal proceedings and in any litigation relating to appeals; and performing any other duties that may be assigned by the county social services director, the county social services board, the BOCC, or state law.[32] A special county attorney for social services may be retained by the county on a contractual basis or hired as a county employee. The compensation for a special county attorney for social services is determined by the BOCC.[33]

In practice, very few attorneys who provide legal services to county social services departments serve as special county attorneys for social services. Instead, counties typically use

- a "county attorney" model, under which the county DSS is represented by the county attorney or an assistant county attorney;
- a "staff attorney" model, under which DSS attorneys are hired by the county DSS director, are employees of the county DSS, and work under the director's supervision; or
- a "contract attorney" model, under which a private attorney is retained to represent the county DSS on a contractual or fee-for-service basis.

Limitations on the Board's Authority

CHS boards have no legal authority to make decisions regarding employees of the county CHSA (other than providing advice and consent to the county manager's appointment of the CHS director). The authority to make decisions regarding CHSA employees lies with the CHS director (and the county manager, who must approve decisions to appoint or dismiss staff).[34] This means that appointed CHS boards do not have the legal authority to

- hire, supervise, promote, discipline, or fire employees of the CHSA;
- establish personnel policies for CHSA employees;
- determine the salary schedule or employment benefits for CHSA employees;
- approve or administer the CHSA's budget; or
- execute contracts involving CHSA employees.

A BOCC that has assumed the powers and duties of a CHS board, on the other hand, does have authority over some of these matters. For example, a BOCC has authority to

- enact personnel ordinances regarding annual leave, sick leave, hours of work, holidays, and the administration of the pay plan for county employees;[35]
- adjust the salary ranges for the CHS director and CHSA employees;[36]
- approve the CHSA's budget;[37] and
- enter into contracts for the provision of health or social services.[38]

Even though appointed CHS boards do not have authority over employment matters within the CHSA, they should be concerned with the compensation, working conditions, training, qualifications, and morale of the CHSA's employees. The compensation, training, and morale of the CHSA's employees all have a direct impact on the quality of the programs and services that the CHSA provides to the community. The CHS board can encourage and support the CHS director and the county manager to ensure that the CHSA has sufficient staff to perform its work and that CHSA staff receive adequate support to do their work. The compensation and working conditions of CHSA employees can make a significant difference in whether a county's CHSA can hire and retain qualified and talented staff.

Notes

1. Chapter 153A, Section 77(a) of the North Carolina General Statutes (hereinafter G.S.).
2. G.S. 153A-77(d); G.S. 108A-15.1; G.S. 130A-43. Additionally, the CHS board may not transmit or present the CHSA budget to the county budget officer.
3. *See* G.S. 153A-76(3).
4. G.S. 108A-9(5). When the Social Services Commission or NCDHHS assigns additional duties and responsibilities to county social services boards, these additional duties and responsibilities may be specified in administrative rules (codified in the North Carolina Administrative Code) or other statements of policy or procedure. When a BOCC assigns additional duties or responsibilities to the county social services board, these additional duties or responsibilities should be specified in a resolution or ordinance adopted by the BOCC.
5. G.S. 153A-77(e).
6. *Id.*
7. G.S. 153A-77(c).
8. *Id.*
9. *Id.*
10. G.S. 153A, § 77(d)(7), 77(e)(5).
11. G.S. 108A-15.1(b); G.S. 130A-43(b).
12. G.S. 153A-77(d)(2).
13. G.S. 153A-77(d)(8).
14. G.S. 153A-77(d)(3).
15. G.S. 153A-77(d)(1).
16. G.S. 130A-130.
17. G.S. 130A-144(e).
18. G.S. 130A-153(a).
19. G.S. 153A-77(d)(10).
20. G.S. 153A-77(d)(13). Under a former version of the CHSA statute, a CHSA could include the functions of the area MH/DD/SA authority. This language regarding dispute resolution procedures in the CHS board statute is likely intended to reflect the responsibility of area authorities to develop dispute resolution procedures (*see* Title 10A, Subchapter 27G, Section .0808 of the North Carolina Administrative Code (hereinafter N.C.A.C.)) but was not omitted or changed when the statute was revised in 2012. Changes made to the law in 2012 now prohibit a BOCC from consolidating an area MH/DD/SA services board into a CHS board (*see* G.S. 153A-76(6)).
21. G.S. 153A-76(6), as amended by Session Law 2012-126, § 2.
22. 10A N.C.A.C. 27G, § .0808.
23. G.S. 108A-15.1.
24. G.S. 130A-39; G.S. 153A-77(d)(4).
25. G.S. 130A-24; G.S. 153A-77(d)(4).
26. G.S. 130A-39(a); G.S. 153A-77(d)(11).
27. G.S. 130A-39(g); G.S. 153A-77(d)(1).
28. *See* G.S. 130A-34.1; 10A N.C.A.C. 48A.
29. G.S. 130A-43.
30. *See generally* G.S. 153A-12.
31. G.S. 108A-16.
32. G.S. 108A-18.
33. G.S. 108A-17.

34. *See* G.S 153A-77(e)(1) (giving CHS director authority to appoint staff of the consolidated human services agency with the county manager's approval).
35. G.S. 126-9(a); G.S. 153A-94.
36. G.S. 153A-92.
37. G.S. 159-13.
38. G.S. 153A-259.

Chapter 6

The Consolidated Human Services Director

Leadership structures within consolidated human services agencies (CHSAs) across North Carolina vary widely from county to county. This is because state law gives counties a great deal of flexibility with respect to who serves as the director of the CHSA, who leads its various divisions, and how duties are delegated among its leaders and staff. In all counties with consolidated agencies, the county manager plays a unique role in personnel decisions regarding the agency's director and staff. This chapter answers common questions about the appointment of the CHSA's director, the various ways a CHSA's leadership may be structured, and personnel decisions regarding the CHS director and CHSA staff.

Who Appoints and Dismisses the Consolidated Human Services Director?

Every CHSA must be led by a consolidated human services (CHS) director, who must be appointed by the county manager.[1] In some counties, this individual is referred to as the "health and human services" (HHS) director or "human services" director, but this book uses the term "CHS director" for consistency. The CHS director is a county employee and a public officeholder who must take an oath of office.[2] By law, the CHS director reports to and is supervised by the county manager, unlike a traditional county social services director or health director who reports solely to their governing board.[3]

The governing board for the CHSA (whether an appointed CHS board or the board of commissioners) must provide advice to the county manager on the CHS director's appointment and must consent to the appointment.[4] The decision to consent to the appointment of a particular individual will require a vote of the CHS board. As a matter of procedure, the county manager should receive consent from the CHS board *before* appointing a candidate to serve as CHS director.

Likewise, the county manager must also receive the CHS board's advice and consent prior to the dismissal of the CHS director.[5] The CHS board will need to take a vote on the dismissal decision in order to collectively provide (or decline to provide) consent to the decision.

All discussions by the CHS board regarding the director's appointment, performance, competence, fitness, character, or dismissal must take place at an official board meeting and may occur during a closed session pursuant to Chapter 143, Section 318.11(a)(6) of the North Carolina General Statutes (hereinafter G.S.). Per North Carolina's open meetings law, "Final action making an appointment or discharge or removal by a public body having final authority for the appointment or discharge or removal shall be taken in an open meeting." Does this mean the CHS board's vote to provide consent to the county manager on the CHS director's appointment or dismissal must occur in an open meeting? Arguably the answer is "no." The CHS board's vote to consent to the director's appointment or dismissal is not the "final action" to appoint or dismiss the director, nor does the board have the "final authority" to appoint or dismiss the director. Accordingly, the board could choose to hold the vote in closed session under G.S. 143-318.11(a)(6). More information about the open meetings law and closed sessions is available in Chapter 10.

How Is Leadership Within a Consolidated Human Services Agency Structured?

Except as otherwise provided by law, the individual appointed as the CHS director acquires all of the powers and duties of a social services director and a local health director (if both social services and public health are consolidated into the CHSA).[6] These powers and duties are primarily found in G.S. 108A-14 (social services director) and G.S. 130A-41 (local health director), though some powers and duties are scattered throughout other portions of the North Carolina General Statutes as well. The CHS director is permitted, but not required, to delegate most of these powers and duties to other staff members within the agency.[7] The county manager and the CHS director have flexibility in deciding how to delegate these powers and duties and in structuring the internal organization of the CHSA. There is a limitation on this flexibility: if the CHS director does not personally satisfy the statutory qualifications for a local health director, the CHS director is required to appoint a qualified individual (with the county manager's approval) to serve as the local health director.[8]

In some counties, the new CHS director was formerly a social services director or local health director prior to consolidation. The CHS director may retain the core responsibilities of their preconsolidation role (as the director of social services or health director) or delegate them to other employees.

In other counties, a separate individual is appointed as the CHS director, with a social services director and public health director reporting to that individual and handling the day-to-day management of their respective divisions.

Figure 6.1. Examples of Management Structures for CHSAs

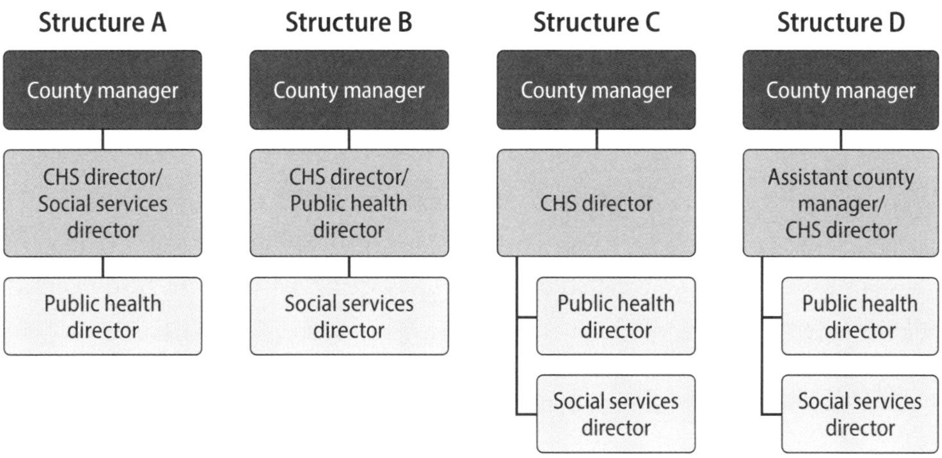

In some cases, an assistant or deputy county manager is appointed as the CHS director, with a social services and public health director reporting to that individual and handling the day-to-day management of their respective divisions.

Figure 6.1 shows several examples of how a CHSA's management could be structured, though it is not an exhaustive representation of all possible organizational structures. For example, at least one county in North Carolina has divided the powers and duties of a social services director between two individuals in the consolidated human services agency, instead of having a single individual serve in that role.

State law imposes an important limitation on how a county structures a CHSA's leadership, specifically regarding the appointment of the local health director (if the local health department has been consolidated into the CHSA). The law requires that the CHS director appoint (with the county manager's approval) an individual who meets the statutory requirements for a local health director (found in G.S. 130A-40(a)) to serve as the local health director.[9] This appointment is only necessary if the director of the CHSA does not already *personally* meet those statutory local health director requirements. There is no equivalent statutory requirement for the CHS director to appoint someone with social services experience or qualifications to serve as a social services director, though it would be prudent for the CHS director to do so.

Regardless of the internal management structure that a county decides to use for a CHSA, the CHS director should ensure that the director's delegation of duties to staff (including to a social services and/or health director, if applicable) is clearly documented in writing. This documentation should be examined and updated from time to time. There is no statute or regulation that specifically addresses documenting these delegations of CHS director authority (or social services or local public health director authority). However, such documentation may become important if an exercise of authority is challenged in litigation. Moreover, clearly documenting the delegation of authority in writing allows staff members to know who is authorized to act on certain matters within the CHSA.[10]

Who May Serve as the Consolidated Human Services Director?

The statute that creates and defines the role of the CHS director, G.S. 153A-77, does not provide any required qualifications or experience for an individual to be appointed to that position. As described earlier, in some cases, counties will want to appoint a preconsolidation county director of social services, public health, or another human services function to fill this role. In other cases, the county may appoint an assistant or deputy county manager to this role, who may or may not have prior experience working with the departments or functions that have been consolidated into the CHSA. Sometimes, the county will want to hire a new individual for the CHS director role, such as someone with a background in leading large or complex agencies.

In some counties, the CHS director is heavily involved in the day-to-day work of the CHSA, while in other counties, the CHS director delegates most of the substantive duties to the director's direct reports (such as a separate social services and/or public health director). In any case, the role of CHS director requires an individual to have skills in the administration and supervision of organizations or agencies with complex budgets and personnel structures. In addition to having supervisory authority over many employees, the CHS director oversees the administration of dozens of different programs and manages a budget with myriad federal, state, and local funding sources.

Though an assistant or deputy county manager may be appointed as the CHS director, the *county manager* may not serve in this role. Under G.S. 153A-77(e), the director of a CHSA must be appointed and dismissed by the county manager, with the advice and consent of the CHS board.[11] That same statute also requires the CHS director to report directly to the county manager.[12] State law contemplates that these are two separate and distinct roles with a clear hierarchy—the CHS director reports to and is supervised by the county manager. Having someone simultaneously serve in both positions arguably violates G.S. 153A-76(3), which prohibits the board of commissioners from "assign[ing] elsewhere a function or duty assigned by law to a particular office [or] position."

Having the county manager serve as the CHS director may also run afoul of the common law doctrine of incompatible office-holding. The doctrine recognizes that in some cases it is simply inappropriate for one person to serve in two official roles that are incompatible.[13] Applying this doctrine, courts have held that it is inappropriate for a person to hold two positions when one of them is subservient to the other.[14] Another way the doctrine is sometimes phrased is that a public employee or official should not "be his own boss." A county manager who serves as the CHS director—a position that must be appointed, supervised, evaluated, and disciplined by the county manager—would be acting as her own boss.

What Role Does the CHS Board Play with Respect to the CHS Director?

Unlike a traditional county board of health or social services board, a CHS board does not have appointment or dismissal authority over the director of the county's CHSA. In the consolidated model, the county manager holds this authority. However, the county manager must receive the "advice and consent" of the CHS board before appointing or terminating the director.[15] This gives the CHS board an important role in appointment and dismissal decisions, even though the board does not have final or sole appointment or dismissal authority.

By statute, the CHS director reports directly to the county manager—not to the CHS board.[16] Accordingly, the CHS board has no formal role in supervising or evaluating the CHS director, though the county manager may choose to seek feedback from the board on the director's performance or otherwise involve the board in the director's evaluation process. Nonetheless, the law still contemplates that the CHS board will work closely with the CHS director, much like a local board of health or social services board works with a county department director. The CHS board has a role in advising the director on human services matters, recommending the creation of new human services programs, helping the director perform public advocacy functions, assisting the director in planning the agency budget, setting fees for certain agency services, adopting local public health rules (if acting as a board of health), and assuring that the agency complies with state and federal law.[17] All of these responsibilities, which will be discussed in more detail in later sections of this book, require good communication and coordination between the CHS board and the CHS director.

What Are the Powers and Duties of the Consolidated Human Services Director?

G.S. 153A-77(e) states that "the human services director or the director's designee shall have the same powers and duties as a social services director [or] a local health director" except as otherwise provided by law.[18] Most counties with CHSAs have consolidated both the local health department and the county department of social services into the CHSA, but some CHSAs only include one of those departments. If a local department does not get consolidated into a CHSA, then it is logical to conclude that the CHS director does not acquire the statutory powers and duties of the director of that nonconsolidated department.[19] For example, if a CHSA does not include the local health department, the CHS director does not acquire and cannot exercise the powers and duties of the local health director.

In many counties, the CHS director chooses to delegate many of these social services and public health powers and duties to other individuals within the CHSA (such as a separate social services director or health director who report to the CHS director).[20] The CHS director should always put any such delegation of authority in writing and clearly document any changes to those delegations that happen over time.

In addition to acquiring the powers and duties of a local health director and social services director, the consolidated human services statute (G.S. 153A-77) establishes some other responsibilities and powers that lie with the CHS director. Specifically, the CHS director has authority and responsibility to

- appoint (and dismiss) staff of the CHSA with the county manager's approval;
- administer state human services programs at the local level;
- administer county human services programs;
- act as secretary and staff to the CHS board under the direction of the county manager;
- plan the budget of the CHSA;
- advise the board of county commissioners through the county manager;
- perform regulatory functions of investigation and enforcement of state and local health regulations, as required by state law;
- act as an agent of and liaison to the state, to the extent required by law; and
- appoint, with the county manager's approval, an individual that meets the statutory requirements for a local health director (found at G.S. 130A-40(a)) to serve as the local health director.[21]

State law gives the county manager a role in some of these responsibilities. The county manager has the authority to approve (or deny) the CHS director's hiring or dismissal decisions regarding CHSA staff (though as a practical matter, a county manager may want to authorize the CHS director to handle hiring and dismissal decisions largely or entirely independently). The statute also states that the CHS director has a responsibility to advise the board of commissioners "through the county manager," indicating that the CHS director's guidance to the commissioners on human services generally flows through the county manager unless the manager wants the CHS director to advise the commissioners directly.

Notes

1. Chapter 153A, Section 77(b)(1) and (e) of the North Carolina General Statutes (hereinafter G.S.).
2. For more information on this topic, see Kristi Nickodem, *Who Is Required to Take an Oath of Office in the Human Services Field?*, Coates' Canons: NC Loc. Gov't L. (blog) (Jan. 3, 2022), https://canons.sog.unc.edu/2022/01/who-is-required-to-take-an-oath-of-office-in-the-human-services-field/.
3. G.S. 153A-77(e).
4. *Id.*
5. *Id.* The statutory authority to dismiss a particular official is inherent in the power to appoint. If the consolidated human services (CHS) director cannot be appointed without the advice and consent of the CHS board, a logical reading of the statute is that the director also may not be dismissed without the advice and consent of the CHS board.
6. *Id.*
7. *See* G.S. 130A-6, regarding the local health director's powers and duties ("Whenever authority is granted by this Chapter upon a public official, the authority may be delegated to another person authorized by the public official."), and G.S. 108A-14, regarding the DSS director's powers and duties ("The director may delegate to one or more members of his staff the authority to act as his representative. The director may limit the delegated authority of his representative to specific tasks or areas of expertise.").
8. *See* G.S. 153A-77(e)(9). The experience and education requirements for a local health director are found in G.S. 130A-40(a).
9. G.S. 153A-77(e).
10. *Id.*
11. *Id.*
12. *Id.*
13. For a comprehensive discussion of the common law doctrine of incompatible office-holding, including applicable case law, please see A. Fleming Bell, II, Ethics, Conflicts, and Offices: A Guide for Local Officials ch. 7 (UNC School of Government, 2d ed. 2011).
14. *See* Bell, *supra* note 13, at 148.
15. G.S. 153A-77(e).
16. *Id.*
17. G.S. 153A-77(d).
18. G.S. 153A-77(e) also states that "the human services director or the director's designee shall have the same powers and duties as . . . a director of an area mental health, developmental disabilities, and substance abuse services authority." However, counties have been prohibited from consolidating an area mental health, developmental disabilities, and substance abuse services authority (LME/MCO) into a CHSA since 2012 (*see* G.S. 153A-76), and these agencies are not part of county government. Accordingly, the CHS director cannot exercise the powers and duties of the director of an area authority.
19. *See* Romulus v. Romulus, 216 N.C. App. 28, 34 (2011) ("It is well settled that in construing statutes courts normally adopt an interpretation which will avoid absurd or bizarre consequences, the presumption being that the legislature acted in accordance with reason and common sense and did not intend untoward results.") (citing Duplin Cnty. Bd. of Educ. v. Duplin Cnty. Bd. of Cnty. Comm'rs, 201 N.C. App. 113, 119 (2009)).
20. *See* G.S. 108A-14(b); G.S. 130A-6.
21. G.S. 153A-77(e).

Chapter 7

Funding the Consolidated Human Services Agency's Programs

Each appointed consolidated human services (CHS) board is responsible for helping the CHS director plan the proposed annual budget for the consolidated human services agency (CHSA).[1] To carry out this responsibility, CHS board members should understand the funding streams for the CHSA's programs and the basic steps in the agency's budgeting process. The CHSA may include multiple departments or functions that have separate funding streams, different requirements attached to that funding, and different administrative processes related to that funding at the state level, which can make budgeting and administration for the agency extremely complex. Where allowed by law, CHS directors sometimes combine funding from different sources to fund a single position that is involved with multiple services or programs across the agency.

Though a CHSA may include a variety of different county human services functions, this chapter focuses on the funding available for social services and public health, which are both included in most CHSAs in North Carolina at the time of this book's publication. Social services and public health financing is complicated by a complex interplay of federal, state, and county funding. The federal government plays a major role in financing many social services programs and specific public health programs. Those programs contribute many federal and state dollars to local economies, but they may also require the expenditure of substantial county funds. In some cases, the North Carolina General Assembly assigns responsibility to counties for a portion of the nonfederal cost of certain federally funded programs. In other cases, county expenditures are required as a condition of receiving other federal and state

This chapter incorporates material about social services funding and the budgeting process from Aimee N. Wall, *Social Services*, in County and Municipal Government in North Carolina 677–88 (Frayda S. Bluestein ed., UNC School of Government, 2d ed. 2014), and John L. Saxon, Social Services in North Carolina (UNC School of Government, 2009), 203–18.

funds. Additionally, counties may need to spend county funds to provide services and programs for which state and federal funds are either unavailable or insufficient.

The Budgeting Process for a Consolidated Human Services Agency

The Local Government Budget and Fiscal Control Act (LGBFCA)[2] governs the budgeting, expenditure, and accounting of all money received or spent by local government agencies, including consolidated human services agencies. Under the LGBFCA, local government agencies that are not independent units of local government or public authorities must have their budgeting, disbursing, and accounting done for them by the unit of local government of which they are a part (i.e., the county). Though the CHS director is responsible for administering funds allocated to the agency, the budget for a CHSA is part of the county budget, and the expenditure of money by a CHSA is subject to oversight by the county. State law requires that all county expenditures—including those made by a CHSA—be made in accordance with the LGBFCA.[3]

The CHS director is responsible, with the assistance of the CHS board, for planning the proposed budget for the CHSA.[4] Under the LGBFCA, the CHS director must submit the agency's proposed budget to the county budget officer no later than April 30 of each year (or an earlier date fixed by the county budget officer).[5]

The agency's proposed budget must include a request for appropriations for the coming fiscal year, an estimate of agency revenues for the coming year (including federal, state, and nonpublic funding), actual and estimated expenditures for each category of expenditure included in the county budget ordinance for the current and immediately preceding fiscal years, actual and estimated amounts realized for each source of revenue for the current and immediately preceding fiscal years, and any additional information requested by the budget officer.[6]

The LGBFCA requires the county budget officer to prepare a proposed budget for the county and submit it to the board of county commissioners (BOCC) by June 1 of each year.[7] The budget officer's proposed budget may increase, decrease, or revise the budget submitted by the CHS director without the approval or consent of the CHS director. After the proposed county budget is submitted, the BOCC must hold a public hearing on the proposed budget.[8] Following the hearing, but no later than July 1,[9] the BOCC must adopt a balanced[10] budget ordinance that accepts or modifies the budget officer's proposed budget; makes appropriations of county revenues for specified purposes, functions, activities, or objectives;[11] appropriates sufficient funds to pay the county's share of mandated public assistance and social services programs;[12] levies the county property tax for the coming fiscal year;[13] and includes the county's estimated revenues for the coming fiscal year.[14]

The Role of the CHS Board in Agency Funding

As described above, each appointed CHS board is responsible for helping the CHS director plan the proposed annual budget for the CHSA.[15] However, an appointed CHS board does not have the legal authority to approve or disapprove the county's human services budget, to determine the size of the budget, to levy the local taxes or provide the funding that will be used to provide human services programs, or to administer the county's human services budget.

An appointed CHS board should work with the CHS director, the county manager, the BOCC, other state and local government officials, and the community to assess whether adequate funding is available for the public health and social services programs that county residents need. The board's statutory duties include "advis[ing] local officials through the county manager" and "perform[ing] public relations and advocacy functions."[16] Among other things, this responsibility may include advocating for sufficient funding for the CHSA's programs and services.

Learning about the various funding streams for social services and public health programs—and other county human services programs—is an important part of serving as a member of the governing board for a CHSA. Understanding the limitations on funding will help board members assist the director in planning the agency budget and identify gaps in federal and state funding that need to be filled to meet the unique needs of their community.

Federal Funding for Social Services

All federal funding for social services comes with certain conditions attached, meaning that recipients of these funds must comply with certain legal requirements. Among other things, these legal requirements may specify who is eligible for assistance under a given program, what types of assistance and services may be provided, how much assistance may be provided, how long assistance may be provided, when confidential program information may be disclosed, and how much states (or, in North Carolina, state and local governments) must contribute to the cost of these programs.

Federal funding constitutes a significant portion of all social services expenditures in North Carolina. For state fiscal year 2024–2025, NCDHHS estimated that the federal government would fund 85.97 percent of total statewide costs for public assistance programs, program assistance administration, and services programs.[17] In that same budget estimate, counties were projected to provide 11.54 percent of total costs, while the state was projected to provide 2.49 percent of total costs.

Some federally funded public assistance programs, such as Food and Nutrition Services (FNS) and Medicaid, are known as *entitlement programs*, meaning that benefits must be provided to every person who applies and meets the program's eligibility requirements. Regardless of how many people qualify for benefits under an entitlement program, the federal government must provide funds sufficient to pay the federal share of benefits for all eligible individuals.

The mix of federal, state, and county funding varies for each entitlement program. In the FNS program, the federal government pays the full cost of the direct benefits but only part of the costs to administer the program.[18] For state fiscal year 2024–2025, NCDHHS estimated that federal funding would provide over two billion dollars in FNS benefits (100 percent of costs) and over 125 million dollars for FNS program administration (50 percent of costs), while counties would fund the remaining 50 percent of FNS program administration costs.[19] In the Medicaid program, the state has an open-ended obligation to provide funds sufficient to pay the nonfederal share of Medicaid-coverage costs for all eligible individuals.[20] While federal and state government bear the vast majority of Medicaid-related costs, counties do provide some funds to pay the nonfederal share of program administration costs. For state fiscal year 2024–2025, NCDHHS estimated that counties would provide over 129 million in Medicaid program administration funding (32.38 percent of costs) while the federal government would cover over 67 percent of administrative costs.[21]

In other programs, such as Work First, the Low Income Energy Assistance Program (LIEAP), and most service programs, the amount of federal funding is capped. Federal appropriations provide a fixed amount of funding, often called a *block grant*. In order to receive these funds, state and local governments must contribute either a specified percentage of "matching" funds or an amount representing a "maintenance of effort" tied to amounts expended or budgeted for the program in a designated prior period. The state must develop comprehensive state plans describing the proposed use of the federal block grant funds and related state and local funds. The General Assembly is responsible for approving the distribution of federal block grant funds to counties.

If the federal funds and the required state and local contributions are insufficient to provide benefits or services to everyone who is eligible for a particular program, the state or local government must either limit the number of people served by the program, limit the amount of benefits or the level of services provided, or provide additional state or local funding for the program. In some cases, the ability to limit eligibility, benefits, or services may be constrained by program requirements associated with federal funds.

State and County Funding for Social Services

The General Assembly has the authority to decide whether and how to divide the nonfederal share of costs for social services programs between the state and counties.[22] North Carolina generally requires counties to pay the bulk of the nonfederal share of administrative costs for public assistance programs, as well as a significant portion of the cost of social services provided to county residents.[23]

Every board of county commissioners is required to levy and collect taxes sufficient to meet its county's share of expenses for mandated social services programs.[24] If a county does not pay or arrange for payment of its full share of the costs, the state budget director is authorized to withhold from the county any state appropriations for public assistance and related administrative costs or to direct the secretary of revenue and the state controller to withhold specified tax revenues owed to the county. The state budget director must notify the chair of the board of commissioners of the proposed action prior to withholding any funds.[25]

The board of county commissioners has discretion as to how much county money (if any) to budget for *nonmandated* social services programs.[26]

In some instances, counties must fill a funding gap with county funds to fulfill a legal mandate that is unfunded or underfunded by state and federal funds. For example, state law requires county departments of social services to provide adult protective services, but there is very little state or federal funding available for such services. In order to fulfill the legal mandate to protect vulnerable adults, a board of county commissioners must appropriate county funds to support a county's provision of adult protective services. Likewise, federal and state funding are sometimes inadequate to support a sufficient number of social workers and attorneys to handle all the child welfare cases in a given county, in which case the county must "fill the gap" in services for these children with county funds.

Federal Funding for Public Health

The federal government advances public health in many ways, but one of its most significant roles in public health is providing funding. Federal funding is distributed via grants and contracts that often require recipients to comply with federal standards and policies in exchange for funds. In this way, the federal government shapes public health at every level, even when it is not directly involved in program administration or service delivery.

Examples of federal funding of state and local public health work in North Carolina include Epidemiology and Laboratory Capacity cooperative agreement funds provided by the United States Centers for Disease Control and Prevention (CDC); Medicaid funding that originates from the Centers for Medicare & Medicaid Services; Title X family planning services funding from the Office of Population Affairs; and funding for a diversity of nutrition services programs that are administered by the United States Department of Agriculture.

Historically, public health funding has followed a boom-and-bust cycle in which public health crises trigger a surge in investments, only for those funds to be reduced again once the immediate threat has subsided. The COVID-19 pandemic provides a recent example of this cycle in public health funding. Before the pandemic began in 2019, investments in public health systems across the United States had reached a relative low. During the pandemic, an influx of emergency funding was distributed to public health agencies nationwide to support rapid capacity building and bolster public health infrastructure.[27]

On May 11, 2023, the national COVID-19 public health emergency declared under the Public Health Service Act came to an end,[28] and that June, the Fiscal Responsibility Act of 2023 was signed into law. Among other things, the Fiscal Responsibility Act of 2023 rescinded approximately $28 billion in unobligated COVID-19 funds that had been disbursed to public health agencies during the pandemic.[29] In its summary of the impact of the Fiscal Responsibility Act of 2023 on public health, the Congressional Research Service noted that "Several [U.S. Public Health Service] agencies and funded [state, local, tribal, and territorial] health agencies are likely to see a funding 'cliff' as pandemic supplemental funding ends."[30]

Another significant challenge for public health is that funders of governmental public health often operate independently, rather than through a single, coordinated effort. For example, although the CDC is the nation's lead public health agency, neither the CDC nor any other specific department, agency, or office of the federal government acts as the primary coordinator of funding for state, territorial, local, and tribal public health systems. It is common for funders, and even different grants or contracts offered by the same funder, to have divergent standards for data collection, reporting timelines, and performance measures. Many federal funding sources are also program- or service-specific and place strict, detailed limits on when, where, how, and by whom the funds may be expended.

Navigating the complex patchwork of public health funding is no small feat and often requires significant resources and staff time from the state and local public health agencies that receive these funds. The practice of allocating funding for specific activities with detailed expenditure restrictions—rather than distributing funds in a more general, flexible manner—can also make it challenging for public health agencies to deliver services and run programs that are tailored and responsive to the unique needs of their communities.

State and County Funding for Public Health

When local health departments are the recipients of federal dollars, the funds typically flow first to NCDHHS, specifically to the Division of Public Health (DPH) or the Division of Child and Family Well-Being (DCFW), and are then distributed to the local agencies. The North Carolina General Assembly also appropriates funding through the state budget and other legislation to support the work of local public health.

The distribution of funds by the state to local health departments is memorialized in the Consolidated Agreement, which is an annual "master" contract that NCDHHS enters into with each local health department that receives funding distributed by NCDHHS.[31] The Consolidated Agreement sets out general terms and conditions that NCDHHS and local health departments must abide by, while the granular details of how various funds must be used are set out in Agreement Addenda to the Consolidated Agreement (often referred to as "AAs"). Each Agreement Addendum outlines the funding amount, scope of work, deliverables, performance measures, and funding guidelines or restrictions for a specific public health program or activity, such as family planning services or communicable disease control.[32] Many of the details of the Agreement Addenda reflect requirements and restrictions established by the North Carolina General Assembly or the federal agency that provided the funding.

Dozens of Agreement Addenda are signed alongside the Consolidated Agreement every year. There are several so-called "legacy" Agreement Addenda, which address public health activities that have historically been funded consistently from year to year (though the amount of funding may change over time). Some Agreement Addenda may relate to new funding streams, such as time-limited funding provided by a federal partner to help local public health agencies respond to an emerging health threat. Other Agreement Addenda outline the terms for funding that has narrow eligibility criteria and is therefore only available to certain local health departments, such as a financial support intended solely for local public health agencies serving rural communities. This means that the total number of Agreement Addenda differs from year to year and across local health departments.[33]

In late summer and early fall, NCDHHS and local health departments come together to begin reviewing the Agreement Addenda for the next fiscal year. Agreement Addenda are typically finalized near the start of the next calendar year, which allows local health departments to advise their counties of the expected amount of federal and state support for local public health as counties begin their own budget processes in the spring.[34]

Once the Consolidated Agreement and Agreement Addenda are signed, county budgets are finalized, and a new fiscal year begins, local health departments access the funds described in the Agreement Addenda for that fiscal year by submitting reports and drawing down funds from the state's electronic "Aid to Counties" system. Failure to comply with the terms and conditions of the Consolidated Agreement or Agreement Addenda can result in a local health department's funding being limited or terminated.

In addition to federal and state dollars, local health departments receive funding through county appropriations. County financial support for local public health varies significantly across the state. According to a 2022 report by the North Carolina Institute of Medicine, in fiscal year 2019 the portion of total annual local health department expenditures that were supported by county appropriations ranged from just 7 percent for some departments to as much as 71 percent for others.[35]

Local health departments may also generate their own fee-based revenue for certain services (subject to restrictions set out in state and federal laws). The authority of a CHS board to approve a fee schedule for the public health services rendered by a CHSA is described further in Chapter 18. Local health departments may also receive reimbursements from Medicaid, Medicare, and other insurers for the health services that they provide.

Funding Estimates for County Social Services and Public Health Programs

Before February 15 of each year, NCDHHS is required to notify the county social services director, the local health director, the county manager, and the BOCC of the amount of state and federal funds estimated to be available to the county for public assistance, social services, and public health programs and related administrative costs for the next fiscal year.[36]

For public health, this requirement is met by NCDHHS's release of finalized Agreement Addenda (discussed in the previous section) to local health departments near the start of each calendar year. Local social services agencies receive an annual written notice from the Division of Social Services within NCDHHS. In contrast to public health funding, federal funding for social services regularly requires counties to match a certain percentage of federal dollars received. The notice to local social services agencies typically states the percentage of county financial participation expected for each social services program.

Periodically, the state revises these estimates to reflect new state-budget figures and actions taken by the General Assembly, Congress, and federal agencies. Accordingly, the budgeting process for county social services and public health programs involves some degree of uncertainty regarding the exact amount of county funds that will be needed to fund a county's share of the cost of mandated programs.

County budgets for social services and public health may estimate expenditures that are higher than the amounts indicated in NCDHHS's estimates. These higher county-level estimates are often due to needing to fill a funding gap, as described above. For example, federal and state funds available to a county for child protective services, along with NCDHHS's estimate of the county's match, may be insufficient to hire the number of social workers necessary to carry out the county's legal responsibility to provide protective services to abused and neglected children. In other cases, counties may need to spend additional funds to comply with state mandates that are not accompanied by state funding.

Additionally, counties may want to provide nonmandated social services or public health programs to meet unique local needs. Those optional, nonmandated programs and services are not reflected in NCDHHS's budget estimates and must be supported by county or other funds if federal and state funding is not available.

Notes

1. Chapter 153A, Section 77(d)(7) of the North Carolina General Statutes (hereinafter G.S.).
2. G.S. 159, art. 3.
3. *See generally* G.S. 159, §§ 8(a), 28.
4. G.S. 153A, § 77(d)(7), 77(e)(5).
5. G.S. 159-10. In counties having the manager form of government, the county manager is the statutory budget officer. *See* G.S. 159-9. However, in some counties, a budget director who reports to the manager (or occasionally to the finance officer) actually performs most of the day-to-day duties of the budget officer.
6. G.S. 159-10.
7. G.S. 159-11(b).
8. G.S. 159-12(b).
9. G.S. 159-13(a).
10. G.S. 159-8(a).
11. G.S. 159-7(b)(2).
12. G.S. 108A-90.
13. G.S. 159, § 7(b)(2), 13(c).
14. G.S. 159, § 13(a), 13(b)(7).
15. G.S. 108A-9(3).
16. G.S. 153A-77(d).
17. *See* N.C. Dep't of Health & Hum. Servs., *County Budget Estimates State Totals—State Fiscal Year 2024–2025*, https://www.ncdhhs.gov/divisions/social-services/county-staff-information/budget-information/dss-budget-estimates (under the heading County Budget Estimates 2024–2025, select Budget Estimates State Totals to access PDF).
18. *See generally* 7 U.S.C. §§ 2014(a), 2025.
19. *See* N.C. Dep't of Health & Hum. Servs., *supra* note 17.
20. *See generally* 42 U.S.C. § 1396b.
21. *See* N.C. Dep't of Health & Hum. Servs., *supra* note 17.
22. G.S. 108A-87.
23. *See* N.C. Dep't of Health & Hum. Servs., *supra* note 17.
24. G.S. 108A-90.
25. G.S. 108A-93.
26. *See* G.S. 153A-255 (giving each county the authority to "undertake, sponsor, organize, engage in, and support . . . social service programs intended to further the health, welfare, education, employment, safety, comfort, and convenience of its citizens"). For more information on the scope of this authority, see Kristi Nickodem, *County Legal Authority to Fund Non-Mandated Social Services Programs*, Coates' Canons: NC Loc. Gov't L. (blog) (June 6, 2023), https://canons.sog.unc.edu/2023/06/county-legal-authority-to-fund-non-mandated-social-services-programs/.
27. Michelle R. Smith, Lauren Weber, & Hannah Recht, *Public Health Experts Worry About Boom-Bust Cycle of Support*, KFF Health News, April 19, 2021, https://perma.cc/94AE-T692.
28. U.S. Dep't of Health & Hum. Servs., "COVID-19 Public Health Emergency," https://www.hhs.gov/coronavirus/covid-19-public-health-emergency/index.html.
29. U.S. House Budget Comm., *H.R. 3746, the Fiscal Responsibility Act of 2023: Frequently Asked Questions*, House Budget Committee (May 31, 2023), https://perma.cc/9LAN-JM2S.
30. Cong. Res. Serv., *Public Health Funding and the Fiscal Responsibility Act of 2023*, July 31, 2023, https://perma.cc/QP6W-JRLC.

31. Title 10A, Chapter 48B, Section .0102(2) of the North Carolina Administrative Code. *See, e.g., FY 2024 Consolidated Agreement* at https://perma.cc/67JL-PRWE.
32. An example of a family planning services addendum, *Division of Public Health Agreement Addendum FY 24–25,* is available online at https://perma.cc/5VJR-EY6H.
33. NCDHHS, Div. of Pub. Health, *Introduction to Consolidated Agreement & Agreement Addenda: New Health Directors' Orientation,* January 21, 2024. A copy of the slides from this presentation is on file with author Kirsten E. Leloudis.
34. *Id.*
35. N.C. Inst. of Med., *Foundations of Health and Opportunity: Investing in the Future of Local Public Health in North Carolina* 19 (Dec. 2022), https://nciom.org/wp-content/uploads/2022/12/FLPH-Final-Report_12.30.2022.pdf.
36. G.S. 108A-88.

Chapter 8

The Role of the Board of County Commissioners

Every county board of commissioners has some involvement and responsibilities with respect to a county's consolidated human services agency (CHSA). Each board of county commissioners (BOCC) is responsible for determining (1) the type of agency that will provide social services and public health in the county and (2) the type of governing board for that agency (or agencies). These options are described in Chapter 1, as well as in Appendixes A and B of this book.

At the time of this book's publication, thirty-four counties have CHSAs. The BOCC serves directly as the governing board for a CHSA in eighteen of those counties. In the other sixteen counties, the BOCC has appointed a consolidated human services (CHS) board to govern the county's CHSA. In those counties with an appointed CHS board, one of the commissioners must also serve on the appointed CHS board.

No matter what governance structure is in place, every BOCC has a number of important duties related to social services and public health, which are discussed later in this chapter.

Direct County Commissioner Governance of County Social Services Agencies

A BOCC can directly assume the powers and duties of a governing board appointed by the BOCC or acting under and pursuant to the authority of the BOCC.[1] In the human services arena, these boards include a county board of health, county board of social services, or CHS board. A BOCC cannot abolish and assume the powers and duties of a board for a multicounty agency, such as a regional board of social services or a district board of health.[2]

If a BOCC plans to serve as the governing board for a county department of social services, a county health department, or a CHSA, it must first hold a public hearing on the matter.[3] The BOCC must give thirty days' notice of the public hearing in a newspaper having general circulation in the county, and it must adhere to any notice requirements that would generally apply to official meetings of the board under North Carolina's open meetings law.[4] Following the public hearing, the BOCC may adopt a resolution "assuming and conferring upon the board of county commissioners all powers, responsibilities and duties" of the applicable governing board(s).[5]

If a board of commissioners decides to assume the powers and duties of a CHS board in a county where the CHSA includes public health, the commissioners must appoint an advisory committee for public health.[6] The differences between an advisory committee and an appointed CHS board are discussed in more depth in Chapter 2. The advisory committee must include members representing all of the required categories of membership for a county board of health, which are found in Chapter 130A, Section 35 of the North Carolina General Statutes.[7]

There is no corresponding legal requirement to create a social services advisory committee when the board of commissioners assumes the powers and duties of a social services governing board. However, a board of commissioners has the *option* of appointing an advisory committee for social services, though doing so is not required by law.[8]

A board of commissioners that abolishes the governing board for social services or public health takes on all the legal responsibilities of those boards, including the responsibilities described in Chapter 5 (and explained in more detail in Chapters 13–20). In a county with a CHSA governed by the board of commissioners, the county manager is responsible for appointing and dismissing the consolidated human services director, though the board of commissioners must provide "advice and consent" regarding these decisions.[9]

Serving Ex Officio on an Appointed CHS Board

In counties with an *appointed* CHS board, the board of commissioners is required to appoint a county commissioner to the board.[10] When the board of commissioners appoints one of its members to serve on the county's CHS board, it is an *ex officio* appointment.[11] This means that a county commissioner is considered to be serving on the CHS board as a part of the commissioner's duties as a commissioner and not as a separate public office. Accordingly, the county commissioner's ex officio service on the CHS board does not "count" as a separate public office for purposes of the multiple-office-holding limit described in Chapter 4.

A county commissioner who serves ex officio on an appointed CHS board may only serve on the board for as long as the member is a county commissioner.[12]

Decisions Related to CHSA Employees and the State Human Resources Act

When a county creates a new CHSA, public health or social services employees who were previously subject to the State Human Resources Act (SHRA) are removed from the coverage of the SHRA and instead become solely subject to county personnel policies, unless the board of commissioners affirmatively elects to keep them under the SHRA.[13] If the resolution creating the CHSA is silent, then by default, all CHSA employees become subject solely to county personnel policies and are removed from SHRA coverage. The board of commissioners can make this decision to remove CHSA employees from SHRA coverage when the CHSA is first created or at a later date (even months or years after the CSHA was created). The vast majority of North Carolina counties with CHSAs have opted *not* to keep the agency's employees subject to the SHRA.

Chapter 2 discusses this decision in more detail, including the federal merit personnel standards that counties must apply with respect to CHSA employees. For a more in-depth discussion of the issues around this decision, please see Kristi Nickodem, *Personnel Decisions for North Carolina's Consolidated Human Services Agencies*, available on the UNC School of Government's website.[14]

Responsibilities of all Boards of Commissioners Regarding the CHSA, Social Services, and Public Health

Even in counties where the board of commissioners does *not* serve directly as the governing board for the county's human services agency, the commissioners have a number of duties regarding the agency, its board, and its programs.

Duties Related to CHSA Funding, Fees, and Compensation

- A primary role of the board of commissioners is ensuring the adequacy of funds for social services, public health, and other human services programs in the county budget. That role is discussed in Chapter 7.
- The board of commissioners has authority to establish per diem rates and a policy for subsistence and travel reimbursement for CHS board members.[15] If the board of commissioners establishes a per diem rate and a policy for reimbursement, it will also need to include funds in the county budget to cover such expenses.
- If a CHS board is serving as the governing board for social services, state law authorizes the board to enter into contracts under which the CHSA will voluntarily render services in exchange for a fee (see Chapter 15).[16] Any fees charged by the board using this contract authority must be based on a plan that is developed by the CHS director (or the social services director, as the CHS director's designee) and approved by

the board of commissioners (and by the appointed CHS board, if the commissioners are not directly serving as the governing board for the CHSA). An appointed CHS board is required to make an annual report to the county commissioners regarding receipt of such fees.

- If a CHS board is serving as the governing board for public health, state law authorizes the board to set fees that are charged by the CHSA for certain public health services. The CHS board must base its fees on a plan proposed by the human services director and any fees adopted by the CHS board must also be approved by the board of commissioners (if the commissioners are not directly serving as the governing board for the CHSA).[17] There are limits on the type of fees that a CHS board may adopt and a local health department may charge for public health services. These limitations are discussed further in Chapter 18.
- The board of commissioners is responsible for approving the compensation of all county employees, including the CHS director and CHSA staff.[18]

Duties Related to Social Services Programs and Administration

- Through its power over the county budget, the board of commissioners has authority to determine what *nonmandated* public assistance programs or services the county will provide. State law requires counties to participate in a number of social services programs but also authorizes counties to "undertake, sponsor, organize, engage in, and support other social service programs intended to further the health, welfare, education, employment, safety, comfort, and convenience of its citizens."[19] Many counties, for example, provide some form of general assistance to help address emergency needs of people not eligible for other benefits.
- State law allows the board of commissioners, with the approval of the CHS board (if the county has an appointed CHS board), to appoint an attorney as the "special county attorney for social service matters" or to designate a county attorney to serve in that role.[20] A county is not required to have a special county attorney for social services, but if it does, that attorney's duties include serving as legal adviser to the board of commissioners, the director of social services, and the CHS board regarding social services matters.[21] The board of commissioners is also responsible for determining the attorney's compensation.[22]
- State law requires counties to operate the State-County Special Assistance program, which is designed to assist needy aged or disabled persons in paying for room and board in adult care homes, special-care units, and in-home living arrangements. The board of commissioners has authority to determine whether this program will also provide

financial assistance for a different category of "certain disabled persons" who are in private living arrangements but may not otherwise qualify for State-County Special Assistance under the eligibility requirements set forth in state law.[23]

- Each county must administer a child support enforcement program.[24] Most county child support enforcement programs are operated by a county department of social services or CHSA. However, each board of commissioners has the option of creating an independent county department for child support enforcement, locating the program in another county department or office, or contracting with a private entity or another county to operate the program.[25]

Duties Related to the Work First Program

State law allows each board of commissioners to indicate to the North Carolina Department of Health and Human Services (NCDHHS) whether the county wants to be a "standard" or "electing" county for purposes of the Work First program (see Chapter 14 for a description of Work First).[26] In a standard county, NCDHHS is responsible for the development and supervision of the Work First program, which is administered by the county department of social services (or CHSA, if the CHSA includes social services).[27] In an electing county, the board of commissioners is directly responsible for the development, administration, and implementation of the Work First program.[28] A board's request to become an electing county must be supported by a three-fifths vote of the commissioners. The General Assembly designates each county as either a standard county or an electing county based on recommendations from NCDHHS.[29]

An electing county has more authority to set eligibility criteria, payment levels, and other program features that the state sets for standard counties.[30] In an electing county, the board of commissioners is responsible for

- establishing outcome and performance goals,
- establishing eligibility criteria,
- entering into Mutual Responsibility Agreements with Work First recipients,
- ensuring that services and resources are available to help participants comply with the agreements,
- monitoring compliance with those agreements,
- ensuring that participants engage in the required hours of work activities,
- developing and submitting to NCDHHS a biennial county Work First plan,
- developing and implementing an appeals process for the county's Work First program, and
- complying with all state and federal laws regarding the Work First program.[31]

A board of commissioners may delegate most of these responsibilities to other public or private entities, but the board ultimately remains accountable for all of them.[32]

In electing counties, the board of commissioners must appoint a committee of individuals to identify the needs of the population to be served by Work First and to assist in developing the county's Work First plan to respond to those needs.[33] The committee membership must include, but is not limited to, individuals from the county board of social services (which may be a CHS board), the board of the area mental health authority, the local board of health, the local school systems, the business community, the board of commissioners, and community-based organizations representative of the population served by the Work First program.[34]

NCDHHS policy also requires standard counties to establish a committee for the biennial Work First planning process and establishes membership requirements for that committee.[35]

Duties Related to Public Health Programs and Administration

As with social services, the board of commissioners can use its authority to set the county budget to inform which nonmandated public health services the county will provide (if any). State law authorizes a county to "provide for and regulate the public health pursuant to Chapter 130A of the General Statutes and any other law authorizing local public health activities."[36]

State law authorizes a board of commissioners to establish sanitary districts and mosquito control districts as necessary to protect and promote the public health.[37]

A board of commissioners may also adopt ordinances to address "conditions detrimental to the health, safety, or welfare" and may abate public health nuisances.[38] However, any such ordinance does not apply to municipalities within the county and does not impede upon a local board of health's authority to adopt local rules to protect and promote the public health.[39] Chapter 19 addresses the relationship between the board of commissioners' ordinance authority and the local board of health's authority to engage in public health rulemaking.

Notes

1. Chapter 153A, Section 77(a) of the North Carolina General Statutes (hereinafter G.S.). Exceptions to this rule are stated in G.S. 153A-76.
2. G.S. 153A-76.
3. G.S. 153A-77(a).
4. *Id.*; *see generally* G.S. 143-318.12 (public notice requirements for official meetings of public bodies).
5. G.S. 153A-77(a).
6. The requirement for a health advisory committee applies only to counties that abolish their health boards after January 1, 2012. This amounts to an exception for Mecklenburg County, which abolished its health boards (a county board of health, and subsequently a CHS board) before that date.
7. This means that the advisory committee must include one physician licensed to practice medicine in North Carolina, one licensed dentist, one licensed optometrist, one licensed veterinarian, one registered nurse, one licensed pharmacist, one county commissioner, one professional engineer, and three representatives of the general public. All members must be residents of the county where the agency is located.
8. *See* G.S. 153A-77(a).
9. G.S. 153A-77(e). The board of commissioners' decision to consent (or to decline to consent) to the county manager's appointment or dismissal of a CHS director should occur through a vote of the board.
10. G.S. 153A-77(c).
11. G.S. 128-1.2. Ex-officio appointments are discussed in greater detail in A. Fleming Bell, II, Ethics, Conflicts, and Offices: A Guide for Local Officials (UNC School of Government, 2d ed. 2010).
12. G.S. 153A-77(c).
13. G.S. 153A-77(d).
14. Kristi Nickodem, *Personnel Decisions for North Carolina's Consolidated Human Services Agencies*, Soc. Servs. L. Bull. No. 49 (UNC School of Government, Dec. 2021), https://www.sog.unc.edu/sites/default/files/reports/SSLB%2049.pdf.
15. G.S. 153A-77(c).
16. G.S. 108A-10; G.S. 153A-77(d).
17. G.S. 130A-39(g); G.S. 153A-77(d)(1).
18. G.S. 153A-92.
19. G.S. 153A-255.
20. G.S. 108A-16.
21. G.S. 108A-18.
22. G.S. 108A-17.
23. Per G.S. 108A-42, a "Certain Disabled" person is a person in a private living arrangement who is at least eighteen but younger than sixty-five, "having a physical or mental impairment which substantially precludes him from obtaining gainful employment, which impairment appears reasonably certain to continue without substantial improvement throughout his lifetime." By contrast, eligibility for State-County Special Assistance requires that the recipient meet certain income criteria, along with being (1) sixty-five years of age or older or (2) between the ages of eighteen and sixty-five and *permanently and totally* disabled or legally blind. G.S. 108A-41. Eligibility requirements for the "Certain Disabled Program" are set forth at Title 10A, Chapter 71P, Section .0805 of the North Carolina Administrative Code.

24. G.S. 110-141.
25. *Id.* Until 2010, about one-third of North Carolina counties chose to have the state operate their child support enforcement programs. That option was eliminated effective July 1, 2010, and now all counties must have their own programs. S.L. 2009-451, § 10.46A(a).
26. G.S. 108A-27(e). When notifying NCDHHS of the county's desire to be designated as electing or standard, the county must submit documentation demonstrating that three-fifths of its county commissioners support the desired designation.
27. G.S. 108A-27.8(a).
28. G.S. 108A-27(f).
29. G.S. 108A, § 27.2(12)–(14).
30. *Compare* G.S. 108A-27.3 (duties of electing counties) *with* G.S. 108A-27.6 (duties of standard counties).
31. G.S. 108A-27.3.
32. G.S. 108A-27.3(b).
33. G.S. 108A-27.3(c).
34. *Id.*
35. *See* N.C. Dep't of Health & Hum. Servs., *The Planning Process for Work First, in* Work First Manual, Policy § 003 (July 1, 2011), https://policies.ncdhhs.gov/wp-content/uploads/wf003.pdf.
36. G.S. 153A-247.
37. G.S. 130A, art. 2, pt. 2 (sanitary district); G.S. 130A, art. 12, pt. 2 (mosquito control district). A sanitary district provides water and wastewater services to communities within its jurisdiction. A mosquito control district is responsible for managing populations of mosquitos and other arthropods, which can be vectors for disease.
38. G.S. 153A, §§ 121, 140.
39. G.S. 153A, §§ 121(c), 122. The governing board of a municipality may, however, adopt a resolution permitting a county ordinance to be applicable within the municipality.

Chapter 9

Ethical Standards and Legal Prohibitions for Consolidated Human Services Board Members

As used in this book, the term *ethics* refers broadly to standards of behavior that the public expects from people who hold public office.[1] When discussing ethical standards related to board service, it is important to distinguish between conduct that is legally prohibited and conduct that merely falls short of ethical norms.

Some conduct by consolidated human services (CHS) board members may violate state or federal laws. That conduct is both *unethical* and *illegal*. Other conduct by board members may violate ethical norms but not actually violate any laws. In other words, that behavior would be *unethical* but not *illegal*.

Board members should not engage in unethical behavior, regardless of whether the behavior violates the law. For purposes of clarity, this chapter will attempt to distinguish between ethical expectations and legal prohibitions.

Ethical Expectations for Public Officials

Basic Standards of Ethical Behavior

The general public expects all public officials, including CHS board members, to act ethically in their public and private lives. Based on basic ethical principles, CHS board members should

- devote adequate time and energy to their board responsibilities;
- make fair, impartial decisions;
- act in the public interest and for the public good;
- not use their offices to benefit themselves, their family members, or their friends;
- exercise sound judgment and discretion in connection with their official duties; and
- act honestly, courteously, and collaboratively when working together as a board.

Conflicts of Interest

The term *conflict of interest* generally refers to a conflict between an individual's personal, family, business, professional, or financial interests and that individual's role, responsibilities, duties, or actions as a public official.[2] Put another way, a conflict of interest occurs when an individual's private interests interfere (or may interfere) with that individual's independence, decision-making, and judgment as a board member.

CHS board members should act in the public interest—not for their own personal benefit—when serving as public officials. They should take reasonable actions to avoid actual and potential conflicts between their personal interests and public responsibilities. When possible, board members should avoid even the *appearance* of acting unethically, inappropriately, or for their own benefit.[3] Avoiding conflicts of interest helps the board maintain the public's trust.

If the conflict between an individual's personal interests and professional responsibilities as a social services board member is significant and unavoidable, it may constitute good cause for requesting the board member's resignation or, if the board member fails to resign, removing the member from the board. More information about the removal of board members may be found in Chapter 4.

In some cases, making or administering certain contracts (or attempting to influence someone who does) when a board member has a conflict of interest is not only unethical but also illegal. The laws related to conflicts of interest in contracting will be discussed later in this chapter.

Political Activities

CHS board members should not use their positions on the board to promote political candidates, parties, or platforms. The CHS board should be seen by the public as a nonpartisan, politically neutral entity. When board members use their positions on the board to promote political parties or candidates, it can cause members of the public to lose trust in the board's motives and impartiality.

Legally Prohibited Conduct

Involvement with Contracts for Personal Benefit

Chapter 14, Section 234 of the North Carolina General Statutes (hereinafter G.S.) addresses conflicts of interest related to contracts. Specifically, this law prohibits public officials, including county social services board members, from the following actions.

- **Prohibition 1:** A board member is prohibited from receiving a direct benefit from a public contract if the board member is involved in *making or administering* the contract.[4]

- **Prohibition 2:** A board member is prohibited from *influencing or attempting to influence* any person involved in making or administering a public contract if the board member will derive a direct benefit from the contract.[5]
- **Prohibition 3:** A board member is prohibited from soliciting or receiving "any gift, favor, reward, service, or promise of reward, including a promise of future employment, in exchange for *recommending, influencing, or attempting to influence* the award of a contract" by the county.[6]

Violating any one of these conflict-of-interest provisions in G.S. 14-234 is a criminal offense (a Class 1 misdemeanor).[7] Moreover, contracts made in violation of the statute are void.[8]

What Is a "Direct Benefit"?

A board member directly benefits from a public contract if the board member or the board member's spouse "(i) has more than a ten percent (10%) ownership or other interest in an entity that is a party to the contract; (ii) derives any income or commission directly from the contract; or (iii) acquires property under the contract."[9]

This means that Prohibitions 1 and 2 relate not only to contracts that may benefit the board member, but also to contracts that may benefit the board member's spouse.

What Does It Mean to "Make or Administer" a Contract?

A public official who "participates in the development of specifications or terms or in the preparation or award of the contract" or who is a member of a board that takes action with respect to the contract (regardless of whether the official participates in the action) is involved in *making* a contract.[10] A public official who "oversees the performance of [a] contract or has authority to make decisions regarding the contract or to interpret the contract" is involved in *administering* a contract.[11]

Appointed CHS boards have no general legal authority to make or administer contracts involving the consolidated human services agency, so they are rarely involved in making or administering public contracts. As a result, Prohibition 1 (described earlier) will rarely apply to appointed CHS board members. It is more common for board members to run afoul of Prohibition 2 or 3, which involve improperly influencing someone else (such as the CHS director or a county commissioner) who is involved in making or administering a contract.

Are There Any Exceptions to These Prohibitions Around Contracts?

There are a number of exceptions to Prohibition 1, in which a board member is prohibited from deriving a direct benefit from a contract that the board member is involved in making or administering.[12]

For example, Prohibition 1 does not apply to an employment relationship between the consolidated human services agency and the spouse of a CHS board member if the board member

1. does not participate in deliberating or voting with respect to the making or administering of the contract and
2. does not attempt to influence any other person (such as the CHS director) who is involved in making or administering the contract.[13]

Prohibition 1 also does not apply to a contract involving payment to a CHS board member or the board member's spouse for services, facilities, or supplies furnished directly to "needy" individuals under any federal or state public assistance program if

1. the program is open generally to all providers of services on a nondiscriminatory basis;
2. neither the consolidated human services agency nor its agents or employees have any control over the selection of participating providers by beneficiaries of the program;
3. the payment for services, facilities, or supplies is in the same amount as would be paid to any other participating provider;
4. the board member does not participate in approving the payment;
5. the board member does not deliberate or vote on the contract; and
6. the board member does not attempt to influence any other person (such as the CHS director or social services director) who is involved in making or administering the contract.[14]

There is also a "small jurisdiction" exception to Prohibition 1 for contracts benefitting some individuals on the CHS board. Specifically, this exception applies to a board member who is a physician, pharmacist, dentist, optometrist, veterinarian, or nurse serving on a governing board for social services or public health in a county where there is no village, town, or city with a population of more than 20,000 people.[15] If a contract provides a direct benefit to a board member who fits that description, the board may still make or administer the contract so long as

1. the contract (or series of contracts) "is approved by specific resolution of the [board] adopted in an open and public meeting, and recorded in its minutes";
2. the amount of the contract "does not exceed twenty thousand dollars ($20,000) for medically related services [or] sixty thousand dollars ($60,000) for other goods or services within a 12-month period";
3. the board member entering into the contract does not participate in any way or vote;
4. the total annual amount of contracts with the board member is "specifically noted in the audited annual financial statement of the village, town, city, or county"; and

5. the board posts "in a conspicuous place in its village, town, or city hall, or courthouse" (e.g., the door of its regular meeting room), "a list of all such officials with whom such contracts have been made," briefly describing the subject matter of the contracts and showing their total amounts (covering the preceding twelve months and updated at least quarterly).[16]

This exception recognizes the reality that in some less populated counties, a medical or dental professional serving on the governing board for social services or public health may be the only person available (or one of few) in the county to provide certain necessary services.

Key Takeaways

Learning about the prohibitions in G.S. 14-234 and the exceptions to those prohibitions can feel confusing. Here are some key takeaways:

- Board members should never, under any circumstances, attempt to influence the CHS director or any other public official or employee involved in making or administering a contract if the board member or board member's spouse will receive a direct benefit from the contract.
- Board members should never, under any circumstances, attempt to influence the CHS director or any other public official or employee involved in making or administering a contract in exchange for any gift, favor, reward, service, or promise of reward (regardless of whether the board member receives any direct benefit under the contract).
- If a board member is involved in any way in making decisions about a contract or overseeing the performance of a contract, and the board member knows that the contract may provide a benefit to the board member or the board member's spouse, then the board member should take a step back and consult with the county attorney prior to taking any action with respect to the contract. The county attorney or other legal counsel will be able to help determine whether the board member's involvement with the contract is permitted under one of the exceptions in the law.

Accepting Gifts and Favors

Another North Carolina statute, G.S. 133-32, makes it a Class 1 misdemeanor for certain public officials and government employees to willfully receive or accept a gift or favor from a contractor, subcontractor, or supplier who has a contract with a governmental agency, has performed under such a contract within the past year, or anticipates bidding on one in the future.[17] Specifically, this prohibition on receiving or accepting gifts or favors applies to any CHS board member, CHS director, or consolidated human services agency employee who is involved in (1) preparing plans, specifications, or estimates for public contracts; (2) awarding or administering public contracts; or (3) inspecting or supervising construction.[18]

This statute does not prohibit public officials or government employees from receiving customary gifts or favors from friends and family members, so long as it is clear that the gifts are motivated by preexisting friendships or familial relationships rather than by a desire to do business with a government agency.[19] Likewise, the statute contains exceptions for honorariums, advertising items of nominal value, meals at banquets, donations to professional organizations to defray meeting expenses, and participation in functions at meetings of professional organizations that are available to all attending organization members.[20]

Other Legally Prohibited Conduct

Willful Failure to Discharge Board Member Duties

If a CHS board member willfully neglects or refuses to discharge the duties of the office to which the board member was elected or appointed, the board member can be charged with a Class 1 misdemeanor as a criminal offense.[21] Under some circumstances, the court may remove the board member from public office as part of the sentence for the offense.

Improper Influence Regarding Hiring and Promotion of CHSA Employees

As described earlier in this chapter, a CHS board member is legally prohibited from influencing or attempting to influence the CHS director (or any other leader within the consolidated agency) to hire or promote the board member's spouse.[22] It is also unethical for a CHS board member to attempt to influence the CHS director to hire, promote, or provide preferential treatment to *any* family member or friend of the board member.[23]

State law does not prohibit the CHS director—or any leader within the CHSA—from hiring a qualified applicant merely because the person is related to a CHS board member. Likewise, an individual is not prohibited from serving on the CHS board merely because a spouse or other relative is employed by the county's consolidated human services agency. Being related to a consolidated agency employee or applicant for employment, in itself, does not create an ethical conflict for a board member. Rather, ethical conflicts are created when board members use their positions on the board to influence or coerce agency leaders to make certain decisions around hiring or promotions.

Board members should also be aware that under State Human Resources Commission rules, the CHS director is prohibited from hiring members of the director's immediate family (spouse, parents, siblings, children, grandparents, or grandchildren) to be employed by the consolidated human services agency.[24]

Improper Use or Disclosure of Confidential Information

If a consolidated human services agency includes social services, state law allows CHS board members to examine certain records of persons who have applied for or are receiving public assistance or social services.[25] This topic is discussed in more detail in Chapter 15. It is unethical and illegal for a CHS board member to use or disclose any information regarding persons who have applied for or are receiving public assistance or social services for any purpose other than discharging the board's responsibilities with respect to administering public assistance and social services programs.[26] Improper use or disclosure of confidential information may violate both state and federal law.

Likewise, state law requires county employee personnel information to be kept confidential, including information regarding job applicants.[27] This means that, except in performance of their board duties, CHS board members should not use or disclose information about a CHS director's application, selection, performance, promotions, demotions, transfers, suspension, other disciplinary actions, evaluations, leave, compensation, or dismissal.[28] Only certain pieces of information from the director's personnel file are a matter of public record, as described in Chapter 11. A public official or employee who knowingly, willfully, and with malice permits any person to have access to county employee personnel-file information in violation of G.S. 153A-98 is guilty of a Class 3 misdemeanor.[29]

Another state statute, G.S. 14-234.1, prohibits board members from using nonpublic information that they learn through board service for purposes of financially benefiting themselves or others. Specifically, this statute makes it a Class 1 misdemeanor for a board member to acquire a pecuniary interest or gain a pecuniary benefit (or intentionally aid someone else in doing so) if the board member is

1. acting in anticipation of the board member's official action as a board member or by the county DSS, and the pecuniary interest or benefit may be affected by this official action; or
2. relying on nonpublic information that the board member obtained in the member's official capacity, and the pecuniary interest or benefit may be affected by that nonpublic information.

Prohibited Participation in Social Services Programs

If a consolidated agency includes social services, there are a couple of unique conflicts of interest related to public assistance and social services that may limit an individual's ability to serve on the CHS board. If one of these conflicts arises after an individual has already been appointed to the board, and the board member refuses to resign or take action to resolve the conflict, it could serve as grounds for removal of the board member.

State law expressly prohibits a board member or the board member's spouse from receiving payments under the State-County Special Assistance or Medicaid programs on behalf of persons who are residents or patients in adult care or nursing homes that are owned or operated, in whole or in part, by the board member or the board member's spouse.[30]

When a consolidated agency includes social services, CHS board members are also prohibited from (1) being licensed as foster parents through the county in which they serve on the CHS board or (2) being supervised or considered as a placement resource by the social services department of the county in which they serve on the social services board.[31]

Outside of these specific conflicts, receiving public assistance or social services from the county social services department does not prohibit an individual from serving on the CHS board. To the contrary, CHS boards are required to have at least four members who are "consumers of human services," which might include receiving public assistance or social services.[32] However, to avoid ethical conflicts of interest, board members should abstain from being involved in board discussions, investigations, or hearings about a public assistance or social services case involving the board member or a relative of the board member.

Holding Too Many Public Offices

Under North Carolina law, an individual is prohibited from holding more than

- two appointive public offices at the same time or
- one elective public office and one appointive public office at the same time.[33]

Serving on an appointed CHS board is an appointive office. But a county commissioner appointed to a CHS board by the board of county commissioners (an *ex officio* appointment) is deemed to be only holding one elective public office (the office of county commissioner)—not an elected and an appointive public office.[34] In other words, service on a CHS board does not count toward the office-holding limit for that commissioner. Ex officio appointments of county commissioners are discussed in more detail in Chapter 8.

Holding Incompatible Offices

In addition to the prohibition on multiple office-holding described above, some older North Carolina case law recognizes a common law doctrine that prohibits incompatible office-holding.[35] This doctrine generally defines offices as "incompatible" when there is a conflict between the functions or duties of the two offices.[36] For example, this would prohibit an individual from holding two offices where one of the offices acts as a supervisor for another (i.e., a superior/subordinate relationship).

For CHS boards, this means that an active board member should never serve as acting or interim director of the consolidated human services agency, since the board is required to provide advice and consent to the director's appointment and dismissal.[37]

Improper Conduct of Board Members Who Are Lawyers

CHS board members who are licensed to practice law in North Carolina must comply with the Rules of Professional Conduct (Rules) adopted by the North Carolina State

Bar.[38] The Rules prohibit a lawyer who has been appointed to a CHS board from considering any matter, participating in any decision, or attempting to influence any issue as a board member in which the lawyer or the lawyer's firm has any direct or indirect interest.[39]

The Rules do not prohibit a lawyer from serving on the CHS board merely because the lawyer's partner, associate, or firm represents the CHS board or the consolidated human services agency, so long as the lawyer who serves on the board refrains from participating in any deliberations or actions related to the firm's legal representation of the board or agency and does not attempt to influence the board's, agency's, or county's actions with respect to the firm.[40]

The Rules also prohibit an attorney who serves on the CHS board from directly participating in a lawsuit or other matter in which the attorney's firm is adverse to the consolidated human services agency, the board, or the CHS director.[41] The attorney's law firm must screen the attorney out from participating in the matter, the CHS board must screen the attorney out from participating in the board's discussions or voting on the matter, and the attorney must make certain disclosures to the board about the attorney's relationship to the matter.[42] The attorney board member must also refrain from any expression of opinion, public or private, or any formal or informal consideration of the matter, including any communication with other board members or the CHS director about the matter. The attorney's *law firm* is not prohibited from representing a client in such a matter, so long as these requirements are met. However, if the attorney board member is a necessary *party* to the litigation or other adverse action (in either an individual or official capacity), the attorney's firm or partner is disqualified from representing *any* party in the action.[43]

Certain Ethics Laws Applicable to the CHS Director

Remember, CHS board members are public officials, not government employees. This means that they are not subject to some of the ethics laws that apply to county employees, such as the Hatch Act (Title 5 of the U.S. Code, Chapter 15) and G.S. 153A-99. However, board members should be familiar with these ethics laws, since they do apply to the CHS director.

The Hatch Act[44] is a federal law that prohibits a state or local government employee from running for partisan political office if the employee works in a position that has duties in connection with programs financed in whole or in part by federal funds.[45]

G.S. 153A-99 is a state statute that prohibits county employees from (1) using their official authority or influence for the purpose of interfering with or affecting the result of an election or nomination for political office; or (2) coercing, soliciting, or compelling contributions for political or partisan purposes by another employee while on duty or in the workplace. This law also prohibits county employees from requiring other county employees to contribute funds for political or partisan purposes.

Adopting a Code of Ethics

What if a board member's conduct is unethical but does not violate the law? This presents a challenging situation for appointed CHS board members, who have no general authority to discipline one another.[46] The board could ask the member to resign or to cease the unethical conduct, but the board member might refuse to do either one. To anticipate such situations, an appointed CHS board may want to consider adopting its own code of ethics, along with rules of procedure that allow for the removal of a board member who violates the board's code of ethics (see Chapter 10 regarding rules of procedure and Chapter 4 regarding removal of board members).

Codes of ethics or rules of procedure adopted by *appointed* CHS boards have no authority to bind the board of county commissioners with respect to decisions to remove (or not remove) board members that it appointed. CHS board members could, however, present information about a fellow board member's unethical conduct to the board of county commissioners and ask that the commissioners consider removing the board member.

More information on the purposes and limitations of ethical codes is available in Chapter 3 of *Ethics, Conflicts, and Offices: A Guide for Local Officials*, by A. Fleming Bell.[47]

Other Laws Applicable to County Commissioners

When the board of county commissioners serves directly as the governing board for a consolidated human services agency, the commissioners may be subject to additional ethics and conflicts of interest requirements (that would not normally apply to appointed CHS boards) due to their roles as elected commissioners. For example, G.S. 153A-44 imposes a duty upon each county commissioner to vote on any matter before the board of county commissioners unless the matter involves certain actual (not merely apparent) conflicts of interest for the commissioner as defined by statute. Appointed social CHS members do not have a similar statutory "duty to vote."

A board of county commissioners exercising the powers and duties of a CHS board also should be mindful of G.S. 14-234.3, which prohibits a county commissioner who serves as a director, officer, or governing-board member of a nonprofit organization from participating in making or administering any contracts between that nonprofit and the county.[48] Specifically, commissioners who are directors, officers, or governing-board members of a nonprofit must recuse themselves from any deliberation or vote by the board of commissioners on a contract (including an award of money) with that nonprofit, and the recusal must be recorded with the board's clerk.[49] A knowing violation of G.S. 14-234.3 is a Class 1 misdemeanor.[50]

For more information on compliance with G.S. 14-234.3, please see *Conflicts of Interest for Public Officials on Nonprofit Boards: An Analysis of North Carolina G.S. 14-234.3*, by Kristina Wilson.[51]

Notes

1. For a more in-depth discussion of ethics for public officials (and other definitions of the term *ethics*), please see A. FLEMING BELL, II, ETHICS, CONFLICTS, AND OFFICES: A GUIDE FOR LOCAL OFFICIALS (UNC School of Government, 2d ed. 2010).
2. Conflicts of interest are discussed in more detail in Chapter 4 and Chapter 5 of BELL, *supra* note 1.
3. When the board of county commissioners is acting as the governing board for a consolidated human services agency, the county commissioners have a duty to vote unless there is an actual conflict of interest as defined under Chapter 153A, Section 44 of the North Carolina General Statutes (hereinafter G.S.). Members of appointed consolidated human services boards do not have a similar statutory duty to vote.
4. G.S. 14-234(a)(1).
5. G.S. 14-234(a)(2).
6. G.S. 14-234(a)(3) (emphasis added).
7. G.S. 14-234(e).
8. G.S. 14-234(f). This statute provides certain exceptions under which the void contract may continue in effect until an alternative can be arranged.
9. G.S. 14-234(a1)(4).
10. G.S. 14-234(a1)(3).
11. G.S. 14-234(a1)(2).
12. G.S. 14-234(b) lists additional exceptions for other types of contracts that are not described in this chapter.
13. G.S. 14-234(b)(3), (b1).
14. G.S. 14-234(b)(4), (b1).
15. G.S. 14-234(d1). Population size is determined according to the most recent official federal census.
16. *Id.*
17. G.S. 133-32(a).
18. *Id.*
19. G.S. 133-32(d).
20. *Id.*
21. G.S. 14-230(a).
22. G.S. 14-234(a)(2).
23. If the board member solicits or receives a gift, favor, reward, service, or promise of reward (including a promise of future employment) in exchange for this influence, it may be a violation of G.S. 14-234(a)(3).
24. *See* Title 25, Chapter 01I, Section .1702 of the North Carolina Administrative Code (hereinafter N.C.A.C.). Specifically, the rule states, "Members of an immediate family shall not be employed within the same agency if the employment results in one member supervising another member of the employee's immediate family, or if one member will occupy a position that has influence over another member's employment, promotion, salary administration, or other related management or personnel considerations." The CHS director occupies a position that has influence over the terms and conditions of all CHSA employees' employment.
25. G.S. 108A-11.
26. G.S. 108A, §§ 11, 80.
27. G.S. 153A-98; *see also* Elkin Trib., Inc. v. Yadkin Cnty. Bd. of Cnty. Comm'rs, 331 N.C. 735 (1992).

28. G.S. 153A-98(a).
29. G.S. 153A-98(e).
30. G.S. 108A, §§ 47, 55(d).
31. 10A N.C.A.C. 70E, § .1105.
32. G.S. 153A-77(c).
33. N.C. Const. art. VI, § 9; G.S. 128-1.1. North Carolina's law limiting multiple office-holding is discussed in detail in A. Fleming Bell, II, *Multiple Office-Holding, in* Ethics, Conflicts, and Offices: A Guide for Local Officials, *supra* note 1, ch. 6.
34. G.S. 128-1.2.
35. For a comprehensive discussion of the common law doctrine of incompatible office-holding, including applicable case law, please see A Fleming Bell, II, *Incompatible Office-Holding, in* Ethics, Conflicts, and Offices: A Guide for Local Officials, *supra* note 1, ch. 7.
36. *See* Bell, *supra* note 1, at 148.
37. G.S. 153A-77(e).
38. The full text of the Rules is available on the North Carolina State Bar's website at https://www.ncbar.gov/for-lawyers/ethics/rules-of-professional-conduct/.
39. N.C. State Bar, Ethics Opinion CPR 290 (Oct. 14, 1981) (overruled in part by N.C. State Bar, Employment of Board Member's Law Firm, Ethics Opinion RPC 130 (Oct. 23, 1992)).
40. N.C. State Bar, Employment of Board Member's Law Firm, *supra* note 39.
41. N.C. State Bar, Implications of Service on a Public Body or Non-Profit Board, 2002 Formal Ethics Op. 2 (July 19, 2002).
42. *Id.*
43. *Id.*
44. 5 U.S.C. §§ 1501–08.
45. *See* Diane Juffras, *What Is the Hatch Act?*, UNC Sch. of Gov't, https://www.sog.unc.edu/resources/faqs/what-hatch-act (last visited March 14, 2025).
46. *See* Bell, *supra* note 1, at 43–44.
47. *Id.* at 33–46.
48. G.S. 14-234.3(a).
49. *Id.* The same exceptions that apply to G.S. 14-234 also apply to this recusal requirement regarding contracts with nonprofits (*see* G.S. 14-234.3(b)), meaning G.S. 14-234.3 does not require a commissioner's recusal from involvement with a contract with a nonprofit if it falls within one of those exceptions. However, the requirements for complying with those exceptions, discussed earlier in this chapter, will generally also mandate the conflicted public official's recusal from involvement with the contract.
50. G.S. 14-234.3(b).
51. Kristina Wilson, *Conflicts of Interest for Public Officials on Nonprofit Boards: An Analysis of North Carolina G.S. 14-234.3*, Loc. Gov't L. Bull. No. 142 (UNC School of Government, Nov. 2022), https://www.sog.unc.edu/sites/default/files/reports/2022-11-21%2020220220%20LGLB%20142.pdf.

Chapter 10

Board Meetings and Procedures

To exercise the consolidated human services (CHS) board's powers and duties, board members must act together as a public body in an official meeting. North Carolina's open meetings law (Chapter 143, Article 33C of the North Carolina General Statutes, hereinafter G.S.) establishes multiple requirements for how these meetings must be conducted, which are discussed in this chapter. Outside of the open meetings law, state law also contains requirements for CHS boards regarding the frequency of board meetings, the role of the board chair, and the board's voting process. This chapter covers these legal requirements, along with other procedural matters.

Board Meeting Procedures

Board Secretary

In a county with an appointed CHS board, state law designates the CHS director as the board's secretary.[1] The CHS director must exercise this responsibility under the direction of the county manager.

Frequency of Board Meetings

Appointed CHS boards are only required to meet on a quarterly basis.[2] However, in some cases, the board may want or need to meet more frequently to accomplish all of its work. Additional meetings of a CHS board may be called by the board chair or by any three board members.[3]

When a board of county commissioners (BOCC) assumes the powers and duties of the CHS board and acts as the governing board for a CHSA (instead of an appointed board), it may conduct CHS board business as part of its regular meetings. In other words, a BOCC is not required to hold separate meetings acting in its capacity as the CHS board, though it may choose to do so. Even if they do not hold separate meetings for CHS board work, commissioners may find it useful to have dedicated time in some or all of their regular meeting agendas devoted to their CHSA-related responsibilities.

Date and Time of Board Meetings

Appointed CHS boards may vote to determine the dates and times of their regular board meetings.[4] Most CHS boards establish a consistent day and time for board meetings. Some boards find it more convenient to meet during the workday, while others choose to meet in the evenings to accommodate the work schedules of board members. When deciding on a schedule for regular meetings, the board should attempt to choose a time slot and day of the week that is mutually convenient for board members and the CHS director.

Election and Role of the Board Chair

State law requires each appointed CHS board to annually elect a member to serve as board chair.[5] This election must not be conducted in closed session.[6] Unless the board's procedures or policies provide otherwise, the board chair should be elected by a majority vote of the board members who are currently serving on the board and are present at the meeting.[7]

Each board chair serves for a term of one year and continues to serve in that role until a new chair is elected by the board.[8] Though the board chair must be elected each year, the same CHS board member could be reelected for additional consecutive one-year terms as chair.

A CHS board may vote to designate another board member as vice-chair, though the board is not required to do so. The board may authorize this individual to exercise the board chair's powers and duties in the event of the chair's absence, death, resignation, or removal from office.

What are the CHS board chair's powers and duties?

- The chair is authorized to call additional meetings of the board, outside of the regular monthly meeting schedule.[9]
- The chair is responsible for appointing a board member to the local multidisciplinary child death review team.[10]
- The chair has the implied authority and responsibility to preside at board meetings; to ensure that board meetings are conducted fairly and in accordance with the board's rules of procedure; to recognize members who wish to speak at board meetings; and to rule on motions and questions of procedure at board meetings.[11]

Other responsibilities of the CHS board chair vary from county to county and person to person. In some counties, for example, the board chair functions as the board's primary spokesperson in the community or acts as a liaison between the CHS board and other public bodies. In other counties, the board chair presides over meetings but does not act as an external spokesperson or liaison. CHS board members should discuss and agree upon their expectations with respect to the chair's role and responsibilities.

Board Meeting Agendas

Preparing and following an agenda for each CHS board meeting can help the board be efficient and effective.

The board has discretion to develop its own procedures and practices regarding the preparation and circulation of agendas. Generally, the board chair will prepare a proposed agenda for each board meeting with input from the CHS director and other board members. The CHS director, acting as the board's secretary, will typically send a copy of the agenda and any additional information related to agenda items to board members at least several days before the meeting. As its first order of business at the meeting, the board decides whether items should be added to or removed from the proposed agenda, make any additional changes to the proposed agenda, and adopt the agenda for the meeting.[12]

Some CHS boards may want the CHS director to determine the agenda for every board meeting. In some cases, allowing or requiring the director to establish every meeting agenda can cause board members to become passive regarding their work. The board should seek input from the director regarding the agenda, but it should also be proactive and involved in agenda-setting.

A CHS board should ensure that adequate time is allotted for every item on the meeting agenda. The board's rules of procedure should address the length of board meetings and what the board will do if there is insufficient time to consider all the items on its agenda.

The board must provide a copy of the meeting agenda to meeting attendees if the board discusses or acts on matters by reference to a number, letter, or other designation of the matter on the board's agenda and attendees would need a copy of the agenda to understand what the board is referring to.[13]

The agendas for CHS board meetings (and all records submitted to the board in connection with its meetings) are public records, meaning they must be made available to members of the public upon request except to the extent that they contain information that is confidential or privileged under state or federal laws. Disclosure of public records is discussed in Chapter 11 of this book.

Quorum

A *quorum* is the minimum number of board members that must be present before the board can take any official action or transact public business. If board members act at a meeting where a quorum is not present, their actions are invalid unless they are subsequently ratified by a majority vote of the board at a meeting where a quorum is present.

For an appointed CHS board, state law defines a quorum as a majority of the board's members.[14] If the board of county commissioners acts as the governing board for a consolidated human services agency, a majority of the board's membership (without regard to vacancies) constitutes a quorum.[15]

Though the CHS director acts as board secretary, the CHS director is not a member of the board, so the director does not count when determining whether a quorum is present.

Voting

Except as otherwise provided by state law or by a board's rules of procedure, all decisions by a CHS board should be made by a majority vote of the members who are present and constitute a quorum at an official board meeting. A board member who presides at a meeting as the chair or vice-chair retains the right to vote on all issues coming before the board.[16] The CHS director may not vote on any matter before the board, since the director is not a board member. Likewise, though the county manager has authority to make certain decisions related to a consolidated human services agency, the county manager is not a board member and therefore may not vote on any matter before the board.

The state's open meetings law prohibits CHS board members from voting by secret ballot.[17] Board members are allowed to vote by written ballot only if each ballot is signed by the member who cast it and the minutes of the meeting show how each member voted.[18] The written ballots also must be retained and made available for public inspection in the office of the CHS director (as the board's secretary) until the minutes of that meeting are approved.[19]

For more information on conflicts of interest that might require board members to recuse themselves from voting, please see Chapter 9 of this book.

Rules of Procedure

Aside from the open meetings law, state law provides little guidance on procedures for CHS board meetings. Accordingly, appointed CHS boards have the discretion to establish their own local rules of procedure, so long as those rules do not contradict requirements established by state or federal law. At a minimum, each appointed CHS board should consider adopting rules regarding

- scheduling board meetings;
- determining and circulating the agendas for board meetings;
- conducting business at board meetings;
- nomination of individuals to fill board member vacancies;
- removal of a board member (in accordance with the requirements of G.S. 153A-77(c));
- electing the board chair;
- public comment periods;
- remote participation in meetings; and
- evaluating the board's work.

The UNC School of Government has developed model rules of procedure for local appointed boards that CHS boards can use as a starting point for adopting their own rules of procedure. For more information, please read *Suggested Procedural Rules for Local Appointed Boards*, by Trey Allen and A. Fleming Bell.[20] These suggested rules incorporate the requirements of the state's open meetings law and include model rules regarding board meetings, adoption of meeting agendas, order of business, the duties of the board chair, quorum, minutes, public hearings, appointments, committees, motions, debate, and voting.

Complying with the Open Meetings Law

A CHS board is considered a "public body" for purposes of North Carolina's open meetings law.[21] North Carolina's open meetings law focuses on two main requirements that promote transparency regarding the meetings of public bodies. First, the public must have *notice* of official meetings of public bodies, and second, the public must have *access* to such meetings. Additionally, the open meetings law requires each public body to keep full and accurate minutes of its official meetings. These requirements, described in more detail in the remaining sections of this chapter, are intended to ensure that members of the public are better informed about how public bodies are carrying out their official responsibilities. As a helpful reference for questions about the open meetings law's requirements, please read *Open Meetings and Local Governments in North Carolina: Some Questions and Answers*, by Frayda Bluestein and David Lawrence.[22]

The open meetings law's requirements regarding public notice and public access are triggered whenever a majority of the board's members meet, assemble, or gather—in person or via simultaneous electronic or telephonic communication—for the purpose of conducting a hearing, participating in deliberations, voting, or otherwise transacting "public business."[23] This means that board members must be careful to discuss and deliberate on matters of public business related to their board duties only in the context of an official meeting that meets the notice and access requirements of the open meetings law. Even group telephone calls, web conferences, and simultaneous online chat or email threads involving the majority of the board's members have the potential to trigger the requirements of the open meetings law.

Board members can still engage in social gatherings without providing public notice or access, so long as they are not engaging in public business during the gathering and the gathering is not called or held to evade the spirit and purposes of the open meetings law.[24] For example, nine members of a fifteen-person CHS board could have a dinner party together without triggering the open meetings law's requirements, but they might violate the law if they use the dinner party as an opportunity to discuss the potential adoption of a new public health rule for the county.

Table 10.1. Types of Board Meetings

Regular meeting	A meeting held on a regular date and at a regular time and place specified in a schedule filed with the clerk of county commissioners.
Special meeting	Any meeting (other than an emergency or recessed meeting) that is held at a date, time, or place other than the regular date, time, or place specified in the schedule of regular board meetings on file with the clerk.
Emergency meeting	A meeting called because of generally unexpected circumstances that require immediate consideration by the board. Only business connected with the emergency may be considered at an emergency meeting.
Recessed meeting	A continuation (reconvening) of an earlier regular, special, or emergency meeting.

Note: See G.S. 143-318.12.

Public Notice of Board Meetings

North Carolina's open meetings law requires a CHS board to give public notice of all of its official meetings (including those where all of the board's business will be conducted in closed session) as well as the official meetings of committees or subcommittees of the board.[25] This means that the board may never hold a secret meeting (one without advance notice to the public), even if the entire meeting will be conducted in closed session.

The type of public notice that must be given for appointed CHS board meetings depends on whether the meeting is a regular meeting, a special meeting, an emergency meeting, or a recessed meeting. Table 10.1 defines each type of meeting.

Each type of meeting has its own notice requirements set forth in the open meetings law.

Notice of Regular Meetings

If an appointed CHS board establishes a regular date, time, and place for its meetings, the board must file a regular meeting schedule with the clerk of the county's BOCC.[26] The CHS board must also post its regular meeting schedule on the county's website.[27] Once the board's regular meeting schedule is filed with the clerk and posted online, the board does not need to give additional public notice for any meeting held at the regular date, time, and location established in the schedule.

If the board wants to change its regular meeting date, time, or location, the CHS director or board chair must file the revised regular meeting schedule with the clerk of the county's BOCC at least seven calendar days before the next regular board meeting under the revised schedule.[28] The revised schedule must also be posted on the county's website.[29]

Notice of Special Meetings

Whenever a CHS board holds a special meeting, the board must provide notice at least forty-eight hours before the time of the meeting, notifying the public of the date, time, place, and *purpose* of the meeting by

1. posting the notice on the principal bulletin board of the consolidated human services agency (if available) or at the door of the board's usual meeting room;[30]
2. mailing, emailing, or delivering the notice to each person, newspaper, wire service, radio station, and television station that has filed a written request for such notices with the clerk or secretary of the board (often called a "sunshine list");[31] and
3. posting the notice on the county's website.[32]

If the building containing the board's usual meeting room is closed to the public continuously for forty-eight hours before the time of the special meeting, the notice that is normally posted on the bulletin board or meeting room door must instead be posted on the door of the building (or on the building in an area accessible to the public).[33]

If the board of commissioners is acting as the governing board for a consolidated human services agency, the commissioners can only discuss subjects in the special meeting that were listed on the notice of the meeting.[34]

Notice of Emergency Meetings

The CHS board must give notice of an emergency meeting immediately after board members have been notified of the meeting.[35] The notice must be given to any local newspaper, wire service, radio station, or television station that has filed a written request for such notices with the clerk or secretary of the board. The board may give notice of an emergency meeting by email, by telephone, or by the same method used to notify the members of the board.

Notice of Recessed Meetings

To continue a meeting at a later time or date, a motion to recess the meeting must be approved by a majority vote of the board. The time and place at which the regular, special, or emergency meeting is to be continued (reconvened) must be announced in open session during the meeting.[36] The time and place of the recessed meeting should also be posted on the county's website.[37]

Public Access to Board Meetings

CHS boards may choose the location of their regular monthly board meetings. However, the board must consider public accessibility when choosing a location, because the open meetings law requires a public body to take reasonable measures to ensure public access to its official meetings.[38] Among other things, this means that the CHS board should take reasonable measures to provide adequate seating for the number of people who typically attend the board's meetings (though the board does not have to provide overflow seating or ensure space for a larger-than-usual crowd).[39] For example, holding a board meeting in a room that is only large enough to provide seating for the board's members may violate the open meetings law if larger rooms are readily available, since using the smaller room would completely exclude members of the public from attending.[40]

The board should also attempt to choose a meeting location that is reasonably accessible to individuals with disabilities and to individuals who must rely on public transportation.[41]

If the board of commissioners is acting as the CHS board, it is generally required to hold all its meetings within the county except in certain circumstances set forth in G.S. 153A-40(c).

Public Comment and Recording at Board Meetings

The open meetings law gives any person the right to attend open sessions of official meetings of a CHS board.[42] However, the open meetings law does not give members of the public a right to address the CHS board during the board meeting or participate in the board's discussions. An appointed CHS board may *choose* to include a public comment period in its meetings but is not required by law to do so. By contrast, if the board of commissioners is acting as the governing board for a consolidated human services agency, it is required by law to provide at least one public comment period per month at a regular meeting of the board.[43]

The board chair may direct any person, including a board member, to leave a board meeting if the person is willfully interrupting, disrupting, or disturbing the meeting.[44] Willfully refusing to leave the meeting after such an order constitutes a Class 2 misdemeanor.[45]

The open meetings law allows any person to photograph, film, tape-record, or otherwise reproduce any part of an open meeting of the CHS board.[46] Any radio or television station may also broadcast all or part of an open board meeting. The board may regulate the placement and use of recording or broadcasting equipment if necessary to prevent undue interference with its meetings.[47]

Closed Sessions in Board Meetings

Every official meeting of the CHS board must be open to the public.[48] However, sometimes the board needs to hold part of the meeting in "closed session," meaning members of the public are excluded when the board is discussing certain matters. Closed sessions must occur within the context of an official meeting—a meeting that the public has received notice of in accordance with the open meetings law.[49] This means that the CHS board cannot hold a secret meeting (one without notice to the public) even if the board intends to conduct all of its business in closed session.

When a CHS board holds a closed session, only the board's members have a right to attend. The board may allow the CHS director, county manager, human services staff, or others to attend a closed session if the board chooses to do so and their participation will be helpful to the board. However, the board should have a logical justification for the individuals it permits to join a closed session instead of making arbitrary decisions about which members of the public (non-board members) are allowed to attend.[50]

Procedure for Going into Closed Session

Even if most or all of the board's business will be conducted in a closed session, the board must start the meeting in open session. In order to go into closed session, a board member must make a motion (in open session) to go into closed session, and that motion must be adopted by a majority of the board members present and voting.[51]

The motion must state the purpose of the closed session, which must be one (or more) of the permissible purposes listed in G.S. 143-318.11(a).[52] If the purpose is to prevent the disclosure of privileged or confidential information, the motion must state the name or citation of the law that makes the information privileged or confidential. If the purpose is to consult with an attorney and preserve attorney-client privilege, the motion must identify the parties in each existing lawsuit about which the board expects to receive advice during the closed session.

During a closed session, the board may not discuss or take action on any matter outside of the purpose(s) specified in the motion to meet in closed session (or outside of the permitted purposes described in G.S. 143-318.11(a)). If the board wants to discuss a different matter in closed session, other than what was specified in the motion, it must reconvene in open session and adopt another motion to meet in closed session for a different permitted purpose.

Permitted Purposes for Closed Sessions

A CHS board is not allowed to go into closed session for any reason or to discuss any topic. Instead, the open meetings law provides a limited list of allowable purposes for entering closed session. This means that a CHS board may meet in closed session only

- to prevent the disclosure of information that is privileged or confidential under state or federal law or is not considered to be a public record under North Carolina's public records law;[53]
- to consult with an attorney employed or retained by the board in order to preserve the attorney-client privilege (but not to discuss general policy matters);[54]
- to consider the qualifications, competence, performance, character, fitness, conditions of appointment, or conditions of initial employment of the consolidated human services director;[55]
- to hear or investigate a complaint, charge, or grievance by or against a particular individual public officer or employee;[56]

- to plan, conduct, or hear reports concerning investigations of alleged criminal misconduct;[57] or
- to consider or take action with respect to other matters listed in G.S. 143-318.11(a).

Prohibited Purposes for Closed Sessions

The CHS board cannot meet in closed session for any purpose other than those listed in the open meetings law at G.S. 143-318.11(a). The open meetings law also explicitly prohibits the board from meeting in closed session for the following purposes.

1. While the board may discuss a *specific* public employee or official (such as the CHS director) in closed session, the board may not discuss issues related to general agency personnel policies or concerns in closed session.[58]
2. A public body may not take final action to appoint or dismiss a public officer or employee in closed session.[59] The CHS board does not have final authority to appoint or dismiss the CHS director, but the county manager's appointment and dismissal decisions must be made with the "advice and consent" of the CHS board, which will ultimately require a board vote.[60] As a best practice, this board vote on whether to provide consent to the appointment or dismissal of a particular individual as director should arguably be taken in open session.[61] However, the board may provide its advice and feedback to the county manager and reach a tentative consensus on such a decision during a closed session.[62]
3. The board may not use a closed session to consider the qualifications, competence, performance, character, fitness, appointment, or removal of a member of the CHS board, or to discuss or evaluate the board's own performance.[63] These matters must be discussed in open session.

Keeping Minutes of Board Meetings

The open meetings law requires each CHS board to keep full and accurate minutes of its official meetings, including closed sessions.[64] Minutes of CHS board meetings are typically recorded in written form, but the board may choose to keep minutes in the form of audio or video recordings.[65] The primary purpose of these minutes is to provide evidence that the board's actions followed proper procedure.[66]

The CHS director, as the board's secretary, should take minutes of CHS board meetings (or delegate this duty to an employee if the director is unavailable). If the director or the employee who has been designated to take minutes is excluded from a closed session of a board meeting, minutes of the closed session should be taken by a board member (or another person designated by the board who is in the closed session).

For more information about requirements related to keeping minutes, including a more in-depth discussion of some of the topics mentioned in this section, please see *"Full and Accurate" Minutes: A Primer*, by Trey Allen.[67]

Contents of the Minutes

The board's minutes must accurately reflect the substance of all official actions taken by the board and the vote by which each action was taken. The board is not required to summarize or quote each member's comments on an issue or to record the names of members who voted for or against a motion (unless the board voted by written ballot).[68] If the board doesn't take any official action at a meeting, the minutes only need to document that a meeting occurred.[69] However, a board may want to include additional detail beyond what is legally required, since the minutes also serve as a historical record of the board's work.[70]

General Accounts of Closed Sessions

If a CHS board meets in closed session, the board must (in addition to recording minutes) prepare a "general account of the closed session so that a person not in attendance would have a reasonable understanding of what transpired."[71] The general account of a closed session may consist of a written narrative or an audio or audiovisual recording of the session.

Approving Meeting Minutes

Though not required by the open meetings law, it is important for CHS boards to officially approve the minutes of their meetings. Among other things, this gives board members the opportunity to correct errors in the record. If the board determines that the proposed minutes are incorrect or incomplete, the board may vote to amend the minutes. The motion to approve minutes from a prior meeting should occur in open session, unless the discussion about the minutes or the general account of a closed session would "frustrate the purpose" of the closed session (for example, by revealing confidential information).[72] In such a case, the board could approve the minutes or general account of the closed session in a subsequent closed session.[73]

Meeting Minutes Are Public Records

The minutes (and proposed or draft minutes) of CHS board meetings are public records, meaning they must be made available to a member of the public upon request under the state's public records law except to the extent that they contain information that is privileged or confidential under state or federal law.[74] General accounts and minutes of closed sessions are also public records but can be withheld from public inspection for "so long as public inspection would frustrate the purpose of a closed session."[75]

The CHS board and CHS director must preserve the minutes of board meetings—along with meeting agendas and copies of supporting documentation submitted and discussed during meetings—until they are authorized to be destroyed pursuant to a records retention and disposition schedule established by the state Department of Natural and Cultural Resources.[76] The official minutes of board meetings, as well as all attachments necessary to understand the board's actions during a meeting, must be retained permanently.[77] For more information on records retention and disposition requirements, please see Chapter 11 of this book.

Remote Meetings and Remote Participation

CHS boards may wish to hold some meetings remotely via teleconference, videoconference, or other electronic means. Under state law, a "remote meeting" is any official meeting with *one or more* members of the public body participating by conference call, conference video, or other electronic means.[78] Before undertaking a remote meeting, a CHS board should carefully consider whether such remote participation will jeopardize quorum requirements. Under current North Carolina law, there is clear authority for boards to engage in remote meetings during state of emergency declarations, but the state of the law is less clear with respect to meetings that occur outside of a state of emergency. The nuances of this distinction are discussed in more detail below.

Remote Meetings During Emergency Declarations

A special set of requirements apply to remote meetings when the governor or the General Assembly has declared a state of emergency and the board is within the emergency area. Under such circumstances, a CHS board should comply with the requirements of G.S. 166A-19.24, which establishes remote-meeting requirements applicable to public bodies during emergency declarations.[79] This statute provides clear authority for a board to meet remotely during an emergency declaration (assuming the board is in the area covered by the declaration), provided that the board complies with the requirements of G.S. 166A-19.24, including those related to notice of the meeting, voting, minutes, online streaming, and public hearings. A member of the board participating remotely as allowed under G.S. 166A-19.24 must be counted as present for quorum purposes while simultaneous communication is maintained for that member.[80] Likewise, votes made during a remote meeting under G.S. 166A-19.24 must be counted as if the member were physically present, so long as simultaneous communication is maintained for that member.[81]

Some of the unique requirements of G.S. 166A-19.24 include the following:

- The method of simultaneous communication used by board members participating remotely must allow for any board member to (1) hear what is said by the other board members, (2) hear what is said by any individual addressing the board, and (3) be heard by the other board members when speaking to the board.
- Any board members participating by a method of simultaneous communication in which they cannot be physically seen by the board must identify themselves (1) when the roll is taken or the remote meeting is commenced; (2) prior to participating in the deliberations, including making motions, proposing amendments, and raising points of order; and (3) prior to voting.
- All documents to be considered during the remote meeting must be provided to each member of the board.

- All votes must be conducted by roll call (voting by secret or written ballots is not permitted).
- The minutes of the remote meeting must reflect that the meeting was conducted using simultaneous communication, which members participated by simultaneous communication, and when such members joined or left the remote meeting.
- All chats, instant messages, texts, or other written communications between board members regarding the transaction of the public business must be treated as public records.[82]
- The remote meeting must be simultaneously streamed live online so that live audio (and video, if any) of the meeting is available to the public. If the remote meeting is conducted by conference call, the board must provide the public with an opportunity to dial in or stream the audio live.

Remote Meetings and Participation Outside of a State of Emergency

What about remote meetings held when the governor or the General Assembly has *not* declared a state of emergency, or when the board is outside of the declared emergency area? The current state of the law with respect to whether remote participation counts toward quorum is unclear. In a 2024 case, *State* ex rel. *Cannon v. Anson County*, the North Carolina Court of Appeals held that only county commissioners who were physically present at a board of county commissioners meeting could be counted toward the quorum "because there was no state of emergency in effect that would have permitted remote participation."[83] However, in March 2025, the North Carolina Supreme Court declared the Court of Appeals' decision in *Anson County* to stand "without precedential value."[84] This means that the *Anson County* decision does not bind future trial courts if the same issues that were decided in *Anson County* arise in future cases.[85]

The CHS board statute states that "[a] majority of the members shall constitute a quorum" (similar to the quorum statute for boards of commissioners), but it does not use the term *present* or indicate that physical presence at meetings is required.[86] This statute—combined with the *Anson County* decision, which stands without precedential value—leaves uncertainty over whether members participating remotely count toward quorum. In the absence of a binding decision from North Carolina's appellate courts or a law from the General Assembly that directly addresses this issue, a cautious approach for CHS boards would be to not count remote participants toward quorum for purposes of voting or otherwise conducting board business, unless the board is meeting under a declared state of emergency as authorized by G.S. 166A-19.24.

Ideally, CHS boards should address the issue of remote participation in their local rules of procedure, including whether to allow remote participation outside a state of emergency and whether to allow remotely participating members to count toward quorum for voting purposes. Given the complicated legal landscape involved, a board with questions about remote participation by board members should consult with legal counsel.

Special Requirements for Remote Meetings

If a CHS board holds a meeting using teleconference or other electronic means, the open meetings law requires the board to provide "a location and means whereby members of the public may listen to the meeting."[87] The board must specify that location information in the notice of the meeting. At a minimum, this means the board must provide an online meeting link or teleconference information to the public in advance of the meeting.[88]

The open meetings law does not require the board to provide a way for members of the public to speak to or communicate with the board during a remote meeting. In other words, members of the public must be able to *hear* the board meeting, but the board does not have to provide a method for the public to *contribute* to the meeting. However, a board may want to provide a way for members of the public to speak during remote meetings if it has decided (in its own rules of procedure) to routinely allow public comment periods during its meetings.

Liability for Violating the Open Meetings Law

Any person who believes that a CHS board has violated the open meetings law may seek injunctive relief in district or superior court.[89] If a judge finds that the board violated the open meetings law, the judge may enjoin the board from threatened or continuing violations of the open meetings law or the recurrence of past violations of the law.[90]

Likewise, any individual may file a lawsuit in superior court requesting the entry of a judgment declaring that an action of the CHS board was taken, considered, discussed, or deliberated in violation of the open meetings law.[91] If a superior court judge makes such a finding, the judge may declare the action taken by the board in violation of the law to be null and void.[92]

If a court finds that the board has violated the open meetings law, the court may order the board to pay the attorney's fees of the person or entity that sued the board.[93] If the court finds that a board member knowingly or intentionally violated the open meetings law, the court may order the board member to *personally* pay all or part of the plaintiff's attorney's fees.[94] However, there is some protection from this potential personal liability: the court may not order a board member to pay the plaintiff's attorney's fees if the board member (or the board as a whole) sought and followed the advice of an attorney with respect to the board's actions.[95] Accordingly, if the board is confused or unclear about the open meetings law's requirements with respect to a certain decision or procedure, it should attempt to consult with an attorney before acting.

Notes

1. Chapter 153A, Section 77(e)(4) of the North Carolina General Statutes (hereinafter G.S.).
2. G.S. 153A-77(c).
3. *Id.*
4. If the board chair or a group of three members calls a special or emergency meeting, the chair or the group calling the meeting may determine the date and time of that meeting. However, the chair or the group of members calling the meeting should attempt (to the extent possible) to choose a reasonable date and time when other board members are likely to be available.
5. G.S. 153A-77(c).
6. *See* G.S. 143-318.11(a)(6) (prohibiting a public body from considering the qualifications or appointment of a member during a closed session of an official meeting). The fact that a board member has been nominated to serve as chair does not disqualify the nominee from participating in the election of the board's chair.
7. This vote should include newly appointed board members if they have taken their oaths of office.
8. Unlike G.S. 108A-7, which prescribes a one-year term for a social services board chair, G.S. 153A-77 does explicitly state a term for a CHS board chair. However, the fact that G.S. 153A-77(c) requires the CHS board chair to be elected annually implies that the chair serves a one-year term.
9. G.S. 153A-77(c) (providing that a special meeting of a CHS board may be called by the chair or by three board members).
10. G.S. 7B-1407(b)(6); *see also* G.S. 7B-1401.
11. Any board member may make a motion to appeal the board chair's decision regarding a procedural matter, and the board may affirm or reverse the chair's decision by majority vote.
12. The agenda may be changed during the meeting after its adoption, but only by a majority vote of the board.
13. G.S. 143-318.13(c).
14. G.S. 153A-77(c).
15. G.S. 153A-43.
16. The board chair or vice-chair cannot, however, cast a *second* vote as a tie-breaker.
17. *See* G.S. 143-318.13(b).
18. *See id.*
19. *See id.*
20. Trey Allen & A. Fleming Bell, II, Suggested Procedural Rules for Local Appointed Boards (UNC School of Government, 2020).
21. *See* G.S. 143-318.10(b) (defining *public body*).
22. Frayda S. Bluestein & David M. Lawrence, Open Meetings and Local Governments in North Carolina: Some Questions and Answers (UNC School of Government, 8th ed. 2017).
23. G.S. 143-318.10(d).
24. *Id.*
25. G.S. 143-318.12.
26. G.S. 143-318.12(a)(2).
27. *See* G.S. 143-318.12(d). The statute imposes this requirement "if a public body has a Web site." Some counties have a web page where notices of board meetings (including local appointed boards) are typically posted. In other counties, information about the CHS

board may be customarily posted to a separate website or county website subpage devoted to the county's consolidated human services agency. The clerk to the board of county commissioners (BOCC) may be able to advise a CHS board on the best location for this web-based notice.

28. *See* G.S. 143-318.12(a).
29. *Id.* See *supra* note 27 regarding this requirement.
30. G.S. 143-318.12(b)(2).
31. *Id.* The board may require each newspaper, wire service, radio station, and television station submitting a written request for notice to renew the request annually. The board may require individual persons (other than the media) to renew their requests for notice quarterly.
32. G.S. 143-318.12(e). See *supra* note 27 regarding this requirement. For special meetings, this notice requirement technically only applies if the website is maintained by an employee of the public body. However, best practice is to provide this online notice regardless of who maintains the website, since many members of the public use county websites to stay informed about meetings of their elected and appointed officials.
33. G.S. 143-318.12(b)(2).
34. G.S. 153A-40(b).
35. G.S. 143-318.12(b)(3).
36. G.S. 143-318.12(b)(1).
37. G.S. 143-318.12(e). See *supra* note 27 regarding this requirement. For recessed meetings, this notice requirement technically only applies if the website is maintained by an employee of the public body. However, best practice is to provide this online notice regardless of who maintains the website, since many members of the public use county websites to stay informed about meetings of their elected and appointed officials.
38. G.S. 143, art. 33C; Garlock v. Wake Cnty. Bd. of Educ., 211 N.C. App. 200, 223 (2011).
39. Hildebran Heritage & Dev. Ass'n v. Town of Hildebran, 252 N.C. App. 286, 294 (2017) (finding that a lack of overflow seating or external speakers, absent more, did not constitute an unreasonable failure of access under the open meetings law).
40. *See Garlock*, 211 N.C. App. at 226–27 (2011).
41. The open meetings law does not require special accommodations at public meetings for a disabled member of the public, as opposed to a nondisabled member of the public. However, other state and federal statutes that govern access to public facilities by persons with disabilities (such as the Americans with Disabilities Act, 42 U.S.C. § 12101–12213, and the Persons with Disabilities Protection Act, G.S. 168A) may impose such reasonable accommodation requirements.
42. G.S. 143-318.10(a).
43. G.S. 153A-52.1. The board of commissioners is not required to provide a public comment period in a month in which it does not hold a regular meeting.
44. *See* G.S. 143-318.17.
45. *Id.*
46. G.S. 143-318.14(a).
47. G.S. 143-318.14(b).
48. G.S. 143-318.10(a).
49. G.S. 143-318.11(c).
50. See Question 87 in Bluestein & Lawrence, *supra* note 22.
51. G.S. 143-318.11(c).
52. *Id.*
53. G.S. 143-318.11(a)(1). *See also* G.S. 108A-80 (making records of persons who have applied for or received public assistance or social services from a county social services department confidential); G.S. 153-98 (making county employee personnel file information confidential).

54. G.S. 143-318.11(a)(3). The mere fact that an attorney retained or employed by a CHS board participates in a board meeting does not in itself justify holding a closed session. To go into closed session, the board must be discussing a legal issue with the attorney that necessitates acting to preserve attorney-client privilege. This could include discussing potential, threatened, or active litigation, but the allowable discussion is not limited to litigation-related matters so long as some legal issue is involved. If the board has approved or considered a settlement in closed session, the terms of that settlement must be reported to the board and entered into its minutes as soon as possible within a reasonable time after the settlement is concluded.
55. G.S. 143-318.11(a)(6).
56. *Id.* A CHS board has no specific authority to investigate or hear complaints, charges, or grievances from human services employees. However, the CHS board does have a responsibility to "assure compliance with laws related to State and federal programs" and to "conduct audits and reviews of human services programs, including quality assurance activities," per G.S. 153A-77, which could theoretically involve hearing or investigating complaints or grievances from a particular public official or employee. The board should involve the county human resources officer and county attorney before conducting any investigation of alleged misconduct by the CHS director or any human services employee.
57. G.S. 143-318.11(a)(7).
58. G.S. 143-318.11(a)(6).
59. *Id.*
60. G.S. 153A-77(e).
61. One could also argue that the vote to provide consent is not required to be made in open session, since it is not a "final action making an appointment or discharge or removal by a public body having final authority for the appointment or discharge or removal," per G.S. 143-318.11(a)(6).
62. *See* Maready v. City of Winston-Salem, 342 N.C. 708, 732 (1996).
63. G.S. 143-318.11(a)(6).
64. G.S. 143-318.10(e).
65. *Id.*
66. See Question 178 in Bluestein & Lawrence, *supra* note 22.
67. Trey Allen, *"Full and Accurate" Minutes: A Primer*, Loc. Gov't L. Bull. No. 140 (UNC School of Government, Jan. 2019), https://www.sog.unc.edu/publications/bulletins/full-and-accurate-minutes-primer.
68. G.S. 143-318.13(b).
69. See Question 178 in Bluestein & Lawrence, *supra* note 22; *see also* Maready v. City of Winston-Salem, 342 N.C. 708, 733 (1996).
70. See Question 178 in Bluestein & Lawrence, *supra* note 22.
71. G.S. 143-318.10(e).
72. *See id.*
73. For more information about the topic of approving confidential closed-session minutes (including other options for doing so), please see Frayda Bluestein, *How to Approve Minutes and General Accounts of Closed Sessions*, Coates' Canons: NC Loc. Gov't L. (blog) (June 5, 2018), https://canons.sog.unc.edu/2018/06/how-to-approve-minutes-and-general-accounts-of-closed-sessions/.
74. G.S. 143-318.10(e).
75. *Id.*
76. *See* N.C. Dep't of Nat. & Cultural Res., General Records Schedule: Local Government Agencies, items 1.47, 1.54 (Oct. 1, 2021), https://archives.ncdcr.gov/media/1066/open.
77. *See id.*, item 1.54.
78. G.S. 166A-19.24(i).

79. If the board's own rules of procedure conflict with the requirements in G.S. 166A-19.24, the board should follow G.S. 166A-19.24.
80. G.S. 166A-19.24(c).
81. G.S. 166A-19.24(d).
82. Like other records created by the board, these electronic communications may be withheld from the public if they were created during a closed session and disclosing them to the public would "frustrate the purpose" of the closed session. *See* G.S. 143-318.10.
83. State *ex rel.* Cannon v. Anson Cnty., 295 N.C. App. 152, 163 (2024), *aff'd, ordered not precedential*, 912 S.E.2d 379 (N.C. 2025).
84. *Cannon*, 912 S.E.2d at 379. The North Carolina Supreme Court denied the plaintiff-appellant's petition for discretionary review, leaving the decision of the Court of Appeals "undisturbed but without precedential value." Accordingly, it is unclear why the Supreme Court decided to order the Court of Appeals decision without precedential value. For a discussion of the procedural issues involved, see the concurring and dissenting opinions in *Molè v. City of Durham*, 384 N.C. 78, 79 (2023).
85. *See generally* John V. Orth, *"Without Precedential Value"—When the Justices of the Supreme Court of North Carolina Are Equally Divided*, 93 N.C. L. Rev. 1719 (2015).
86. G.S. 153A-77(c); *see also* G.S. 153A-43 (defining *quorum* for a board of county commissioners as "[a] majority of the membership of the board of commissioners.").
87. G.S. 143-318.13.
88. In light of modern technological advances, it is unclear whether the requirement to "provide a location and means whereby members of the public may listen to the meeting" is satisfied by simply providing an online link or teleconference-access information, or whether a public body is still required to provide a physical space and equipment for the public to listen to the remote meeting. A cautious approach would be to provide access to a room in a county building with a telephone, computer, or projector where members of the public could listen to the meeting.
89. G.S. 143-318.16; G.S. 143-318.16A.
90. G.S. 143-318.16(a).
91. G.S. 143-318.16A.
92. G.S. 143-318.16A(a).
93. G.S. 143-318.16B.
94. *Id.*
95. *Id.*

Chapter 11

The Public Records Law

Members of the general public have a right to inspect or copy any record that a consolidated human services (CHS) board member, CHS director, or county human services employee makes or receives "in connection with the transaction of public business," unless an exception applies.[1] This broad right of access is established by North Carolina's public records law (Chapter 132 of the North Carolina General Statutes (hereinafter G.S.)). The scope of the public's right of access to records, limitations on public access to records, and records retention requirements are all discussed in this chapter.

What Is a Public Record?

Public record refers to any document, paper, letter, map, book, photograph, film, sound recording, tape recording, electronic data-processing record, email, text message, artifact, or other documentary material that is made or received in connection with the transaction of public business by any agency of North Carolina government or its subdivisions (including CHS boards and consolidated human services agencies).[2]

It is the content and purpose of a record—not its location—that determines whether it is subject to the public records law.[3] For example, text messages or emails sent or received by board members on their personal cell phones or through their personal email accounts may be public records if they involve the transaction of public business.

The Right to Access Public Records

Any member of the public has a right to inspect and examine public records "at reasonable times and under reasonable supervision."[4] Likewise, any member of the public has the right to obtain copies of public records, which must be furnished "as promptly as possible" following a request for such copies.[5] The public records law does not provide any hard-and-fast rule for promptness, meaning that the time frame for responding to a request for copies likely depends on factors such as the nature of the request and the personnel capacity of the agency.[6] A public agency or board's obligation to fulfill requests for inspection or copies of public records can be satisfied by making a record available online in a format that allows someone to view it and to print it or save it.[7]

The public records law does not define "reasonable times" or "as promptly as possible," which leaves some ambiguity about how much time public officials have to respond to records requests. This will depend on factors such as the nature of the request, the availability of personnel to respond, the location of the records, and whether the records need to be redacted before being produced.[8]

Limitations on the Right to Access Public Records

The right to access public records is not absolute. Many state laws create exceptions to the public's right to access public records, either by making the records confidential or by exempting them from public access. The CHS board must not disclose any record in response to a public records request if that record is confidential under state or federal law.

What if a requested record contains some information that is confidential and other information that is public? Unless an exception in the law prohibits the disclosure of an *entire* record, the board should redact any confidential or nonpublic information and then disclose the public (nonredacted) parts of the record in response to a records request.[9] Whenever possible, the board should consult with legal counsel before disclosing any records to ensure that the information being disclosed is public and not confidential.

Some of the exceptions to the right of access that are most relevant to CHS boards are described below.

Closed-Session Minutes or General Accounts

Meeting minutes and general accounts recorded by the board during a closed session may be withheld from the public "so long as public inspection would frustrate the purpose of a closed session."[10]

Personnel Records

Except in limited circumstances described in G.S. 153A-98, the board may not disclose any personnel file information regarding a current or former CHS director (or any other county employee).[11] However, G.S. 153A-98(b) establishes a list of particular information about a county employee that *is* a matter of public record and must be disclosed upon request.

Social Services Records

Any record concerning a person applying for or receiving social services or public assistance is confidential and may not be disclosed to the public.[12]

Attorney-Client Communications

The board may withhold from the public any communications by an attorney made within the scope of the attorney-client relationship concerning (1) any claim by or against the board, the consolidated human services agency, or the county; or (2) the prosecution, defense, settlement, or litigation of any judicial action or administrative proceeding to which the board is a party or by which the board may be directly affected.[13] However, these communications become public records three years after the date they are received by the board.

Sensitive Identifying Information

The board may not disclose information that can be used to access a person's financial resources, such as a person's social security number, tax identification number, driver's license or state identification card number, passport number, checking or savings account number, credit or debit card number, PIN (personal identification number), digital signature, biometric data, fingerprints, or passwords.[14]

Other exemptions exist in state law for criminal investigation information, trial preparation materials, medical records, contract bid documents, and records involving public security, among others.

Records Versus Information

It is important to remember that the public records law gives the public a right to access existing *records*, not *information*. This means that if a member of the public asks for a record that does not already exist, the board is not obligated to compile information or create a *new* record in response to the request.[15]

There is one important exception to this general rule, which relates to county personnel information. As described earlier in this chapter, G.S. 153A-98 makes most personnel file information confidential but also establishes a list of personnel information (not just records) that must be made available upon request. The following information is a matter of public record about any county employee (including the CHS director) and must be provided upon request even if it is not part of an existing record:

- the employee's name;
- the employee's age;
- the date of the employee's original employment or appointment;
- the terms of any employment contract, whether written or oral;
- the employee's current position, title, and salary;

- the date and amount of each increase or decrease in the employee's salary (including pay, benefits, incentives, bonuses, and deferred and all other forms of compensation);
- the date and type of the employee's most recent promotion, demotion, transfer, suspension, separation, or other change in position classification;
- the date and general description of the reasons for each promotion;
- the date and type of each dismissal, suspension, or demotion for disciplinary reasons (if the disciplinary action was a dismissal, the written notice of the final decision setting forth the basis of the dismissal is also a matter of public record); and
- the office or station to which the employee is currently assigned.[16]

Given that the CHS director reports directly to the county manager, not the CHS board, it would be prudent for CHS board members to involve the county manager before responding to any public records requests regarding the CHS director.

Responsibility for Responding to Public Records Requests

Who is responsible for responding to public records requests on behalf of an appointed CHS board? The public records law states that the "custodian of public records" is responsible for responding to such requests and defines the custodian as "[t]he public official in charge of an office having public records."[17] The CHS director is the ultimate records custodian for all records created or maintained by the consolidated human services agency. It is less clear who should act as the custodian of records created or maintained by an appointed CHS board.[18]

In some counties, the clerk to the board of commissioners may serve (either by policy or practice) as the custodian of records created by appointed county boards. In a county where this is not the case, the CHS board could designate its board chair to serve as the board's custodian of records in its rules of procedure. In either case, each CHS board member is a public official and retains responsibility for preserving any records that are in the board members' custody. CHS board members should work together to respond to public records requests, and they should seek counsel from the county clerk and the county attorney when they are unsure if a record can or should be disclosed to the public.

Liability for Denial of Access to Records

Any person who is denied access to public records or copies of public records may seek a court order compelling disclosure or copying of the records.[19] If a party successfully compels the disclosure of public records from the board, the court must

Framework for Responding to Public Records Requests

UNC School of Government professor Frayda Bluestein created a four-step framework that CHS board members may find useful for analyzing public records requests.[a]

1. **Does a record exist that corresponds to the request?**
   a. If not, no disclosure is required.
   b. If so, continue to question 2.
2. **Is the record "made or received in the transaction of public business"?**
   a. If not, no disclosure is required.
   b. If so, continue to question 3.
3. **Is there an exception in the law that applies (for example, is this a confidential record)?**
   a. If not, the requested access must be provided.
   b. If so, continue to question 4.
4. **Does the exception apply to the entire record or only to certain information? Does the exception prohibit disclosure or merely deny the right of access?**
   a. If a prohibition applies to the entire record, do not disclose. If it applies only to certain information, redact that information and then disclose.
   b. If there is no right of access to some or all of the information, but releasing the record is not prohibited, determine whether or not to release the entire record or a redacted record.

[a] *See* Frayda S. Bluestein, Public Records in North Carolina, UNC School of Government (2012), https://www.sog.unc.edu/sites/default/files/course_materials/public_records_overview.pdf (updated and revised from a previous paper authored by David M. Lawrence).

allow that party to recover its reasonable attorneys' fees from the county.[20] However, the court may not assess attorneys' fees against the county if the court finds that the board acted in reasonable reliance on

- a court judgment or order applicable to the board;
- the published opinion of a North Carolina appellate court, an order of the North Carolina Business Court, or a final order of a North Carolina superior or district court; or
- a written opinion, decision, or letter of the North Carolina Attorney General.[21]

A board member may be found *personally* liable for all or part of the attorneys' fees owed to a plaintiff if the court finds that the board member knowingly or intentionally committed, caused, permitted, suborned, or participated in a violation of the public records law. However, a board member cannot be held personally liable for such fees if the board member sought and followed the advice of an attorney with respect to the public records request at issue.[22] Because of this potential shield from personal liability, it is prudent for board members to consult with an attorney when deciding whether to withhold records in response to a public records request.

Records Retention Requirements

Public officials, including CHS board members, are prohibited from destroying, selling, loaning, or disposing of any public record except as allowed by a records retention and disposition schedule established by the North Carolina Department of Natural and Cultural Resources (NC DNCR).[23] These schedules determine how long certain categories of records must be retained and when they may be disposed of or destroyed. The current retention and disposition schedules for local governments are available on NC DNCR's website.[24]

Many of a CHS board's records (such as meeting minutes) fall under categories described in the general records schedule for local government agencies. That schedule must be approved by the board of commissioners. Appointed CHS board members and the CHS director should obtain a copy of the county's approved general records schedule to ensure that CHS board members are properly preserving and disposing of records.

The records of various divisions and programs within a consolidated human services agency may fall under different records retention schedules. Specifically, there are separate schedules for county social services agencies, local health departments, and county veterans services programs available on NC DNCR's website.[25] If a consolidated human services agency includes any of these functions, its records for that function will be subject to the applicable records retention schedule. The records retention schedules for social services and public health must be signed by the chair of the agency's governing board to acknowledge that the board agrees to comply with each schedule's requirements.[26] That acknowledgment should be made in a regular meeting and recorded as an action in the board's meeting minutes. A signed copy of the signature page must be sent to the NC DNCR Records Analysis Unit, Government Records Section, 4615 Mail Service Center, Raleigh, NC 27699-4615 or faxed to 919-715-3627.

If board members are unsure whether NC DNCR has a signed copy of the applicable records retention schedules for their county on file, they may contact a records management analyst at NC DNCR for confirmation.[27]

Notes

1. Chapter 132, Section 1 of the North Carolina General Statutes (hereinafter G.S.).
2. G.S. 132-1(a).
3. *See* Frayda S. Bluestein, Public Records in North Carolina, UNC School of Government (2012), https://www.sog.unc.edu/sites/default/files/course_materials/public_records_overview.pdf (updated and revised from a previous paper authored by David M. Lawrence).
4. G.S. 132-6(a).
5. *Id.*
6. Kristi A. Nickodem & Kristina Wilson, *Responding to First Amendment "Audits" in the Local Government Context*, Loc. Gov't L. Bull. No. 141 (Nov. 2022), 62, https://www.sog.unc.edu/sites/default/files/reports/2022-11-09%2020220124%20LGLB%20141.pdf.
7. G.S. 132-6(a1).
8. *See* Bluestein, *supra* note 3.
9. *See* G.S. 132-6(c).
10. G.S. 143-318.10(e).
11. G.S. 153A-98(a).
12. *See* G.S. 108A, §§ 80, 11. Other statutes and regulations also make specific types of social services and public assistance information confidential.
13. G.S. 132-1.1(a).
14. G.S. 132-1.10(b)(5).
15. *See* G.S. 132-6.2(e).
16. G.S. 153A-98(b).
17. G.S. 132, §§ 6(a), 2.
18. For a discussion of problems with the records-custodian concept as it is defined in the public records law, see Frayda Bluestein, *Custodians of Public Records*, Coates' Canons: NC Loc. Gov't L. (blog) (Dec. 19, 2014), https://canons.sog.unc.edu/2014/12/custodians-of-public-records/.
19. G.S. 132-9(a).
20. G.S. 132-9(c).
21. *Id.*
22. *Id.*
23. G.S. 132-3(a); G.S. 121-5.
24. *Local Government Agencies*, State Archives of N.C. (last visited Apr. 14, 2025), https://archives.ncdcr.gov/government/local.
25. *See id.* Animal services programs, which may be included in some consolidated human services agencies, have records retention requirements under the schedule entitled "Program Records Schedule: Local Government Agencies."
26. Per G.S. 121-5, the schedule should also be approved by "the head of the governmental unit or agency having custody of the records." The social services schedule is formatted to be signed by the county social services agency director, while the public health schedule is formatted to be signed by the local health director. Depending on the leadership structure and delegation of authority within a consolidated agency, the CHS director might sign one or both schedules, or individuals identified as the social services director and local health director (if different from the CHS director) may sign their respective schedules.
27. *See Directory of Records Management Analysts for Local Government Agencies*, State Archives of N.C. (last visited Apr. 14, 2025), https://archives.ncdcr.gov/government/local/analysts.

Chapter 12

Legal Liability and Immunity

The actions of a consolidated human services agency (CHSA) or its governing board may subject a county to liability in a variety of ways. In many cases, it is the county itself that is liable for legal claims involving CHSA officials and employees. However, in some cases, a lawsuit may also seek to hold individual consolidated human services (CHS) board members, the CHS director, or CHSA employees personally liable for their conduct.

This chapter discusses the ways in which liability can arise from lawsuits related to human services, the types of immunity available to the county and board members, and the board's role in helping to reduce the risks of such liability for the county.[1]

Lawsuits Against Board Members

An individual may file a civil lawsuit against CHS board members in either their official capacities or their individual capacities. Alternatively, an individual may bring legal claims against board members in *both* their official and individual capacities. The difference between *official capacity claims* and *individual capacity claims* is significant. The type of claim determines who is potentially liable for damages in the lawsuit and what types of immunity are available to the named board members.

Official Capacity Claims

If a person sues a CHS board member in the member's official capacity based on the board's alleged violation of state or federal law, the lawsuit is, in essence, a lawsuit against the *county*.[2] Even though individual board members are named as defendants, an official capacity lawsuit does not seek to hold the individual board members liable. This means that if a monetary judgment is entered against board members in their official capacities, the legal responsibility for paying the judgment lies with the county and not with the individual board members. Likewise, if the

CHS director is sued in the director's official capacity, the lawsuit seeks to recover monetary damages from the county, not the director personally.

If an official capacity lawsuit is filed against CHS board members, the board and the affected members should immediately contact the county attorney regarding the lawsuit.

Individual Capacity Claims

By contrast, a lawsuit that names a CHS board member in the member's individual capacity alleges that the board member is *personally* liable.[3] This means that if a monetary judgment is entered against the board member, the legal responsibility for paying the judgment lies with the individual board member, not the county. Likewise, if the CHS director is sued in the director's individual capacity, the lawsuit is seeking to hold the director personally liable for a violation of the law.

If a lawsuit names a board member as a defendant in the member's individual capacity, the board member may want to consider seeking advice from independent legal counsel.

Lawsuits Against the County

In North Carolina, a CHSA is a subdivision of a county government, not a separate or independent legal entity.[4] Consequently, if a lawsuit is brought against a CHSA, it is the county, not the CHSA itself, that is the proper defendant.[5] This means that counties may, in some circumstances, be subject to liability based on the acts or omissions of CHSA employees, including the CHS director.

Liability Under the Open Meetings Law and Public Records Law

Please refer to Chapter 10 for information about liability under the open meetings law and Chapter 11 for information about liability under the public records law. If a CHS board member knowingly and intentionally violates the open meetings law or the public records law, a court may order the board member to personally pay all or part of a plaintiff's attorneys' fees.[6] However, a board member cannot be held personally liable for such fees under either law if the board member sought and followed the advice of an attorney with respect to the action or request at issue.[7]

Liability and Immunity for Tort Claims

Sometimes lawsuits involving human services agencies turn on a question of tort liability. A tort is a wrongful act or omission (other than a criminal act or breach of contract) that causes some form of harm or injury and for which courts will provide a remedy (typically in the form of monetary damages).[8]

To succeed in a tort lawsuit, the injured party (the plaintiff) must generally demonstrate that a defendant violated a duty owed to the plaintiff and that the violation caused harm to the plaintiff or the plaintiff's property.[9]

Categories of Torts

There are two primary categories of torts.[10]

Negligence torts involve a failure to exercise the standard of care that a reasonably prudent person would have exercised in a similar situation.[11] A person may only be liable for negligence if that person had a duty to act according to a particular standard of care, failed to do so, and thereby caused harm to another person or property. For example, a CHSA and its employees might face a lawsuit based on alleged

- negligent placement of a child in a foster or adoptive home,[12]
- negligent assessment of a report of abuse or neglect,[13]
- negligence in acting as a guardian for a legally incompetent adult,[14]
- negligence in approving a septic system,[15]
- negligent misrepresentation as to whether a property was suitable for supporting a septic tank,[16]
- negligent infliction of emotional distress,[17] or
- negligent hiring, retention, or supervision of an employee.[18]

Intentional torts, by contrast, are committed by someone acting with intent to engage in a wrongful act.[19] Examples of intentional torts include battery (nonconsensual touching of the body of another with the intent to cause harmful or offensive contact), intentional infliction of emotional distress, and defamation.

Governmental Immunity for Tort Claims Against the County

In North Carolina, when a lawsuit is brought against a county, a legal doctrine known as *governmental immunity* protects the county from liability for tort claims so long as (1) the claim arises from the performance of governmental (as opposed to proprietary) functions, and (2) the county has not waived its immunity through the purchase of liability insurance.[20] Most of the activities performed by CHSA employees and CHS board members are governmental in nature, meaning that the county will generally be shielded from liability for tort claims arising from those activities.[21]

As discussed earlier in this chapter, legal claims against the CHSA, the CHS director, or CHS board members in their "official capacities," are all in essence lawsuits against the county itself.[22] This means that governmental immunity applies to tort claims against any of these parties as long as the claims arise from the performance of governmental functions, unless the county has waived such immunity.[23] Governmental immunity does not apply to CHS board members in the rare instances when they are sued in their *individual* capacities, but as discussed in the following section, "public official" immunity may apply to those claims.[24]

Public Official Immunity from Tort Claims Against Board Members and CHS Directors

If a CHS board member or CHS director is sued in their individual capacity, a legal doctrine known as "public official immunity" may apply. It protects a public official from personal liability for claims alleging negligence in the exercise of the judgment and discretion with which the official is invested by virtue of the office.[25] However, this immunity is not absolute.

Public official immunity does not apply if the board member's or CHS director's "act, or failure to act, was corrupt or malicious" or if the board member or CHS director "acted outside of and beyond the scope of his duties."[26] Additionally, some North Carolina Court of Appeals decisions have held that public official immunity applies only to mere negligence claims, meaning it does not protect board members or CHS directors who are sued in their individual capacities for *intentional* torts.[27]

Limitations to Governmental Immunity and Public Official Immunity

It is important to remember that governmental immunity and public official immunity apply only to tort claims. These immunity doctrines do not protect the county, a board member, or a CHS director from legal claims alleging

- breach of a valid contract;[28]
- violations of a person's rights under the United States Constitution (see below);
- violations of federal law, such as Title VII of the Civil Rights Act of 1964, the Americans with Disabilities Act, the Age Discrimination in Employment Act, or federal criminal laws; or
- violations of state law, such as the public records law, the open meetings law, social services confidentiality statutes (e.g., Chapter 108A, Section 80 of the North Carolina General Statutes (hereinafter G.S.)), public health laws found in G.S. 130A, or state criminal laws.

Liability and Immunity for Claims Under 42 U.S.C. § 1983

Sometimes a lawsuit involving a CHSA may allege violations of an individual's rights under the United States Constitution. In such a case, the claim is typically brought under 42 U.S.C. § 1983 (often called *Section 1983*), a federal statute that authorizes a person to sue and receive injunctive relief or monetary damages from a local government or local government official if the government's conduct or public official's conduct violates the person's rights under the United States Constitution or certain federal statutes.[29]

County human services officials and employees may be sued for prospective injunctive relief under Section 1983 (typically meaning the suit seeks a court order stopping the agency's officials and employees from engaging in certain conduct in the future). Under certain circumstances, counties may also be held liable for monetary damages in Section 1983 lawsuits that involve the conduct of county human services officials or employees.[30] Section 1983 lawsuits frequently allege violations of federal constitutional rights, such as the First Amendment right to free speech or the Fourteenth Amendment right to due process.

Section 1983 claims may be brought against public officials or public employees in their individual capacities. Board members and CHS directors, like other public officials, may be held personally liable for monetary damages under Section 1983 when sued in their individual capacities. However, a legal doctrine known as *qualified immunity* frequently protects them from personal liability. Qualified immunity protects public officials and employees from personal liability under Section 1983 so long as their conduct "does not violate clearly established statutory or constitutional rights of which a reasonable person would have known."[31] A right is clearly established when it is "sufficiently clear that every reasonable official would have understood that what he is doing violates that right."[32] This means that qualified immunity generally protects CHS board members, CHS directors, and CHSA employees from personal liability under Section 1983 unless they are "plainly incompetent or . . . knowingly violate the law."[33]

Criminal Liability

CHS board members and CHS directors are subject to generally applicable federal and state criminal laws, as well as to certain criminal laws that specifically govern the conduct of public officials. For example, a CHS board member or CHS director may be held criminally liable for

- unlawfully disclosing confidential information regarding persons who have applied for or are receiving public assistance or social services from the CHSA;[34]
- unlawfully receiving a direct benefit from a contract that involves the CHSA (see Chapter 9);[35]
- receiving a gift, service, favor, or reward in return for attempting to influence the award of a contract by the CHSA (see Chapter 9);[36]
- willfully disrupting an official meeting of the CHS board or another public body;[37]
- assaulting other CHS board members, the CHS director, CHSA employees, or other individuals;[38]
- embezzling or willfully and corruptly misapplying county funds;[39]
- making a false statement under oath in the context of a lawsuit;[40] or
- willfully failing to discharge duties as a public official.[41]

Legal Challenges to Local Board of Health Rules

A CHS board or CHSA may also encounter legal challenges related to local public health rules promulgated by the board.[42] Every local board of health in North Carolina—including every CHS board for a CHSA that includes public health—has authority to adopt local rules as necessary to protect and promote public health.[43] Local public health rules adopted by the CHS board (acting as the board of health) apply throughout the county (including in all municipalities).[44] For more information about local public health rulemaking, see Chapter 19.

A person who wishes to challenge the enforcement of a local public health rule has thirty days from when the enforcement action at issue was taken to give notice of their appeal to the local health director.[45] Within five working days of receiving such a notice, the local health director must transmit the notice (along with documentation showing the basis for the challenged enforcement action) to the CHS board (if the CHS board has assumed the powers and duties of a board of health).[46] The CHS board must hold a hearing on the appeal and issue a written decision that affirms, modifies, or reverses the challenged action based on evidence presented at the hearing.[47] For more information about this process (known as "adjudication"), see Chapter 20. If the person who challenged the enforcement action is dissatisfied with the outcome of the CHS board's adjudication, they may contest the board's decision through an appeal to district court.[48]

Some legal challenges to local public health rules may arise in the form of declaratory judgment actions filed in superior court, in which a party seeks a declaration from the court that a rule adopted by the CHS board is not legally valid.[49] These cases generally focus on whether the board had authority to adopt a certain rule, not how the rule was enforced against a specific party.

Legal Representation and Indemnification of County Officials

Legal Representation

A county is authorized, but not required, to provide legal representation for a CHS board member in connection with any civil or criminal action brought against the board member on account of alleged acts or omissions committed in the scope and course of the board member's service on the board.[50] Likewise, a county is authorized, not required, to provide legal representation for a CHS director in connection with any civil or criminal action brought against the director on account of alleged acts or omissions committed in the scope and course of the director's employment.

The county may provide this representation through its own attorney, through a private attorney, or by purchasing insurance that requires the insurer to provide the defense.[51] The board of county commissioners is responsible for deciding whether or not to provide such legal representation to an individual public official.

Liability Insurance

State law authorizes counties to purchase insurance to protect any of their officers, agents, or employees from civil liability for damages arising from acts or omissions within the scope of their authority and the course of their employment.[52] The board of county commissioners has discretion to determine what claims and which public officials and employees will be covered by this liability insurance.[53] This means that counties may choose to purchase insurance that protects CHS board members from individual civil liability in connection with their board service (or that protects the CHS director from individual civil liability in connection with the director's employment), but counties are not required to purchase such insurance.

Paying Settlements or Judgments

Each county is authorized, but not required, to pay all or part of any settlement or judgment entered in a lawsuit brought against a current or former county official (including a CHS board member) on account of alleged acts or omissions within the scope of the official's public office if the following conditions are met:

1. notice of the legal claim or litigation is given to the board of county commissioners prior to the time that the claim is settled or civil judgment is entered;
2. the county has adopted a set of uniform standards (made available for public inspection) under which settlements or judgments against county officials will be paid; and
3. the board of county commissioners determines that the county official did not act or fail to act because of actual fraud, corruption, or actual malice.[54]

Lawsuits Against the State

In some instances, the actions of CHSA employees who work in public health or social services may result in liability for the State of North Carolina under the State Tort Claims Act.[55] For example, the State Tort Claims Act allows the North Carolina Department of Health and Human Services (NCDHHS) to be held liable based on the negligence of a county social services director or employee if the director or employee was acting as an "agent of the State" when the alleged negligence occurred.[56]

The actions of CHSA employees who work in environmental health may likewise result in liability for the state under the State Tort Claims Act. A person who works for CHSA as a registered environmental health specialist (REHS), a REHS intern (REHSI), or a registered environmental health associate (REHA) may be authorized to act on behalf of the state by enforcing certain environmental health rules promulgated by the North Carolina Commission for Public Health (CPH).[57]

Although an REHS, REHSI, or REHA is typically an employee or contractor of a local health department, these professionals act as agents of the state when they conduct inspections and enforce environmental health rules adopted by CPH.[58] As of 2024, each local health department is required to enter into an annual agreement with NCDHHS to provide environmental health services as set forth in G.S. 130A. The agreement must include language regarding quality assurance for all the environmental health services rendered under the agreement. If a CHSA (acting as the local health department) enters into the required annual agreement with NCDHHS, then a REHS, REHSI, or REHA who is employed or contracted by the CHSA will be defended by the North Carolina Office of the Attorney General (AG) in lawsuits brought against them in their official or individual capacities (or both) for acts or omissions made in the scope and course of enforcing CPH rules. However, the state may refuse to defend the REHS, REHSI, or REHA if it determines that

1. the act or omission was not within the scope and course of the REHS, REHSI, or REHA's duties as an authorized agent of the state;
2. the REHS, REHSI, or REHA acted or failed to act because of actual fraud, corruption, or actual malice on the part of the REHS, REHSI, or REHA;
3. defense of the REHS, REHSI, or REHA by the state would create a conflict of interest between the state and the REHS, REHSI, or REHA; or
4. defense of the REHS, REHSI, or REHA would not be in the best interests of the state.[59]

If the AG does provide legal representation and a settlement is reached in the case, then NCDHHS and the CHSA must each pay half of the settlement costs. Under certain circumstances, NCDHHS may opt to exercise its discretion to pay a larger portion of the settlement based on the unique facts of the case.[60] Recovery under the State Tort Claims Act is capped at a maximum of one million dollars.[61] For claims arising out of an REHS, REHSI, or REHSA's enforcement of *local* environmental health rules, legal representation by the AG is not provided and no portion of a settlement will be paid by NCDHHS.[62]

What happens if a CHSA fails to enter into the required annual agreement with NCDHHS? In this situation, any REHS, REHSI, or REHA who works for or is contracted by that CHSA would not be entitled to legal representation by the AG in lawsuits that arise from acts or omissions that occurred while the REHS, REHSI, or REHA was working for that CHSA and enforcing CPH rules. As described earlier in this chapter, the county served by the CHSA could (but is not required to) defend the REHS, REHSI, or REHA.[63] NCDHHS would also not be responsible for paying any portion of a settlement reached in a case involving an REHS, REHSI, or REHA who worked for a CHSA that failed to execute the required annual agreement.[64]

Notes

1. The legal liability and immunity of North Carolina local governments, officials, and employees is discussed in more detail in Kristi A. Nickodem, *Civil Liability and Immunity of Local Governments, Public Officials, and Public Employees*, *in* County and Municipal Government in North Carolina ch. 6 (Chris McLaughlin ed., UNC School of Government, 2025 ed.).
2. *See* Meyer v. Walls, 347 N.C. 97, 110 (1997) ("A suit against a defendant in his individual capacity means that the plaintiff seeks recovery from the defendant directly; a suit against a defendant in his official capacity means that the plaintiff seeks recovery from the entity of which the public servant defendant is an agent.").
3. *Id.*
4. *See, e.g.*, *Meyer*, 347 N.C. at 104 ("[A]n action against a county agency which directly affects the rights of the county is in fact an action against the county."); Malloy v. Durham Cnty. Dep't of Soc. Servs., 58 N.C. App. 61 (1982).
5. *See* Chapter 153A, Section 11 of the North Carolina General Statutes (hereinafter G.S.) (authorizing counties to "sue and be sued"); see also *Meyer*, 347 N.C. at 104; Johnson v. Marrow, 228 N.C. 58, 59 (1947) ("Where a county is the real party in interest, it must sue and be sued in its name."); Wade v. Alamance Cnty. Dep't of Soc. Servs., No. 1:19-CV-619, 2020 WL 3846336, at *5 (M.D.N.C. July 8, 2020) (compiling cases in which federal district courts in North Carolina have dismissed claims against county departments of social services); West v. Buncombe County, No. 1:14-CV-00088-MOC-DSC, 2014 WL 4384021, at *3 (W.D.N.C. Sept. 3, 2014) (dismissing claims asserted against a consolidated human services agency on grounds that the entity lacked legal capacity for suit).
6. G.S. 132-9(c); G.S. 143-318.16B.
7. *Id.*
8. *Tort*, Black's Law Dictionary (12th ed. 2024).
9. *See* Nickodem, *supra* note 1.
10. A third category of torts, known as strict-liability torts, is beyond the scope of this chapter.
11. *See Negligence*, Black's Law Dictionary (12th ed. 2024).
12. White v. Stokes Cnty. Dep't of Soc. Servs., 207 N.C. App. 378 (2010); Hobbs *ex rel.* Winner v. N.C. Dep't of Hum. Res., 135 N.C. App. 412 (1999).
13. *See, e.g.*, Hunter v. Transylvania Cnty. Dep't of Soc. Servs., 207 N.C. App. 735 (2010); Whitaker v. Clark, 109 N.C. App. 379 (1993).
14. Meyer v. Walls, 347 N.C. 97 (1997).
15. *See* Block v. County of Person, 141 N.C. App. 273 (2000).
16. *See* Tabor v. County of Orange, 156 N.C. App. 88 (2003).
17. *See* McConnell v. Watauga County, No. 5:17-CV-195-MOC-DCK, 2019 WL 2344223 (W.D.N.C. May 31, 2019), *aff'd*, 790 F. App'x 543 (4th Cir. 2020).
18. *See* Christmas v. Cabarrus County, 192 N.C. App. 227 (2008); Block v. County of Person, 141 N.C. App. 273 (2000); Carter v. Stanly County, 123 N.C. App. 235 (1996).
19. *See Tort*, Black's Law Dictionary (12th ed. 2024).
20. *See* Trey Allen, Local Government Immunity to Lawsuits in North Carolina 2 (UNC School of Government, 2018).
21. Nickodem, *supra* note 1.
22. G.S. 153A-11 establishes that a county is a legal entity which may be sued, but there is no state statute authorizing lawsuits against a consolidated human services agency or consolidated human services board. *See, e.g.*, Johnson v. Marrow, 228 N.C. 58, 59 (1947) ("Where a county is the real party in interest, it must sue and be sued in its name.");

Meyer v. Walls, 347 N.C. 97, 110 (1997); Malloy v. Durham Cnty. Dep't of Soc. Servs., 58 N.C. App. 61, 67 (1982); Avery v. Burke County, 660 F.2d 111, 114 (4th Cir. 1981) ("Neither the Board of Health nor the Board of Social Services is a legal entity separate and apart from the county. Both boards are created by, and are extensions of, the county.").

23. For more information about the waiver of governmental immunity, please see Allen, *supra* note 20, ch. 4.
24. *See* Wright v. Gaston County, 205 N.C. App. 600 (2010) ("Plaintiff's complaint also alleges claims against the [defendants] in their individual capacities, for which governmental immunity is not applicable.").
25. Hart v. Brienza, 246 N.C. App. 426, 431 (2016) (quoting Smith v. State, 289 N.C. 303, 331 (1976)); *see also* Kitchin *ex rel.* Kitchin v. Halifax County, 192 N.C. App. 559, 568 (2008) (finding a local health director to be a public officer entitled to public official immunity); Hunter v. Transylvania Cnty. Dep't of Soc. Servs., 207 N.C. App. 735, 738 (2010) ("The director of social services has long been recognized as a public official.").
26. Doe v. Wake County, 264 N.C. App. 692, 695, (2019) (quoting Hobbs *ex rel.* Winner v. N.C. Dep't of Hum. Res., 135 N.C. App. 412, 422 (1999)).
27. *See* McCullers v. Lewis, 265 N.C. App. 216, 222 (2019); Wells v. N.C. Dep't of Corr., 152 N.C. App. 307, 320 (2002). For a more comprehensive discussion of this topic, please see Trey Allen, *Do Intentional Tort Claims Always Defeat Public Official Immunity?*, Loc. Gov't L. Bull. No. 139 (UNC School of Government, Sept. 2016), https://www.sog.unc.edu/publications/bulletins/do-intentional-tort-claims-always-defeat-public-official-immunity; *see also* Trey Allen, *Public Official Immunity for Intentional Torts? The Split Continues*, Coates' Canons: NC Loc. Gov't L. (blog) (June 20, 2019), https://canons.sog.unc.edu/2019/06/public-official-immunity-for-intentional-torts-the-split-continues/.
28. *See* Wray v. City of Greensboro, 370 N.C. 41, 47 (2017). Entering into a valid contract constitutes a waiver of governmental immunity.
29. The legal liability of North Carolina local governments and local government officials and employees under Section 1983 is discussed in Nickodem, *supra* note 1.
30. *See* Monell v. Dep't of Soc. Servs. of N.Y., 436 U.S. 658 (1978); *see also* Hogan v. Cherokee County, 519 F. Supp. 3d 263 (W.D.N.C. 2021).
31. Mullenix v. Luna, 577 U.S. 7, 11 (2015) (citing Pearson v. Callahan, 555 U.S. 223, 231 (2009)).
32. *Id.* at 11 (quoting Reichle v. Howards, 566 U.S. 658 (2012)).
33. *Id.* at 12 (quoting Malley v. Briggs, 475 U.S. 335, 341 (1986)).
34. G.S. 108A-80.
35. G.S. 14-234. Chapter 9 discusses this statute in more detail.
36. *Id.*
37. G.S. 143-318.17.
38. *See, e.g.*, G.S. 14, §§ 33, 34.2, 32.4.
39. G.S. 14-92.
40. G.S. 14-209.
41. G.S. 14-230(a).
42. *See, e.g.*, Phillips v. Orange Cnty. Health Dep't, 237 N.C. App. 249 (2014); Craig v. County of Chatham, 356 N.C. 40 (2002); City of Roanoke Rapids v. Peedin, 124 N.C. App. 578 (1996).
43. G.S. 130A-39(a).
44. G.S. 130A-39(c).
45. G.S. 130A-24(b).
46. *Id.*
47. G.S. 130A-24(c).
48. G.S. 130A-24(d).
49. *See* Craig v. County of Chatham, 356 N.C. 40 (2002); City of Roanoke Rapids v. Peedin, 124 N.C. App. 578 (1996).
50. *See* G.S. 160A-167(a); G.S. 153A-97.

51. G.S. 160A-167(a).
52. G.S. 153A-435.
53. G.S. 153A-435(a).
54. G.S. 160A, § 167(b), (c).
55. The North Carolina State Tort Claims Act is codified at G.S. 143, art. 31.
56. *See* Gammons v. N.C. Dep't of Hum. Res., 344 N.C. 51 (1996); Vaughn v. N.C. Dep't of Hum. Res., 296 N.C. 683 (1979); G.S. 108A-14 (responsibility of DSS director to act as an agent of NCDHHS with respect to certain work).
57. G.S. 130A-4(b); Title 15A, Chapter 010, Section .0100 of the North Carolina Administrative Code.
58. *See* G.S. 130A-4(b), (d); G.S. 143-300.8. In the past, an REHS, REHSI, or REHA working for a local health department was entitled—subject to certain limitations—to legal representation by the North Carolina Office of the Attorney General (AG) for lawsuits related to acts or omissions that occurred in the scope and course of enforcing CPH rules. In 2024, the law governing state and local responsibility for providing legal representation and paying out settlements for lawsuits involving REHS, REHSI, and REHA conduct was amended. *See* S.L. 2024-49, § 4.7, amending G.S. 143-300.8.
59. G.S. 143-300.4(a).
60. G.S. 143-300.8(b)–(c).
61. G.S. 143-299.2(a).
62. G.S. 143-300.8(e).
63. G.S. 153A-97.
64. G.S. 143-300.8(d).

PART 2
Social Services

Chapter 13

Social Services in North Carolina

Consolidated human services (CHS) boards in North Carolina function within a large and complex social services system. In a county where the consolidated human services agency (CHSA) includes social services, CHS board members need to have a basic knowledge of this system to understand the broader legal framework around the agencies they govern. This chapter will introduce the legal roles and responsibilities of North Carolina counties, North Carolina state government, and the federal government with respect to social services policy, administration, and funding.

What Are Social Services?

The term *social services* refers to a diverse mix of programs and services intended to help individuals and families in need. In some cases, social services address personal safety needs by providing protection to a child or adult who has been abused or neglected. In other cases, social services address financial needs by connecting low-income individuals and families with programs that can help them buy food or pay for heat in the winter. Some of these services and programs are offered by local public agencies, including county departments of social services, CHSAs, and agencies serving senior citizens, veterans, or survivors of domestic violence. Private organizations, including nonprofits and religious institutions, also offer many social services programs in North Carolina communities.

Social Services Programs and Agencies

Social services programs and agencies address a range of economic and social problems that impair the ability of individuals to function and thrive in society. These problems include poverty, hunger and food insecurity, lack of medical care, homelessness and unstable housing, child abuse and neglect, abuse and neglect of

Table 13.1. Examples of Social Services Programs

Means-Tested	Not Means-Tested
Food and Nutrition Services	Child protective services
Medicaid	Adult protective services
Work First (Temporary Assistance for Needy Families)	Public guardianship
Child Care Subsidy	Child support enforcement

vulnerable adults, and unemployment. Such problems affect the general well-being and stability of society as a whole, not just the individuals and families experiencing them directly. When county social services agencies address these problems, they are making an investment in the long-term flourishing and stability of the community.

North Carolina counties are required by state law to provide certain social services within their jurisdictions. Many counties also offer additional services tailored to community needs. Each county social services agency administers dozens of social services programs, and each of these programs has its own rules regarding eligibility, assistance, services, administration, and funding. The services and programs provided by county social services agencies can be divided into two primary categories: economic services and social work services.

Economic services, also referred to as public assistance programs, assist eligible people through monetary payments and other economic supports. This category includes programs such as Food and Nutrition Services, Medicaid, and Low-Income Energy Assistance. Most economic services programs are *means-tested*, meaning that eligibility is determined based on a person's or family's income and resources.[1]

Social work services, on the other hand, are typically provided without regard to income. Social work services provided by a county social services agency include protecting children and vulnerable adults from abuse and neglect, acting as a public guardian to individuals adjudicated incompetent by a court, and helping families navigate the licensing process for foster care and adoption. Table 13.1 lists some examples of programs that are means-tested and some that are not.

Overview of North Carolina's Social Services System

North Carolina has adopted a county-administered, state-supervised social services system under which social services programs are *administered* primarily by county agencies under the *supervision* of various state-level entities.[2] North Carolina is one of only a small number of states in which social services programs are directly administered by counties rather than by the state.[3] In most states, the state directly administers social services programs through a centralized administrative system.[4] This means that in most states, local governments have "little or no role in administering or financing state and federal social services programs."[5] North Carolina's unique model has implications for counties related to funding, governance, liability, staff, and program administration.

Each county social services agency exists at a complex intersection of federal, state, and county involvement with the agency's funding, policy, and operations. The federal government funds many of the programs offered by county social services agencies and attaches specific requirements to the administration of those programs. That federal funding is received by the state, which in turn allocates that funding to the counties. The state is responsible for ensuring that counties comply with applicable federal and state law related to mandated social services programs, as well as allocating state funding to counties and establishing policies for county agencies.

Each North Carolina county is responsible for establishing a social services agency, determining a governance structure for the agency, hiring and supervising social services staff, funding part of the cost of social services programs, and administering social services programs in compliance with state and federal law.

The unique roles of federal, state, and county government in North Carolina's social services system are described in more detail in the following sections of this chapter.

The Federal Government's Role and Responsibilities

Federal law does not require any state to operate particular social services programs. Rather, Congress appropriates funds available to states that agree to operate certain social services programs in accordance with applicable federal law. In other words, the federal government provides funding to states that choose to operate certain programs, but that funding comes with strings (legal requirements) attached.

The level of federal financial participation varies from program to program. With respect to the costs of programs that involve federal or state financial participation or both—that is, excluding programs funded only by counties—the North Carolina Department of Health and Human Services (NCDHHS) estimated that for state fiscal year 2024–2025, federal funds would provide

- over 95 percent of the direct costs of public assistance programs,
- over 62 percent of associated administrative costs for public assistance programs, and
- over 56 percent of the costs of services programs.[6]

Though the federal government does not require states to provide particular social services programs, the federal government offers significant financial incentives for states to make federally supported social services programs available to their residents.[7]

The federal executive agency with primary responsibility for overseeing most social services programs is the U.S. Department of Health and Human Services.

The U.S. Department of Agriculture oversees food and nutrition programs. These agencies promulgate regulations to carry out federal laws, issue policies to the states, and monitor state compliance with federal requirements. They can impose financial sanctions on states for failing to meet these requirements. Federal laws and regulations may dictate many different aspects of program administration, including eligibility, benefit amounts, duration of assistance or services, and confidentiality of program information.

There is no direct relationship between the federal government and counties with respect to federally funded social services programs. The federal government provides funding for these programs to each state and holds the *state* accountable for complying with federal requirements and conditions. However, counties are still required to comply with the federal laws associated with these programs because the federal mandates that are imposed on the state are passed on to counties along with federal funding for social services programs.[8]

The State's Role and Responsibilities

The North Carolina Constitution recognizes the state's duty to provide "beneficent provision for the poor, the unfortunate, and the orphan"[9] and requires the state to establish and operate "such charitable [and] benevolent . . . institutions and agencies as the needs of humanity and the public good may require" in a manner to be determined by the North Carolina General Assembly.[10]

The North Carolina General Assembly

The General Assembly is primarily responsible for determining the extent and scope of the state's responsibility for social services and how the state will discharge that responsibility. The General Assembly has enacted laws that require counties to carry out a substantial portion of the state's responsibility for social services.[11]

Among other things, laws enacted by the General Assembly

- authorize the state to participate in federal-state social services programs;[12]
- designate NCDHHS as the single state agency responsible for supervising the administration of federal-state social services programs;[13]
- appropriate state funding for social services programs;
- allocate federal social services funds received by the state;
- establish the role, authority, and responsibility of county governments with respect to social services; and
- determine how the state and counties will share responsibility for the nonfederal portion of the cost of federally supported programs.[14]

Much of the social services legislation enacted by the General Assembly is codified in Chapter 108A of the North Carolina General Statutes, which includes laws regarding county administration of social services programs, confidentiality of social services records, and financing of social services programs.[15] However, many details regarding the funding, administration, and supervision of social services programs do not appear in the General Statutes. Some are addressed by administrative rules and policies promulgated by NCDHHS and the state Social Services Commission, while others are decided by the General Assembly when it appropriates funds for public assistance and social services programs.[16]

The North Carolina Department of Health and Human Services

NCDHHS is the state agency that is responsible for supervising the administration of state and federal-state social services programs.[17] This includes issuing policies for use by county social services agencies in interpreting and implementing the various laws and regulations governing social services programs. NCDHHS also handles some administrative functions directly or through contracts with private vendors, such as processing and paying Medicaid claims, operating the child support enforcement program in certain counties, making medical determinations for Social Security and state Medicaid Disability claims, and hearing administrative appeals involving eligibility for certain social services programs.

In addition to creating policies and providing technical assistance, NCDHHS has the authority to take corrective action in the event that a county social services agency is noncompliant with the law.[18] Each county social services agency is required to enter into an annual written *memorandum of agreement* with NCDHHS (sometimes referred to as a memorandum of understanding, or MOU) that sets out specific performance requirements and administrative responsibilities for all mandated social services programs, with the exception of Medicaid.[19] When a county social services agency fails to comply with the terms of the written agreement, the mandated performance measures, or other applicable laws, NCDHHS has the authority to provide technical assistance, create and implement a corrective action plan, divest the county director of social services of service delivery powers, and ultimately control county service delivery directly or through a contract with a public or private agency.[20] If NCDHHS determines that a county social services agency is not providing child protective services, foster care services, or adoption services in accordance with state law and regulations, NCDHHS may act on an emergency basis to temporarily take over the delivery of child welfare services in that county, and it may withhold state and federal funding for child welfare services from the county.[21]

State Commissions

Three state commissions play a significant role in the state's social services programs: the Social Services Commission, the Child Care Commission, and the State Human Resources Commission. These commissions adopt rules found in the North Carolina Administrative Code, which have the force and effect of law.

Social Services Commission

This commission has broad authority to adopt rules that govern most of the state's social services programs.[22] The commission is also authorized to establish standards for inspecting and licensing maternity homes, adult care homes for aged or disabled persons, and residential child care facilities. The commission may authorize investigations of social problems, subpoena witnesses, and compel the production of documents.[23] In counties with an appointed board of social services, the Social Services Commission appoints either one or two members (depending on whether the county has a three- or five-member board).[24] The governor appoints the commission's members, one from each congressional district, for four-year terms.[25]

Child Care Commission

This commission adopts standards and rules for the licensing and operation of child care facilities.[26] It also is charged with making rules for responding to child abuse or neglect in child care facilities.[27] The commission has seventeen members—nine appointed by the governor and eight by the General Assembly—that serve for two-year terms.[28]

State Human Resources Commission

This commission, in conjunction with the Office of State Human Resources, establishes policies and rules related to many aspects of the State Human Resources Act (SHRA).[29] All employees of a (nonconsolidated) county department of social services are subject to the SHRA and to the State Human Resources Commission's rules for local government employees.[30] Most counties with CHSAs have opted to remove their CHSA employees from SHRA coverage, and consequently, the State Human Resources Commission's rules do not apply to their personnel processes. The commission has nine members—four appointed by the General Assembly and five by the state governor—that serve for four-year terms.[31]

The Counties' Roles and Responsibilities

As discussed above, North Carolina is an outlier in the national social services landscape because of the amount of responsibility placed on counties for the funding and administration of social services programs. The role of counties with respect to social services in North Carolina is based on state laws that authorize or require counties to administer or fund social services programs and require counties to establish social services agencies and governing boards.[32]

Under North Carolina's state-supervised and county-administered system, county social services agencies are primarily responsible for administering social services programs, under the supervision of NCDHHS.[33] Under this system, county social services agencies are part of county government and employees of county social services agencies are county employees. In addition, North Carolina counties

Table 13.2. Division of State and County Responsibility for Social Services in North Carolina

State	County
• Accept federal funding for social services programs; transmit federal and state funding to counties • Develop state law and policy • Provide oversight and supervision of county-level administration of social services programs • Provide technical assistance to county agencies	• Allocate county funding to social services agency; pay county's share of nonfederal costs for federally funded programs • Administer programs locally in compliance with federal and state laws and state policy • Hire, train, and supervise local staff to administer and deliver social services programs • Determine agency structure and governance model

must pay part of the administrative costs associated with social services programs and part of the cost of the direct assistance and services provided under many social services programs.

For instance, NCDHHS estimated that for state fiscal year 2024–2025, county funds would provide

- 1.85 percent of the direct costs of public assistance programs;
- 37.84 percent of associated administrative costs for public assistance programs; and
- 38.71 percent of the costs of social services programs (such as child protective services, adult protective services, and child support enforcement).[34]

More information about the county's role in financing social services programs may be found in Chapter 7.

North Carolina's unique social services system reflects the state's long history of county responsibility for social services. It provides counties with a high level of flexibility and control over the structure, governance, and internal operations of their social services agencies. However, the state-supervised, county-administered nature of North Carolina's social services system continues to generate concerns among some stakeholders, as evidenced by ongoing debates regarding intercounty collaboration, county funding obligations, information sharing between counties, child welfare reform, and the nature of state supervision over county operations.[35]

As shown in Table 13.2, North Carolina counties have a substantial amount of responsibility for the administration and funding of social services programs. The powers and duties of county commissioners, county social services agencies, directors of social services, and social services governing boards are defined by and subject to state law and state supervision. In some instances, these powers and duties are also constrained by federal law, including federal confidentiality laws and federal requirements attached to funding for social services programs.

Each board of county commissioners is responsible for establishing an agency to provide social services and choosing a governance structure for that agency.[36] The agency and governance structure a county chooses will affect the hiring process for the agency director and agency staff, who are all recruited and hired at the local level.

Organization

A county has three options for organizing the local agency that delivers social services. The county may

- operate a county department of social services,
- establish a CHSA that includes social services,[37] or
- establish a regional (multicounty) department of social services.[38]

At the time of publication, no North Carolina counties have opted to create a regional department of social services. More information about regional departments and boards of social services is available in *Local Social Services Boards in North Carolina*, by Kristi A. Nickodem (UNC School of Government, 2023).

Governing Board

State law requires every county in North Carolina to have a governing board for social services, which may be

- an appointed county board of social services,
- an appointed consolidated human services board,
- a regional board of social services, or
- a board of county commissioners that exercises the powers and duties of a county board of social services or a consolidated human services board.[39]

The governance options available to each county depend in part on the organizational model that the county has chosen for providing social services. For more information about how the organization and governance options fit together, refer to Chapter 1 of this book.

Director

Regardless of the type of organization that administers social services programs in a county, someone must be appointed to serve in the role of director of social services.[40] The director administers the public assistance and social services programs directly and through social services staff.[41] The person or entity with authority to appoint the director differs based on the agency structure a county has in place.

In a county with a CHSA, the *county manager* must appoint a CHS director, who in turn assumes all of the powers and duties of a social services director.[42] The CHS director may delegate some or all of these social services powers and duties to another employee (sometimes called the "DSS director"), but the CHS director retains the ultimate responsibility for ensuring that all obligations and functions involving social services programs and policies are carried out.[43] In a county with a nonconsolidated county DSS, the *social services board* must appoint a director of social services for the DSS.[44]

If counties form a regional department of social services, the *regional board of social services* must appoint a regional director of social services for the department.[45]

Staff

Employees of a county DSS or a CHSA are county employees. Different rules and policies may apply to social services agency employees based on the agency structure a county has in place.

- In a CHSA, the agency's employees are hired by the CHS director with the approval of the county manager.[46] When creating a CHSA, county commissioners can choose to keep the CHSA's employees subject to the SHRA or opt to remove them from SHRA coverage, making them subject solely to county personnel policies and procedures.[47]
- In a county DSS or regional DSS, the agency's employees are hired by the DSS director and are subject to the SHRA and certain State Human Resources Commission rules.[48]

For more information on the role of a board of county commissioners in choosing a county's organization and governance model for social services, funding social services programs, making decisions regarding social services programs, and appointing a special attorney for social services matters, please see Chapter 8 of this book.

Notes

1. The federal poverty guidelines (sometimes called the "federal poverty level") provide one important measure for determining whether an individual or family qualifies for means-tested services. The federal poverty guidelines are established by the U.S. Department of Health and Human Services. They are adjusted each year, vary based on the number of persons in the household, and attempt to provide a rough measure of the income a family needs to obtain adequate housing, food, and other necessities. In 2022, the federal poverty guideline for a family of three living in North Carolina was $23,030 per year. Various social services programs have different rules regarding whether and how the federal poverty guidelines are used to determine eligibility for services.
2. John L. Saxon, Social Services in North Carolina, 5 (UNC School of Government, 2008).
3. For example, the majority of states have state-administered child welfare programs. Only nine states can be described as county-administered: California, Colorado, Minnesota, New York, North Carolina, North Dakota, Ohio, Pennsylvania, and Virginia. Two "hybrid" states, Nevada and Wisconsin, are partially administered by the state and partially administered by counties. *State vs. County Administration of Child Welfare Services*, Child Welfare Info. Gateway (2018), https://www.childwelfare.gov/pubs/factsheets/services/.
4. N.C. Gen. Assembly, Program Evaluation Div., Statutory Changes Will Promote County Flexibility in Social Services Administration, Rep. No. 2011-03 (May 2011), https://sites.ncleg.gov/ped/wp-content/uploads/sites/11/2022/07/DSS_Report.pdf.
5. *Id.* at 3.
6. N.C. Dep't of Health & Hum. Servs., *County Budget Estimates State Totals—State Fiscal Year 2024–2025,* https://www.ncdhhs.gov/divisions/social-services/county-staff-information/budget-information/dss-budget-estimates (scroll to the heading County Budget Estimates 2024–2025 and select Budget Estimates State Totals to access PDF).
7. *See* Kristi A. Nickodem, *Social Services, in* County and Municipal Government in North Carolina ch. 38 (Chris McLaughlin ed., UNC School of Government, 2025 ed.).
8. Saxon, *supra* note 2, at 41.
9. N.C. Const. art. XI, § 4.
10. N.C. Const. art. XI, § 3.
11. *See* Martin v. Bd. of Comm'rs, 208 N.C. 354 (1935) (care of indigent sick and afflicted poor is a proper function of state government, but the General Assembly may require counties, as administrative agencies of the state, to perform this function within their territorial limits); Bd. of Managers of James Walker Mem'l Hosp. v. City of Wilmington, 237 N.C. 179 (1953); Craven Cnty. Hosp. Corp. v. Lenoir County, 75 N.C. App. 453 (1985).
12. *See* Chapter 108A, Section 71 of the North Carolina General Statutes (hereinafter G.S.).
13. G.S. 108A-71.
14. For example, for many years the state and counties shared responsibility for paying for the nonfederal share of the cost of Medicaid services. In 2007, the General Assembly enacted legislation that ultimately phased out the county's share for Medicaid services but still requires counties to help pay for costs of administering the program (S.L. 2007-323, § 31; S.L. 2007-345, § 14). Another example is found in G.S. 108A-49.1, which provides that the nonfederal share of foster care and adoption assistance payments will be divided equally between the state and county.

15. Other laws regarding social services agencies, employees, and programs are codified in G.S. Chapters 7B (Juvenile Code), 48 (Adoptions), 110 (Child Welfare), 126 (State Human Resources Act), and 153A (Counties).
16. Nickodem, *supra* note 7, 823–25. Some social services policy decisions are included in uncodified session laws, such as uncodified provisions of the state's biennial appropriations act, which specifies who is eligible for Medicaid and what services will be provided under the state's Medicaid program. The state's biennial appropriations act also allocates federal funding received by the state under the Social Services Block Grant, the TANF Block Grant, the Child Care and Development Block Grant, and the Low-Income Energy Assistance Block Grant, and it appropriates money from the state's General Fund for social services agencies and programs.
17. G.S. 108A-71; G.S. 143B, art. 3.
18. G.S. 108A-74 (authorizing NCDHHS to take various remedial measures when a county or a regional social services agency fails to comply with its mandated performance requirements or applicable law, ranging from a corrective action plan to an NCDHHS takeover of the agency, in which the director of social services is divested of service delivery powers).
19. *Id.* G.S. 108A-74 also sets forth the procedures for NCDHHS intervention, including notice requirements.
20. G.S. 108A, § 74(a)–(c).
21. G.S. 108A-74(h).
22. G.S. 143B, art. 3, pt. 6. The secretary of NCDHHS, rather than the Social Services Commission, has rulemaking authority for the Medicaid program.
23. G.S. 143B-153.
24. G.S. 108A-3.
25. G.S. 143B-154.
26. G.S. 143B-168.3.
27. G.S. 110-88.
28. G.S. 143B-168.4.
29. G.S. 126-4. Prior to 2013, the Office of State Human Resources was named the Office of State Personnel and the commission was named the State Personnel Commission. S.L. 2013-382.
30. *See* G.S. 126 (State Human Resources Act); Subchapter 1I of Title 25 of the North Carolina Administrative Code. Even though the director and staff of county social services departments are county employees, their employment is governed by the SHRA unless (1) the county's personnel system, or a portion of it, has been approved by the State Human Resources Commission as being "substantially equivalent" to the SHRA or (2) the county has incorporated the social services department into a consolidated human services agency and elected to remove the agency's employees from the SHRA.
31. G.S. 126-2.
32. North Carolina counties are political subdivisions of the state and may exercise only those powers conferred on them by state law.
33. *See* G.S. 108A, §§ 1, 14(3), 25.
34. *See* N.C. Dep't of Health & Hum. Servs., *supra* note 6. These estimated totals group together many different programs, which may receive highly differing levels of county funding (for example, adult services often receive much lower county funding than child welfare services).
35. For more information on these issues, see, e.g., Ctr. for the Support of Fams., Social Services Reform Plan (May 6, 2019), https://www.osbm.nc.gov/documents/files/socialservicesreform-finalplan/download; Soc. Servs. Reg'l Supervision & Collaboration Working Grp., Stage One Final Report (UNC School of Government, March 2018); and Soc. Servs. Reg'l Supervision & Collaboration

WORKING GRP., STAGE TWO FINAL REPORT (UNC School of Government, December 2018). Both of the working group's final reports are available at https://www.sog.unc.edu/resources/microsites/social-services/reports.

36. *See* G.S. 108A-1.
37. This option is only available to counties with a county manager. *See* G.S. 153A-77(b).
38. *See* G.S. 108A-15.7 (regional departments of social services).
39. G.S. 108A-1.
40. G.S. 108A-12.
41. G.S. 108A-14.
42. G.S. 153A-77(e); G.S. 108A-15.1(c). The county manager's decision to appoint the director must be made with the advice and consent of the CHSA's governing board (which may be an appointed CHS board or the board of county commissioners).
43. For more information on the delegation of authority within a CHSA, please see Kristi A. Nickodem, *Personnel Decisions for North Carolina's Consolidated Human Services Agencies*, SOC. SERVS. L. BULL. No. 49 (UNC School of Government, 2021), https://www.sog.unc.edu/publications/bulletins/personnel-decisions-north-carolinas-consolidated-human-services-agencies. At least one North Carolina county with a CHSA has delegated the social services director's powers and duties between two different employees, instead of having a single employee in this role.
44. *Id.*
45. G.S. 108A-15.8(a).
46. G.S. 153A-77(e).
47. G.S. 153A-77(d). To date, the majority of counties that have created CHSAs have opted to remove employees from the coverage of the SHRA, in favor of making them subject solely to county personnel policies and procedures. For more information on this decision regarding SHRA coverage, please see Nickodem, *supra* note 43.
48. G.S. 108A, §§ 14(a)(2), 15.10; G.S. 126-5(a)(2).

Chapter 14

Social Services Agencies, Programs, and Services

This chapter introduces some of the many programs and services that local social services agencies provide in their communities. Consolidated human services board members should familiarize themselves with the programs and services offered in their county, as many counties offer unique human services programs that are not mandated by state law and may not be described in this chapter.

Types of Local Social Services Agencies

North Carolina counties may choose to provide social services programs through a county department of social services (DSS), a consolidated human services agency (CHSA) that includes social services, or a regional (multicounty) department of social services.[1] At the time of this book's publication, thirty-four counties provide social services through a CHSA and sixty-six counties provide social services through a nonconsolidated county DSS. To date, no North Carolina counties have opted to create a regional department of social services. Table 14.1 shows some key differences between these agency-organization models.

Each county is required to provide adequate physical facilities for the offices of the county's social services agency. All facilities occupied by county social services agencies must meet certain state standards with respect to the types and amount of office space, privacy, accessibility, and storage. These state standards (found in Title 10A, Chapter 67A, Section .0103 of the North Carolina Administrative Code) include, among other things,

- private offices for the county director and each supervisor, and
- private offices or interviewing rooms available to all staff who interview clients.

Table 14.1. Options for Organization of Local Social Services Agencies

	County DSS	CHSA	Regional DSS
Structure	Single county	Single county	Multicounty
Governance options[a]	Appointed county board of social services (3 or 5) or BOCC	Appointed CHS board (up to 25) or BOCC[b]	Appointed regional board of social services (12–18)
Employees subject to	SHRA	County personnel policies unless county opts in to SHRA	SHRA
Director appointed by	Governing board[c]	County manager, with advice and consent of governing board[c]	Governing board

Note: CHS = consolidated human services, CHSA = consolidated human services agency, BOCC = board of county commissioners, SHRA = State Human Resources Act.

[a] Numbers in parentheses represent the number of members on each appointed board.

[b] Advisory committee must be appointed if CHSA includes public health.

[c] This governing board may be a BOCC.

Programs and Services Offered by Social Services Agencies

State law requires counties to administer or assist in the administration of a number of social services and economic services programs, including

- Medicaid,[2]
- Health Choice for Children,[3]
- Work First,[4]
- Food and Nutrition Services,[5]
- Low-Income Energy Assistance,[6]
- State-County Special Assistance,[7]
- Foster Care and Adoption Assistance,[8]
- child protective services,[9]
- adult protective services,[10]
- guardianship services,[11] and
- child support enforcement services.[12]

If a county identifies a need in the community that is not addressed by these programs, state law authorizes each county to undertake, sponsor, organize, engage in, and support any other social services program that will further the health, welfare, education, employment, safety, comfort, and convenience of its citizens.[13]

Several of the largest programs provided by county social services agencies are described below. However, this list is by no means exhaustive.[14]

Food and Nutrition Services

State law requires every county to operate the federally funded Supplemental Nutrition Assistance Program (SNAP), known in North Carolina as the Food and Nutrition Services (FNS) program.[15] This was previously referred to as the "food stamp" program. Through this program, counties issue electronic benefit transfer (debit) cards to eligible recipients for the purchase of food products.[16] Eligibility is based on federal income and resource guidelines. The federal government pays the full cost of SNAP benefits. The federal government also pays half of the administrative costs for the program, while in North Carolina, counties pay the other half.[17] In December 2024, the FNS program provided assistance to more than 1.5 million individuals in North Carolina.[18]

Medicaid

Medicaid is a public assistance program that covers most of the cost of medical care and services for several categories of people who cannot afford these costs.[19] Those who may receive Medicaid include low-income aged, disabled, or blind persons; needy children; pregnant women; individuals who receive federal Supplemental Security Income benefits; and others with low incomes who meet eligibility requirements. In state fiscal year 2024, the federal government provided 67.9 percent of North Carolina's Medicaid funding.[20] As of December 2024, over 3 million North Carolinians were enrolled in Medicaid.[21]

Work First

The federal Temporary Assistance for Needy Families (TANF) program is called "Work First" in North Carolina.[22] The federal government provides a set amount of TANF funding (a *block grant*) to each state to implement programs intended to support families who are in need.[23] Work First focuses on providing eligible families with short-term assistance to help them achieve self-sufficiency through employment.[24] The program provides cash assistance as well as assistance with child care, transportation, job searches, and job training. In December 2024, this program was providing cash assistance to more than 11,000 individuals in North Carolina.[25]

Counties must notify the North Carolina Department of Health and Human Services (NCDHHS) as to whether they desire to be designated as either "electing" or "standard" counties for purposes of administering the Work First program.[26] The General Assembly makes these designations based on recommendations from NCDHHS.[27]

- In an electing county, the board of county commissioners is responsible for the development, administration, and implementation of the Work First program in the county.[28]
- In a standard county, the county social services agency is responsible for administering and implementing the Standard Work First program (which is established, developed, and monitored by NCDHHS) in the county.[29]

Chapter 8 contains more information on the differences between standard and electing counties with respect to Work First.

Other Public Assistance Programs

Social services agencies are also involved with administering other public assistance programs, such as the Child Care Subsidy Program, the Low-Income Energy Assistance Program (LIEAP), the State-County Special Assistance for Adults Program, the Foster Care and Adoption Assistance Programs, and the Refugee Assistance Program (RAP).

Child Support Enforcement Program

The Child Support Enforcement program assists parents in establishing and enforcing child support obligations, including locating absent parents for the purpose of obtaining child support and establishing paternity of dependent children.[30] In most counties the program is administered by the county DSS or a CHSA, but in some counties it is administered by another department of county government or by a contracted provider.[31] Child support agencies must seek support on behalf of dependent children who receive public assistance through certain programs and must also provide services to anyone else who applies and pays a low application fee.[32]

Protective Services for Children

State law requires that cases of suspected child abuse, neglect, dependency, and death from maltreatment be reported to a county social services agency.[33] The North Carolina Juvenile Code, which includes this reporting requirement, is designed to protect children under age 18 from neglect and abuse by parents or other caregivers.[34] The Juvenile Code also requires that protective services be provided for any child who either has no parent, guardian, or custodian responsible for the child's care or supervision or whose parent, guardian, or custodian is unable to provide such care or supervision and lacks an appropriate alternative child care arrangement.[35] When a county social services agency receives a report of suspected abuse, neglect, or dependency, it must conduct a prompt assessment and take appropriate action to protect the child.[36] Each agency provides a wide range of supportive services to children and their families in these cases, often while the children remain in the home, since one purpose of the law is to keep families intact unless the risk of harm to a child requires the child's removal from the home.[37] When necessary, a county social services agency may file a petition in district court seeking either legal custody of a child or some other court order to protect the child.[38]

Permanency Planning Services

Permanency planning services are provided by every county social services agency to children who are separated from their parents or caregivers and are in the custody of the social services agency.[39] The goal of permanency planning services is to provide all children with permanent homes, preferably with their own families of origin, as early as possible. While the emphasis is on preserving or reunifying families, there is a complementary focus on moving children into long-term plans like adoption or guardianship when returning them to their own homes is not possible.

Adoptions

Adoption placement services are designed to find safe and permanent homes for children whose parents have relinquished them for adoption or had their parental rights terminated. In some cases, children may be abused, neglected, or dependent and have adoption designated as a permanent plan by the court hearing the child protection case. Every county social services agency has an adoption program that includes accepting children for placement, recruiting and screening adoptive parents, and arranging and supervising placements.[40] State adoption law requires that either a county social services agency or a licensed child-placing agency conduct a preplacement assessment of every prospective adoptive home and report to the court on almost every adoptive placement.[41] NCDHHS's Division of Social Services supervises county adoption programs and provides resources for families interested in adoption.

Protective Services for Adults

Each county social services agency is charged with receiving and responding to reports regarding the abuse, neglect, or exploitation of disabled adults.[42] When a county social services agency receives a report, it must conduct a prompt assessment and take appropriate action to protect the vulnerable adult.[43] In some cases, the agency may need to petition the district court for an order authorizing the provision of protective services to the vulnerable adult.[44]

Services to Aged or Disabled Adults

In addition to the protective services described above, county social services agencies provide a number of services to older adults and adults with disabilities that include in-home services, community-based services, and institutional care. Some of these services are mandatory, while others are optional.[45] An example of a mandated service is the agency's duty to conduct regular inspections of adult care homes to ensure their compliance with state licensing requirements and other state laws and regulations concerning the care and treatment of elderly or disabled residents.[46] An example of an optional service is the operation of an adult day care program, which is a supervised program offered to individuals with cognitive or physical impairments to promote their social, physical, and emotional well-being.[47] Some counties house these services and programs within the county DSS or CHSA, while other counties offer some of these services through a different county department.

Notes

1. *See* Chapter 108A, Section 15.7 of the North Carolina General Statutes (hereinafter G.S.) (regional departments of social services); G.S. 153A-77 (CHSAs). The option to create a CHSA is only available to counties with a county manager. *See* G.S. 153A-77(b).
2. G.S. 108A-25(b).
3. G.S. 108A, §§ 70.26(a), 70.20.
4. G.S. 108A-27(f), (g).
5. G.S. 108A, §§ 25(a)(3), 51.
6. G.S. 108A-25(a)(5).
7. G.S. 108A, §§ 25(a)(2), 40.
8. G.S. 108A-25(a)(4).
9. G.S. 7B-302.
10. G.S. 108A-103.
11. G.S. 108A-15.
12. G.S. 110-141.
13. G.S. 153A-255. For examples of some potential limitations on this authority, see *Hughey v. Cloninger*, 297 N.C. 86 (1979) and *Stam v. State*, 302 N.C. 357 (1981).
14. The authors are grateful to Aimee Wall for her descriptions of social services programs, upon which this section is based. *See* Wall, *Social Services, in* County and Municipal Government in North Carolina ch. 39 (Frayda S. Bluestein ed., UNC School of Government, 2d ed. 2014). For a more detailed discussion of services and programs, see John L. Saxon, Social Services in North Carolina (UNC School of Government, 2009), 161–201.
15. G.S. 108A-51.
16. G.S. 108A, §§ 51–53.
17. *See* N.C. Dep't of Health & Hum. Servs., *County Budget Estimates State Totals—State Fiscal Year 2022–2023*, https://www.ncdhhs.gov/divisions/social-services/county-staff-information/budget-information/dss-budget-estimates (under the heading County Budget Estimates 2022–2023, select Budget Estimates State Totals to access PDF).
18. *See* N.C. Dep't of Health & Hum. Servs., *FNS Caseload Statistics Reports: FNS Cases and Participants*, https://www.ncdhhs.gov/divisions/social-services/program-statistics-and-reviews/fns-caseload-statistics-reports (click on the link FNS Cases and Participants to download Excel file).
19. G.S. 108A, §§ 54–70.16.
20. *See* N.C. Dep't of Health & Hum. Servs., *State Fiscal Year 2024 Medicaid Annual Report Tables*, https://medicaid.ncdhhs.gov/reports/annual-reports-and-tables.
21. *See* NCDHHS, *NC Medicaid Enrollment Reports*, medicaid.ncdhhs.gov/reports/nc-medicaid-enrollment-reports#FiscalYear2024EnrollmentReports-2073.
22. G.S. 108A-25(b1).
23. 42 U.S.C. § 601.
24. G.S. 108A-27.
25. *See* N.C. Dep't of Health & Hum. Servs., *Work First Caseload Statistics: Work First Cash Assistance and Participants*, https://www.ncdhhs.gov/divisions/social-services/program-statistics-and-reviews/work-first-caseload-statistics (click on the link Work First Cash Assistance Cases and Participants to download Excel file).
26. G.S. 108A-27(e). When notifying NCDHHS of the county's desire to be designated as electing or standard, the county must submit documentation demonstrating that three-fifths of its county commissioners support the desired designation.

27. G.S. 108A, § 27.2(12)–(14).
28. G.S. 108A-27(f). Electing counties must develop biennial Work First plans and submit them to NCDHHS for approval. *See* G.S. 108A, §§ 27.3(a)(12), 27.4(a).
29. G.S. 108A, §§ 27(g), 27.8(a).
30. G.S. 110, art. 9.
31. *See* G.S. 110-141 (requiring all counties to administer a child support enforcement program).
32. *See* G.S. 110-130.1; 42 U.S.C. §§ 608(a)(2), 654(29); 42 C.F.R. § 433.145–.148.
33. G.S. 7B-301.
34. G.S. 7B, subch. I.
35. G.S. 7B, §§ 101(9), 300.
36. G.S. 7B-302.
37. G.S. 7B-100.
38. G.S. 7B, art. 5.
39. N.C. Div. of Soc. Servs., *Permanency Planning Services Policy, Protocol, and Guidance*, *in* NC Child Welfare Manual (updated Aug. 2024), https://policies.ncdhhs.gov/wp-content/uploads/Permanency-Planning-Manual-August-2024-v2.pdf.
40. G.S. 108A, § 14(a)(6), (13).
41. G.S. 48-1-109; *see generally* G.S. 48.
42. G.S. 108A, §§ 14, 15. “Disabled adult,” the term used in the reporting statute, means any person 18 years of age or over or any lawfully emancipated minor who is present in North Carolina “and who is physically or mentally incapacitated due to an intellectual disability, cerebral palsy, epilepsy or autism; organic brain damage caused by advanced age or other physical degeneration . . . or due to conditions incurred at any age which are the result of accident, organic brain damage, mental or physical illness, or continued consumption or absorption of substances.” G.S. 108A-101.
43. G.S. 108A, §§ 103–106.
44. G.S. 108A, §§ 104–106.
45. Local governments, both cities and counties, have the authority to “undertake programs for the assistance and care of its senior citizens” but are not required to do so. G.S. 160A-497.
46. G.S. 131D-2.11(b); *see also* Title 10A, Chapter 13F, Section .1212 of the North Carolina Administrative Code (hereinafter N.C.A.C.).
47. *See* N.C. Div. of Aging & Adult Servs., Adult Day Care and Adult Day Health Services Procedures Manual (updated Jan. 2020), https://www.ncdhhs.gov/adc-adhs-policy-procedure-manual/open; *see also* 10A N.C.A.C. 06P, § .0502.

Chapter 15

The CHS Board's Responsibilities Regarding Social Services Policy and Administration

In a county where the consolidated human services agency (CHSA) includes social services, consolidated human services (CHS) board members are responsible for some decisions around social services policy and program administration. County social services agencies are subject to a significant amount of state and federal regulation regarding how social services programs are administered. Each county is responsible for administering and staffing these social services programs at the local level, while complying with a multitude of federal and state requirements for program administration. At the state level, the North Carolina Department of Health and Human Services (NCDHHS) has an important role in developing policy for local agencies, allocating federal and state funding, and exercising oversight over many of these programs. The Social Services Commission also plays a significant role through adopting rules that govern most of the state's social services programs.

The complex legal requirements for operating social services programs, the significant authority granted to the county director of social services, and the role of the state in developing law and policy for social services all leave very little room for local social services boards (including CHS boards) to make decisions about program administration. Accordingly, local social services boards in North Carolina have relatively limited authority and responsibility regarding social services policy and administration. However, state law does give local social services boards some responsibility and authority to advise local public officials, make certain decisions regarding public assistance programs, monitor and evaluate social services programs, review some social services records, and enter into certain types of contracts. This chapter discusses those powers and duties of the CHS board when it acts as the governing board for a CHSA that includes social services.

In some places, this chapter refers to the county director of social services. In the CHSA model, this individual may serve simultaneously as the CHS director or may instead report to the CHS director, depending on how the county has configured leadership in the CHSA. These different leadership structures are discussed in more detail in Chapter 6.

Monitoring and Evaluating Social Services Programs

Under state law, the CHS director, the county director of social services, and the director's staff—not the governing board for social services—are primarily responsible for administering public assistance and social services programs for county residents. The CHS board should generally focus on the impact that public assistance and social services programs have on community well-being, not the day-to-day administrative procedures regarding the operation of those programs.

However, even though the CHS board has very little direct authority over social services programs, the board is responsible for consulting with the CHS director regarding problems affecting the department (which may include problems related to service delivery or program administration), assuring the CHSA's compliance with laws related to state and federal programs, and assisting the CHS director in planning the CHSA's budget.[1] Each of these duties requires the board to have some level of knowledge regarding the administration of social services programs within the CHSA.

Advising Local Public Officials

When acting as the governing board for social services, the CHS board is responsible for "advis[ing] county and municipal authorities in developing policies and plans to improve the social conditions of the community."[2] This is an important responsibility that is sometimes overlooked and ignored. To effectively advise local government officials about social services policies and plans, CHS board members must educate themselves about the social and economic issues affecting people in their communities. Board members can advise local officials more effectively when they are familiar with the services and programs offered by the CHSA, as well as health and human services programs administered by other agencies and nonprofit organizations in the community. Understanding the services and programs that are available in the local area will help board members identify unmet needs in the community, gaps in available funding for social services, and gaps in service delivery to county residents.

Ideally, board members will seek to educate themselves about issues such as unemployment, homelessness and housing insecurity, domestic violence, child abuse and neglect, abuse and neglect of elderly adults and adults with disabilities, hunger and food insecurity, substance-use disorders, and mental health problems. This includes seeking out information about the organizations and agencies that are addressing these problems at the local and state levels, as well as learning about how the CHSA addresses these issues or works with community partners to address them. Through doing this research and talking with community members, board members may learn about the causes of social and economic problems, identify resources that are available (or not available) to solve those problems, and identify the officials and agencies that may have the authority or resources to address them.

This information will help board members advocate at the local, state, and federal level for the adoption, implementation, and funding of plans and policies to address the social and economic problems facing their communities.

Establishing Local Social Services Policies

In addition to the mandated programs that a county social services agency is required to provide under state law, the board of county commissioners (BOCC) has authority to fund additional (nonmandated) county social services programs and attach conditions to the use of county funding for those programs.[3] State law authorizes a CHS board (acting as the governing board for social services) to adopt policies regarding county-funded programs for "the care of indigent persons."[4] The CHS board's authority to establish policies for county-funded programs does not extend to mandated state or federal-state social services programs that are only funded *in part* by county tax revenues.

For a CHSA that includes social services, state law technically gives the CHS board authority to establish local policies for the State-County Special Assistance program, the Food and Nutrition Services program, the Foster Care and Adoption Assistance Programs, and other public assistance and social services programs established by Chapter 108A of the North Carolina General Statutes (with the exception of Medicaid).[5] Practically speaking, however, the board's authority to establish policies for these programs is *extremely* limited. The federal and state laws that govern social services programs are highly detailed and comprehensive, meaning there is very little room for the board to make policy decisions about them. Federal and state laws and regulations generally dictate these programs' administration, their eligibility criteria, their confidentiality requirements, and the nature, scope, and duration of the assistance and services they provide. Any policy the board adopts regarding these programs must comply with federal and state laws, conform to Social Services Commission rules, and adhere to NCDHHS policies.[6]

Though a CHS board's authority to establish policies for public assistance and social services programs is quite limited, state statutes and rules do authorize the board to make certain decisions regarding the Work First program, the State-County Special Assistance program, and services funded through the Social Services Block Grant, as described below. **The CHS board only has the authority described in the remainder of this chapter if it is acting as the governing board for a CHSA that includes social services** (in other words, this does not apply if the county CHSA includes only public health and other human services functions, but not social services).[7] **References to the role of the CHS board in the remainder of this chapter assume that the CHS board is acting as the governing board for social services in the county.**

Making Decisions Regarding the State-County Special Assistance Program

The State-County Special Assistance program provides a cash supplement for older adults or adults with disabilities to help pay for room and board in adult care homes, special-care units, or in-home living arrangements. The CHS board is responsible for approving determinations made by the county director of social services about whether to grant assistance to an individual and the amount of assistance to be given.[8] However, the CHS board may delegate the authority to approve or reject all applications for State-County Special Assistance to the county director of social services.[9]

Making Decisions Regarding Services Funded Through the Social Services Block Grant

The Social Services Block Grant (SSBG), a major source of federal funding for social services, is a capped entitlement program that provides funding to assist states in delivering social services.[10] SSBG is a flexible funding source that can be used for many different types of social services programs[11] and is the primary source of federal funding for programs such as adult day care and adult protective services. Rules adopted by the Social Services Commission give the CHS board (serving as the governing board for social services) the following responsibilities with respect to SSBG-funded services.

Transportation

The types of transportation that will be provided to people who receive SSBG-funded transportation services, community living services, adult day care services, employment and training support services, and health support services from a county department of social services (including within a CHSA) must be documented in the local transportation development plan.[12] In the absence of a local transportation development plan, the CHS board is responsible for documenting and approving the types of transportation the CHSA will make available to people who receive these services.[13] In such a case, the description of the available types of transportation should be documented in the minutes of a CHS board meeting, and the minutes should reflect the board's approval of that description.[14] Subject to certain driver qualifications and insurance requirements, transportation services may be provided directly by the CHSA, through purchase of service contracts, by vendor payment, by cash payment to a client, through reimbursement to a client's friend or relative, or through volunteers.[15]

Waiting-List Policy

The CHS board has authority to approve a local waiting-list policy for services funded through the SSBG.[16] Local SSBG waiting-list policies must

- designate whether the waiting list is used for meeting prompt provision requirements,[17] responding to inquiries about services, or both;
- ensure that all individuals are treated equitably in terms of how they are advised of the upcoming availability of services;
- ensure that an individual's name does not remain on the waiting list indefinitely without the individual being notified of the status of the request and the anticipated availability of the service; and
- designate a reasonable time period, not to exceed ninety days, that an individual's name can remain on the waiting list prior to providing the service or notifying the individual that the service cannot be provided.[18]

Method for Establishing Financial Eligibility

The CHS board is responsible for determining whether the CHSA will use the "verification method" or "declaration method" of establishing financial eligibility for SSBG-funded services when eligibility for such services is based on income.[19]

Verification Method

The verification method requires the CHSA to verify an individual's stated eligibility status by obtaining evidence that supports the statement.[20] This evidence may be gathered by reviewing copies of documents, through phone conversations, or by identifying existing social services records that may confirm the required information.

Declaration Method

Under the declaration method, the individual provides a statement about their status as a public recipient or the sources and amount of their family's gross income, and the CHSA accepts that statement.[21] However, when the CHSA has reason to believe that the individual's declaration may be inaccurate, it must use the verification method.[22]

Making Decisions Regarding the Work First Program

The federal Temporary Assistance for Needy Families (TANF) program is called "Work First" in North Carolina. Work First focuses on providing eligible families with short-term assistance to help them achieve self-sufficiency through employment.[23] Based on recommendations from NCDHHS, the General Assembly designates each county as either a "standard" county or an "electing" county (described in more detail in Chapter 14).[24] In electing counties, the BOCC must appoint a committee of individuals, including representatives from the county board of social services, to assist in developing the county's Work First plan to respond to community needs.[25]

CHS boards in counties where the CHSA includes social services also have the following responsibilities with respect to the Work First program.

Investigative Assistance

If requested by a district attorney, state law requires CHS boards to provide investigative assistance regarding reports of the abandonment or neglect of certain dependent children, refusal to support those children, or misuse of Work First Family Assistance.[26]

Hardship Exemptions from Federal Lifetime Limit

Work First families that include an adult are subject to a sixty-month lifetime limit on the receipt of assistance under the TANF Block Grant, which includes Work First cash assistance.[27] The sixty-month time limit is a cumulative total and includes the months TANF assistance was received in other states. A family may request a hardship exemption from the sixty-month time limit if it has experienced circumstances beyond its control that have made leaving the Work First program difficult.[28] The time period of the hardship exemption can extend up to six months.

The CHS board is responsible for designating a committee to review requests for hardship exemptions. NCDHHS policy recommends that the committee include a Work First case manager, a child-welfare social worker, a vocational-rehabilitation counselor, a Food and Nutrition Services caseworker, a child support agent, and a qualified substance-use-disorder professional.[29] The committee designated by the CHS board must hold "hardship hearings" to approve or deny hardship status to families that have requested exemptions.[30]

Time-Limit Extensions and Appeals

Unless otherwise stated, the material in this section is drawn from the guidelines on federal and state time limits in the NCDHHS *Work First Manual*.[31]

In addition to the sixty-month lifetime limit on receiving TANF assistance, most families in North Carolina that include a work-eligible adult and are receiving Work First employment services are also subject to a twenty-four-month time limit on receiving Work First cash assistance.[32] Electing counties may establish different time limits on cash assistance, so long as they comply with federal time limits.[33] The family may request an appeal when it believes that there are still months remaining on the time limit. If the family agrees that the months on the time clock are correct and wants to ask for additional months of assistance, it must request an extension.

Extension hearings are held before the CHS board (as the board of social services) or its designee. The CHS board must maintain confidentiality regarding the extension-hearing process, which means that all extension hearings must be held in closed session.[34] The county must complete the extension-hearing process and issue benefits or send a denial notice within forty-five days from the date of the extension request. The family seeking the extension

- may request information from the case file to help prepare its case for the extension hearing (this does not include confidential information from third parties);
- may choose to attend or not to attend the extension hearing (the family's choice not to attend the extension hearing does not prevent the hearing from being held);
- may delay the extension hearing one time, or more than once if the delays are related to the provision of reasonable accommodations;
- may have anyone present at the extension hearing, such as legal counsel obtained at the family's expense;
- may present new information at the hearing, even if it was not previously provided to the county department of social services; and
- must provide the information needed to determine the family's current eligibility within ten calendar days of the county's request for information.

Unless it has delegated its authority to hold extension hearings, the CHS board must evaluate each case to determine whether the family's net household income meets the income test to be eligible for an extension. The method for these calculations is described in NCDHHS policy.

The CHS board may *grant* an extension to an eligible family if it determines that

- the Work First active participant substantially complied with all provisions of their Mutual Responsibility Agreement Plan of Action, considering certain "good cause" exceptions listed in NCDHHS policy (including incapacity, disability, family crisis, or lack of child care, among others); and
- the Work First active participant, through no fault of their own, is unable to obtain or maintain employment that provides a net income of at least the state's maximum Work First payment for the family size.

Conversely, the CHS board must *deny* an extension if it determines that the Work First participant

- failed to substantially comply with the Mutual Responsibility Agreement Plan of Action without good cause;
- was dismissed from a job or demoted from a position with cause;
- voluntarily quit a job without good cause; or
- failed to accept a bona fide job offer without good cause.

The CHS board must also determine the length of the extension (anywhere from one to six months) and specify when the extension begins and ends. The board must complete an Extension Hearing Request form (DSS-5301) and return it to the Work First supervisor as soon as possible after reaching a decision. A family may request a state-level appeal if the CHS board or its designee denies the family's request for an extension.

Reviewing Cases of Suspected Public Assistance Fraud

State rules give county boards of social services—including CHS boards in a county where the CHSA includes social services—authority to review cases of suspected fraud by applicants or recipients of assistance from Work First, the State-County Special Assistance program, the Crisis Intervention Program (CIP), and the Low-Income Energy Assistance Program (LIEAP).[35] NCDHHS policy also authorizes county boards of social services to review cases of suspected Medicaid fraud.[36] For each of these programs, the CHS board may choose to delegate this authority to the county social services director, if desired.[37] In many counties, social services boards (and CHS boards exercising social services powers and duties) have chosen to delegate the responsibility for conducting these fraud reviews to the director of social services.

If the CHS board chooses to delegate its responsibility to review cases of suspected fraud to the social services director, the delegation should be clearly documented in writing. Since the people on the board and the person filling the director position will change from time to time, having written documentation memorializing any of the board's decisions to delegate its duties helps maintain continuity and role clarity. If the board has not delegated this duty to the county social services director, then the director must present cases of suspected fraud to the board for review. The review process established by state rules and policies differs slightly for different types of public assistance programs, as described below.

Case Review Procedures

Work First, CIP, and LIEAP

If the CHS board has not delegated its duty to review fraud cases for Work First, CIP, or LIEAP, the board must review all cases of suspected fraud in these programs presented to the board by the director of social services.[38] The board must determine whether a person *willfully* and *knowingly* (1) provided incorrect or misleading information in response to oral or written questions; (2) failed to report changes that might have affected the amount of payment; or (3) failed to report the receipt of benefits that the person knew they were not entitled to receive.[39] If the board determines that fraud was the reason for an overpayment of assistance, there must be physical evidence to substantiate that determination.[40]

If the board determines that it suspects fraud, it must instruct the CHSA to (1) seek administrative recoupment, (2) initiate an administrative disqualification hearing or referral for prosecution, (3) pursue civil court action, and/or (4) pursue criminal charges.[41] These options are described in more detail in Title 10A,

Chapter 71W, Section .0606(c)(4) of the North Carolina Administrative Code (hereinafter N.C.A.C.).

If the board directs the CHSA to initiate an administrative disqualification hearing, the board must designate either the director of social services or an impartial county employee to act as the hearings officer.[42] NCDHHS policy defines an impartial employee as "one that is not a fraud Investigator, is not directly connected with the case, does not supervise an employee directly connected with the case, and has not discussed the facts of the case with any DSS staff outside of the hearing."[43]

State-County Special Assistance

If the CHS board has not delegated its duty to review fraud cases for State-County Special Assistance, the board must review all cases of suspected fraud that are presented to the board by the director of social services.[44] The board must determine whether the applicant or recipient *willfully* and *knowingly* (1) misstated or provided incorrect or misleading information in response to oral or written questions; (2) failed to report a change in situation affecting eligibility for the State-County Special Assistance Program or the amount of payment; or (3) failed to report the receipt of payments to which the recipient knew he or she was not entitled.[45]

If the board determines that an applicant or recipient engaged in intentional misrepresentation, it must direct the CHSA to pursue certain administrative actions (as described in 10A N.C.A.C. 71P .0508(e)(2)), civil court action, and/or criminal charges.[46] The state rules also allow the board to direct the CHSA not to pursue any action against the applicant or recipient if there are unusual or hardship circumstances, as set forth in 20 C.F.R. § 404.508(a) and 20 C.F.R. § 416.553(a), in which a payment reduction would deprive the applicant or recipient of necessary income for certain expenses.[47]

Medicaid

The board's role in reviewing certain cases of suspected Medicaid beneficiary fraud is set forth in NCDHHS policies.[48] After an investigation of suspected Medicaid fraud, the investigative summary must be presented to the board of social services or its designee for a decision on whether to refer the case for prosecution or use administrative procedures for collection.[49]

The board or its designee must consider the following factors when deciding what action should be taken regarding the case:[50]

- whether there was a violation of policy;
- whether the violation of policy was against the law;
- whether the elements of criminal action were present; and
- whether a beneficiary willfully and knowingly, with intent to deceive,
    - made a false statement or representation,
    - failed to disclose a material fact, and as a result,
    - obtained, attempted to obtain, or continued to receive Medicaid for the beneficiary or others.

The board or its designee must also consider the following mitigating factors:

- the beneficiary's history of prior and repeat offenses;
- the beneficiary's physical and mental state;
- the recommendation of the district attorney; and
- any other factors pertinent to the case, such as the relevant statutes of limitations on available claims (some claims may be time-barred).

Examining Social Services Records

All information concerning individuals applying for or receiving public assistance or social services that may be directly or indirectly derived from the records, files, or communications of the CHSA (as the local department of social services) or the CHS board is confidential under state law.[51] Many federal confidentiality laws and regulations also apply to various types of information held by a county social services agency.

A state statute, Chapter 108A, Section 11 of the North Carolina General Statutes (hereinafter G.S.), authorizes county social services board members to examine the county social services department's records regarding applications for and provision of public assistance and social services.[52] The CHS board holds this authority when a county's CHSA includes social services.[53] However, there are other state and federal confidentiality laws that significantly narrow the board's right of access to records, particularly with respect to child protective services information and certain public assistance information.[54] For example, a 1995 advisory opinion issued by the North Carolina Attorney General's Office concluded that social services board members do not have any right to access child protective services records because these records are subject to provisions of North Carolina's Juvenile Code[55] that do not allow access by governing boards.[56] The county social services director, in consultation with the director's staff or contract attorneys, is responsible for determining which records may be properly inspected by board members under state and federal confidentiality laws.

CHS board members should only use their authority to access social services records to discharge their official board responsibilities. It is unethical for a board member to request or examine records in which the board member has a personal interest, such as records regarding the member's own relatives or friends.[57]

State law prohibits board members from using, disclosing, or publicizing any information regarding individuals applying for or receiving public assistance or social services, including any information a board member may learn through examining social services records.[58]

Approving Social Services Contracts

G.S. 108A-10 authorizes the county social services board to enter into contracts with any public or private agency or individual under which the county department of social services will voluntarily render services to or for the agency or person in exchange for a fee to cover the cost of the services.[59] The CHS board holds this authority when a county's CHSA includes social services.[60] However, contracts under G.S. 108A-10 are relatively rare. Any fees to be charged by the board using this contract authority must be based on a plan that is developed by the social services director and approved by both the BOCC and the appointed CHS board (or merely by the BOCC, if it is serving as the CHS board).[61] An appointed CHS board must annually report to the BOCC regarding any fees the CHSA has received pursuant to the board's authority to enter into contracts for fee-based services under G.S. 108A-10.

The board has no authority to charge a fee for a particular service if

- charging such a fee is specifically prohibited by statute or regulation,
- the county department of social services is required by law to render the service, or
- the recipient of the service is required by law to obtain the service from the county department of social services.[62]

Apart from its authority under G.S. 108A-10, an appointed CHS board generally has no legal authority to enter into any type of contract on behalf of the board or the CHSA. Except as otherwise provided by law, the county's authority to enter into contracts must be exercised by the BOCC.[63] As a general rule, all contracts that involve the county, county agencies, or county boards must be approved by the BOCC or a public official designated by the BOCC (such as the county manager, the county purchasing officer, or county department heads). The BOCC could authorize an appointed CHS board to approve certain contracts that involve the county CHSA. But if the BOCC has not granted such authority, an appointed CHS board has no role or responsibility with respect to the approval of contracts other than those made pursuant to G.S. 108A-10.

Likewise, state statutes do not expressly authorize county CHS directors or social services directors to enter into contracts on behalf of a CHSA. However, the county CHS director or director of social services may enter into or execute a contract on behalf of the county if authorized to do so under a county ordinance or policy.

Involvement with the Local Multidisciplinary Child Death Review Team

If the CHS board is serving as the governing board for a CHSA that includes social services, the CHS board chair must appoint a member of the CHS board to the local multidisciplinary child death review team.[64] Each local multidisciplinary child death review team is responsible for reviewing certain types of child deaths in the county or counties comprising the team.[65] At the request of a director of a local department of social services, the team may elect to review an active case in which a child or children are being served by child protective services.[66] The county director of social services must report quarterly to the CHS board, or as required by the board, on the activities of the multidisciplinary child death review team.[67]

Notes

1. Chapter 108A, Section 9 of the North Carolina General Statutes (hereinafter G.S.); G.S. 153A-77(d).
2. G.S. 108A-9(2); *see also* G.S. 153A-77(d)(9).
3. G.S. 153A-255.
4. G.S. 108A-14(4).
5. *See* G.S. 108A-1. Note that Work First is one of the programs established by Chapter 108A. In a county designated by the General Assembly as an "electing" county under G.S. 108A-27.3, the board of county commissioners (BOCC) is authorized to adopt local policies for the county's Work First program. In standard counties, policies are largely determined by NCDHHS through the Standard Work First program. For a description of the differences between "standard" and "electing" counties, please see Chapter 8 of this book.
6. G.S. 108A-1.
7. *See generally* G.S. 153A-77(d) ("Except as otherwise provided, the consolidated human services board shall have the powers and duties conferred by law upon a board of health, a social services board, and an area mental health, developmental disabilities, and substance abuse services board.").
8. G.S. 108A-43(a).
9. *Id.* Directors who have been delegated this authority by their boards are not required to report their actions (regarding approving or rejecting applications) to their boards.
10. *See Social Services Block Grant*, Benefits.gov, https://www.benefits.gov/benefit/775 (updated Mar. 2, 2023).
11. For a list of services that may be reimbursed with SSBG funds, see Title 10A, Chapter 71R, Section .0101 of the North Carolina Administrative Code (hereinafter N.C.A.C.).
12. 10A N.C.A.C. 71I, § .0101. Per G.S. 136-66.2(b3), each county, with the cooperation of the Department of Transportation, may develop a comprehensive transportation plan. This plan may be adopted by both the BOCC and the Department of Transportation. For portions of a county located within a metropolitan planning organization, the development of a comprehensive transportation plan must take place through that organization.
13. 10A N.C.A.C. 71I, § .0101.
14. *Id.*
15. 10A N.C.A.C. 71I, § .0102.
16. 10A N.C.A.C. 71R, § .0803(b)(1).
17. Requirements for prompt provision of services are set forth at 10A N.C.A.C. 71R, § .0803(a).
18. *Id.*, § .0803(b).
19. *Id.*, § .0701.
20. *Id.*, § .0702.
21. *Id.*, § .0703.
22. *Id.*
23. G.S. 108A-27.
24. G.S. 108A, § 27.2(12)–(14).
25. G.S. 108A-27.3(c).
26. G.S. 15-155.2(a)(1).
27. *See* 45 C.F.R. § 264.1.

28. N.C. Dep't of Health & Hum. Servs., *Federal and State Time Limits, in* Work First Manual, § 105 (April 1, 2021), https://policies.ncdhhs.gov/divisional-n-z/social-services/work-first/wf-policies-manuals/.
29. *Id.*
30. *Id.*
31. *Id.*
32. G.S. 108A-27.1(a).
33. G.S. 108A-27.1(b).
34. *See* G.S. 143-318.11(a)(1) (authorizing public bodies to hold closed sessions when necessary to prevent the disclosure of information that is privileged or confidential pursuant to state or federal law).
35. *See* 10A N.C.A.C. 71W, § .0606(b) (Work First); 10A N.C.A.C. 71P, § .0508(e) (State-County Special Assistance); 10A N.C.A.C. 71V, § .0107 (LIEAP); 10A N.C.A.C. 71V, § .0204 (CIP).
36. N.C. Dep't of Health & Hum. Servs., Aged, Blind and Disabled Medicaid Manual § MA-2900 (Feb. 9, 2021), https://policies.ncdhhs.gov/wp-content/uploads/ma-2900-1.pdf; N.C. Dep't of Health & Hum. Servs., Family and Children's Medicaid Manual § MA-3535 (Feb. 10, 2021), https://policies.ncdhhs.gov/wp-content/uploads/ma-3535-2.pdf.
37. 10A N.C.A.C. 71W, § .0606(b)(3), (c)(1) (Work First); 10A N.C.A.C. 71P, § .0508(d)(2), (e)(1) (State-County Special Assistance). The fraud case review procedures for Work First, including the authority to delegate this responsibility to the director, are incorporated by reference in rules related to LIEAP (10A N.C.A.C. 71V, § .0107) and CIP (10A N.C.A.C. 71V, § .0204).
38. 10A N.C.A.C. 71W, § .0606(b)(3).
39. *Id.* at (2).
40. *Id.* at (3).
41. *Id.* at (4).
42. *Id.* at (4)(B)(II).
43. N.C. Dep't of Health & Hum. Servs., *Fraud and Intentional Program Violations, in* Work First Manual, Policy § 207 (Oct. 1, 2024), https://policies.ncdhhs.gov/wp-content/uploads/WF-207_10.1.24.pdf.
44. 10A N.C.A.C. 71P, § .0508(e)(1).
45. *Id.*
46. *Id.* at (2).
47. *Id.* at (2)(D).
48. N.C. Dep't of Health & Hum. Servs., Aged, Blind and Disabled Medicaid Manual, *supra* note 36; N.C. Dept. of Health and Hum. Servs., Family and Children's Medicaid Manual, *supra* note 36.
49. *Id.*
50. *Id.*
51. G.S. 108A-80(a).
52. G.S. 108A-11.
53. G.S. 153A-77(d) (stating that "the consolidated human services board shall have the powers and duties conferred by law upon . . . a social services board").
54. For more analysis on this topic, see Aimee Wall, *Access to Confidential Client Records by Social Services Governing Boards,* Coates' Canons: NC Loc. Gov't L. (blog) (UNC School of Government, Apr. 26, 2016), https://canons.sog.unc.edu/2016/04/access-confidential-records-social-services-governing-boards/.
55. The Juvenile Code is found in Chapter 7B of the North Carolina General Statutes. Provisions in the Juvenile Code that restrict the disclosure of child protective services records include G.S. 7B-302(a1) and G.S. 7B-2901.

56. N.C. Dep't of Justice, Office of the Att'y Gen., Advisory Opinion: Access to Records by Social Services Boards, Op. N.C. Att'y Gen. (Apr. 20, 1995), https://ncdoj.gov/opinions/access-to-records-by-social-services-board/.
57. *Id.* ("A social services board member who examines and reviews files in which he has a personal interest places himself in conflict with his public duties. He is in effect serving two masters, i.e., himself and the public. This is unethical and serves to undermine the public's trust in its officials.").
58. G.S. 108A, §§ 11, 80.
59. The language of the statute refers to "the board of social services agree[ing] to render services," but this statute has historically been interpreted as applying to contracts for services that will be voluntarily provided by the county department of social services (not the board itself). The legislative history for H.B. 66 (Session 1979), which originally enacted this statute, shows that the General Assembly's intention was to allow county departments of social services to charge fees for certain services in a similar fashion to local health departments.
60. G.S. 153A-77(d) (stating that "the consolidated human services board shall have the powers and duties conferred by law upon . . . a social services board").
61. G.S. 108A-10.
62. Social Services, Adoptions, Fees for Services by County Departments of Social Services, Op. N.C. Atty. Gen., 1984 WL 182160 (Office of the N.C. Att'y Gen. Jan. 26, 1984).
63. G.S. 153A-11.
64. G.S. 7B-1407(b)(6); *see also* G.S. 7B-1401(2) (defining *Local Team*).
65. G.S. 7B-1406.5(c).
66. G.S. 7B-1406.5(e).
67. G.S. 7B-1410(b)(3).

PART 3
Public Health

Chapter 16

Public Health in North Carolina

At the time of publication, most counties that have created a consolidated human services agency (CHSA) have elected to include public health in the CHSA.[1] In addition to their public health-specific powers and duties, it is important that these agencies' governing boards be familiar with the larger public health system within which they and the CHSA operate. This chapter introduces the legal roles and responsibilities of North Carolina counties, North Carolina state government, the federal government, and tribal government with respect to public health functions, administration, and funding.

What Is Public Health?

Public health is the work of promoting and protecting health at the population level. The oldest and most traditional concerns of public health are disease control and sanitation, and the public health system continues to carry out those functions today. Public health's leading role in communicable disease surveillance, prevention, and response was recently on full display during the COVID-19 pandemic. The pandemic pushed public health into the limelight, making visible the otherwise often invisible work that is constantly being carried out to make the public safer and healthier.

As the understanding of determinants of health has evolved beyond disease and sanitation alone, the governmental public health system has expanded its focus over the centuries to include additional duties and embrace other roles. For example, public health agencies today may be responsible for monitoring trends in disease and injury, administering public benefit programs, engaging in community outreach and education, operating health promotion programs, providing clinical health services, conducting research, supporting emergency preparedness and response, developing policy, and enforcing public health laws.

Public health is often associated with, and sometimes conflated with, health care. Although some public health agencies provide direct clinical services, the two fields—public health and health care—are different in important ways. While health care typically involves addressing the needs of individual patients one at a time, public health is concerned with the health, safety, and well-being of entire communities. Public health's focus on the collective, rather than the individual, is part of why public health has historically been a function of government. There are private entities that engage in certain public health-related activities, particularly research and the delivery of direct health services, but it is federal, state, territorial, local, and tribal governments that are responsible for the lion's share of public health work in the United States.

At the federal level, multiple agencies that compose the United States Public Health Service (USPHS) work to advance public health nationwide.[2] At the state level, North Carolina has a decentralized[3] public health system that is composed of two parts: (1) state government entities led by state employees and officials who oversee statewide public health services and programs and (2) eighty-six local health departments (LHDs), which are led by local government officials and employees who oversee public health services and programs in their counties. The North Carolina General Assembly is primarily responsible for determining the extent and scope of the state's and local governments' responsibilities for public health services and how those responsibilities will be carried out. The Eastern Band of Cherokee Indians (EBCI), a federally recognized tribe in western North Carolina, also operates a Division of Public Health and Human Services that serves enrolled tribal members.[4] North Carolina's public health system does not include a formal regional structure, although some state and local public health programs are coordinated by region for the purposes of emergency preparedness and response; consulting services related to environmental, child, and school health; and grant administration.

The roles and responsibilities of the federal government and the state, local, and tribal public health agencies in North Carolina are discussed further in the following sections of this chapter.

The Federal Government's Roles and Responsibilities

The United States Public Health Service (USPHS)

The United States Department of Health and Human Services (HHS) is the cabinet-level department in the executive branch of the federal government that is tasked with protecting health and delivering essential human services to people in the United States.[5] HHS is also home to the USPHS, which traces its origins to 1798, when President John Adams signed the Act for the Relief of Sick and Disabled Seamen to establish marine hospitals throughout the United States' waterways.[6]

The mission and size of the USPHS has evolved over time. Today, the USPHS comprises eight agencies: the Centers for Disease Control and Prevention (CDC), the Agency for Toxic Substances and Disease Registry, the Agency for Healthcare

Research and Quality, the National Institutes of Health, the Health Resources and Services Administration, the Indian Health Service, the Substance Abuse and Mental Health Services Administration, and the Food and Drug Administration.[7] In addition to these eight agencies, USPHS has its own Commissioned Corps, a uniformed services branch that is committed to advancing the nation's health.[8] Although the Commissioned Corps and each of the eight USPHS agencies have their own distinct missions and conduct their work in different ways, they all support the delivery of essential public health services nationwide.

The CDC serves as the nation's lead public health agency and works to increase the country's health security through the control and prevention of disease.[9] The CDC conducts scientific research, tracks trends in disease and injury, engages in disease prevention and response, develops clinical guidance, provides funding, and offers technical assistance and other support to state, territorial, local, and tribal public health agencies. As part of its mission to control disease, the CDC is authorized to prevent the entry of certain communicable diseases into the United States and the spread of those diseases across state lines by detaining, medically examining, and releasing individuals arriving in the country or traveling between states who may carry such diseases.[10] The CDC may also issue federal isolation and quarantine orders pursuant to authority delegated to the CDC Director by the HHS Secretary.[11]

If the CDC is the nation's lead public health agency, then what do the other agencies within the USPHS do? The Agency for Toxic Substances and Disease Registry works closely with the CDC to protect the public from exposure to hazardous substances by "responding to environmental health emergencies; investigating emerging environmental health threats; conducting research on the health impacts of hazardous waste sites; and building capabilities of and providing actionable guidance to state and local health partners."[12] The Agency for Healthcare Research and Quality supports and conducts research on the quality and safety of health care services.[13] Similarly, the National Institutes of Health is a research-oriented agency that focuses on medical research.[14]

The Health Resources and Services Administration, the Indian Health Service, and the Substance Abuse and Mental Health Services Administration each directly provide or support the delivery of health services to specific populations, including those who are geographically isolated and economically or medically vulnerable (Health Resources and Services Administration), American Indians and Alaska Natives (Indian Health Service), and individuals living with mental health and substance use disorders and their families (Substance Abuse and Mental Health Services Administration).[15] The Food and Drug Administration protects public health through counterterrorism efforts and the regulation of food, drugs, medical devices, cosmetics, tobacco products, and devices that emit radiation.[16]

Additional Federal Government Partners in Public Health

There are other departments, agencies, and offices within the federal government that also help advance public health. For example, within HHS, the Office of Population

Affairs administers Title X grant funding for family planning services, while the Centers for Medicare and Medicaid Services oversees major national health care coverage programs.[17] Outside of HHS, the United States Environmental Protection Agency is responsible for federal regulations aimed at reducing childhood lead exposures, and the United States Department of Agriculture administers the Special Supplemental Nutrition Program for Women, Infants, and Children (WIC), which provides food to low-income women, infants, and young children.[18] While these departments, agencies, and offices are not part of the USPHS, their work contributes to a national framework that helps protect and promote the nation's health.

State Government's Roles and Responsibilities

In North Carolina, state-level public health work is led by the North Carolina Department of Health and Human Services (NCDHHS) and its Division of Public Health, the North Carolina Commission for Public Health, and the North Carolina Local Health Department Accreditation Board. The authority for these entities to carry out their work is primarily derived from Chapter 130A of the North Carolina General Statutes (hereinafter G.S.).

North Carolina Department of Health and Human Services and Division of Public Health

NCDHHS is led by a secretary, appointed by the governor, who oversees all the department's activities.[19] The NCDHHS secretary is responsible for implementing and enforcing many of the state's public health laws.[20] For example, the secretary is granted a right of entry "upon the premises of any place where entry is necessary" to enforce public health laws set out in G.S. 130A and the North Carolina Administrative Code and may seek injunctions for violations of these laws.[21] The secretary is also authorized to issue orders for the abatement of public health nuisances[22] and imminent hazards.[23]

Some of the secretary's public health duties and powers may be delegated to the North Carolina state health director, a position appointed by the NCDHHS secretary that must be held by a physician licensed to practice medicine in North Carolina.[24] In addition to any delegated duties, the state health director has a slate of statutorily assigned powers and responsibilities. For example, the state health director is authorized to issue temporary orders requiring health care providers to report certain information related to communicable diseases or conditions that may present a danger to the public's health;[25] to inspect medical and other records as necessary to prevent, control, or investigate certain diseases and health hazards;[26] and to issue orders for isolation and quarantine.[27]

The Division of Public Health (DPH) is located within NCDHHS. DPH is the lead agency for state-level public health work in North Carolina and is overseen by an assistant secretary for public health who reports to the NCDHHS Secretary.

In the past, the state health director and the assistant secretary for public health positions were often held by the same person, but in recent years, the two roles have more frequently been assigned to separate individuals. DPH is organized by sections, which are further subdivided into branches, programs, and units. It is responsible for a wide variety of statewide public health services and programs related to epidemiology, chronic disease and injury prevention, oral health, public health nursing, women's and children's health, environmental health, health equity, and more. DPH is also home to the North Carolina State Center for Health Statistics, the Office of Vital Records, the State Laboratory of Public Health, and the Office of the Chief Medical Examiner.

North Carolina Commission for Public Health

The North Carolina Commission for Public Health (CPH) is the primary rulemaking body for public health in North Carolina.[28] State law grants CPH general authority to adopt rules to protect and promote the public's health, as well as authority to adopt rules that are necessary to implement specific public health programs established under G.S. 130A.[29] State statute also gives CPH the authority to create metropolitan water districts, sanitary districts, and mosquito control districts.[30]

CPH members are appointed to serve four-year terms.[31] CPH's work is supported by DPH employees who provide subject matter expertise, assist with fiscal analyses, and offer other administrative support throughout the rulemaking process. CPH is required to hold four regular meetings per year, with the option to call special meetings as needed. One of the meetings must be held conjointly with the North Carolina Medical Society's annual meeting, during which the state health director is required to deliver an annual report on the state of public health in North Carolina.[32]

North Carolina Local Health Department Accreditation Board

In North Carolina, every agency that operates as an LHD[33] must obtain and maintain accreditation by the North Carolina Local Health Department Accreditation (NCLHDA) Board to be eligible to receive state and federal funds.[34] The NCLHDA Board is established within the North Carolina Institute of Public Health (NCIPH) at the University of North Carolina at Chapel Hill and is composed of seventeen members who are appointed by the NCDHHS secretary. The seventeen-person board must include four members recommended by the North Carolina Association of County Commissioners, four members of a local board of health as recommended by the Association of North Carolina Boards of Health, three LHD directors, three DPH employees, and three at-large members. Members serve staggered four-year terms. CPH is responsible for consulting with the NCLHDA Board and adopting rules that establish accreditation standards.[35] LHDs that have obtained accreditation must be reaccredited every four years.[36]

Additional State Government Partners in Public Health

In addition to DPH, CPH, and the NCLHDA Board, many other state government entities contribute to statewide public health efforts. These include, but are not limited to, other agencies within NCDHHS such as the Division of Child and Family Well-Being, the Division of Social Services, the Division of Health Benefits, the Office of Rural Health, and the Office of Minority Health and Health Disparities. Entities outside of NCDHHS that have a role in promoting and protecting the public health include the state's Department of Environmental Quality, Department of Agriculture, Department of Public Safety, and Department of Labor, among others.

Local Government's Roles and Responsibilities

The Local Health Department

Every county in North Carolina is required to operate a county health department, establish a consolidated human services agency that includes public health, participate in a district health department, or contract with the state to provide public health services.[37] These different types of agencies are captured in the general term *local health department* or *LHD.*[38] LHDs in North Carolina serve as the boots on the ground of public health because of their direct role in administering programs and delivering public health services within the communities they serve. LHDs are often people's primary, and sometimes only, point of contact with the larger public health system.

There is no single law that specifies the types of public health services that an LHD must provide. Instead, the scope and range of local public health services are informed by multiple state laws, contracts between LHDs and NCDHHS, and federal laws. While these laws and legal agreements serve as a starting point for understanding local public health services, they do not paint the complete picture. LHDs, often in partnership with community organizations, area health systems, and other government agencies, may offer additional services based on the unique needs of their communities and the availability of funding or other resources.

The mission of North Carolina's governmental public health system is to promote and contribute to the highest level of health possible for the people of North Carolina.[39] In the furtherance of this mission, each LHD must ensure that the following ten essential public health services are available and accessible to the population in every county served by the LHD:

1. Monitoring health status to identify community health problems.
2. Diagnosing and investigating health hazards in the community.
3. Informing, educating, and empowering people about health issues.
4. Mobilizing community partnerships to identify and solve health problems.

5. Developing policies and plans that support individual and community health efforts.
6. Enforcing laws and regulations that protect health and ensure safety.
7. Linking people to needed personal health care services and ensuring the provision of health care when it is otherwise unavailable.
8. Ensuring a competent public health workforce and personal health care workforce.
9. Evaluating the effectiveness, accessibility, and quality of personal and population-based health services.
10. Conducting research.[40]

This set of ten essential public health services comes from work conducted at the national level by the Core Public Health Functions Steering Committee (the "Committee") in 1994. The Committee was convened by the Assistant Secretary for HHS and included representatives from agencies within HHS and other major public health organizations. It was tasked with creating a framework that would capture all core public health activities. The list of ten essential public health services was the result of the Committee's work.[41] It was formally adopted in North Carolina in 2012, when the legislature codified the ten essential public health services as the statutory framework for the key responsibilities of LHDs.[42]

In addition to codifying the ten essential public health services, the legislature authorized CPH to establish reasonable standards governing the nature and scope of the services provided by LHDs.[43] The standards created by CPH are known as the "mandated services rules."[44] The mandated services described in the rules must be provided in every county in North Carolina. They are divided into two categories: (1) services that an LHD must provide directly and (2) services that must either be provided by the LHD, contracted out to another entity, or delivered through other means (as long as the LHD can certify that the service is available to all individuals in the county it serves).[45]

The services that an LHD must provide directly include regulation and sanitation inspections for on-site water supplies; regulation of sewage collection, treatment, and disposal; regulation and inspections of food and lodging establishments, institutions, and public swimming pools; control of communicable disease; and vital records registration. LHDs must also directly provide, contract for, or certify the availability of child health, maternal health, family planning, dental public health, home health, adult health, and public health laboratory services in their jurisdiction.[46]

Finally, state law identifies a small number of services that LHDs must provide at no cost to the person seeking care. This includes sickle cell syndrome testing and counseling,[47] examination and treatment for tuberculosis or sexually transmitted diseases,[48] administration of certain vaccines to children in low-income families who meet specific criteria,[49] and testing and counseling for HIV.[50]

LHDs may be required to conduct additional activities under the terms of the Consolidated Agreement, a contract that LHDs enter into with two divisions within

NCDHHS: DPH and the Division of Child and Family Well-Being. The Consolidated Agreement details the requirements that LHDs must satisfy as a condition of receiving certain federal, state, and other funds through NCDHHS.[51] The requirements of the Consolidated Agreement may be enforced by NCDHHS and under the accreditation rules adopted by CPH, which mandate compliance with the Consolidated Agreement's terms.[52]

LHDs may also need to perform certain activities to comply with federal law. For example, LHDs in North Carolina that provide clinical health services are usually subject to the Health Insurance Portability and Accountability Act of 1996 (HIPAA) and its implementing regulations. To comply with HIPAA, LHDs must develop and maintain numerous forms, notices, and policies and procedures for protecting, securing, and responding to requests for individuals' health information.[53] Other examples of services or activities that may be required by federal law include the provision of interpreter services for individuals with limited English proficiency.[54]

The Local Health Director

LHDs are led by a local health director who is granted specific powers and responsibilities under North Carolina law. North Carolina law states that a local health director shall be the administrative head of an LHD and shall perform the public health duties prescribed by and under the supervision of the local board of health and NCDHHS.[55] Much of a local health director's authority at the local level mirrors the state-level authority assigned to the state health director or the NCDHHS secretary. The authority granted to a local health director can only be exercised within the county or counties served by the LHD that the director oversees.[56]

Some of the duties and powers given to the local health director are broad in scope, such as the responsibility to administer public health programs, enforce rules adopted by the local board of health, disseminate public health information and promote good health, and advise local officials on public health matters.[57] Other responsibilities are more concrete and specific, such as the requirement that the local health director serve as the local registrar (which involves oversight of vital records)[58] or the mandate to assist in developing and approving the jail health plan for local confinement facilities in the county.[59]

State law also assigns authority and responsibility for addressing certain threats to the public health to the local health director. For example, the local health director is charged with preventing, investigating, and controlling venereal disease, tuberculosis, rabies, and other diseases.[60] Additionally, a local health director can enforce the immunization requirements set forth in state law;[61] access protected medical and other records as necessary to diagnose, treat, or prevent a communicable disease or condition or to investigate an outbreak of a communicable disease or condition;[62] and order quarantine and isolation.[63] The local health director may also order the abatement of public health nuisances[64] and imminent hazards,[65] as well as the embargo of food and drink in certain establishments.[66] These examples of local health directors' duties and powers under law are not exhaustive.

Local Health Department Staff

The number of staff employed by an LHD can vary greatly across jurisdictions but all LHDs must satisfy the minimum staffing requirements set out in state law. Specifically, every LHD must employ a full-time local health director, a full-time public health nurse, a full-time registered environmental health specialist, and a full-time administrative assistant.[67] Every LHD is also required to ensure that the LHD has access to adequate medical consultation by a physician licensed to practice medicine in North Carolina.[68]

An LHD may also employ staff in other roles and positions to help carry out the agency's public health work, including but not limited to a medical director, a director of nursing, nursing staff with various areas of expertise (e.g., communicable disease and epidemiology, family planning, school nursing), physician assistants, laboratory technicians, dentists, dental assistants, public health dental hygienists, registered dietitians, mental and behavioral health specialists, health educators, community health workers, information technology and security staff, billing specialists, language interpreters, and staff with other areas of expertise such as program administration, quality assurance, care management, animal control, industrial hygiene, legal and regulatory compliance, data analysis, and more.

In a CHSA that includes public health, all CHSA employees (including the public health staff) are county employees. CHSA employees are hired by the CHS director with the approval of the county manager.[69] When creating a CHSA, the board of county commissioners can choose to keep the CHSA's employees subject to the North Carolina State Human Resources Act (SHRA) or remove the employees from SHRA coverage and make them solely subject to county personnel policies and procedures.[70]

The Local Board of Health

Each LHD has a governing board called a "board of health." For a CHSA that includes public health, the governing board is the CHS board, which inherits all of the powers and responsibilities of a local board of health. A local board of health is responsible for local public health rulemaking, establishing policies for the LHD, setting certain fees charged by the LHD for public health services, and more.[71] The composition, powers, and duties of a CHS board that is acting as the local board of health are discussed in further detail in the remaining chapters of this book.

Additional Local Government Partners in Public Health

LHDs may work with a diversity of other local government entities to carry out their mission of protecting and promoting the public's health. These local government partners may include, but are not limited to, the sheriff's department, county departments of social services, animal services, county and municipal leadership, local detention centers, and public utilities. LHDs also work closely with NCDHHS and its Division of Public Health, the CDC, and—for some counties in the western part of the state—the Eastern Band of Cherokee Indians to advance public health in their communities.

Tribal Public Health in North Carolina

Eastern Band of Cherokee Indians

The Eastern Band of Cherokee Indians (EBCI) is a federally recognized tribe in western North Carolina. The EBCI owns more than 56,000 acres of land that is held in trust by the federal government and overlaps geographically with five North Carolina counties: Jackson, Swain, Cherokee, Graham, and Haywood. This area of land is called the Qualla Boundary and is home to the majority of the EBCI's approximately 13,400 enrolled tribal members.[72] The Division of Public Health and Human Services (PHHS) serves as the lead public health agency for the EBCI. The public health director is selected by the PHHS secretary.[73]

The PHHS secretary has the authority to seek an injunction for violations of tribal public health laws[74] and to impose isolation and quarantine.[75] Both the PHHS secretary and the public health director are authorized to issue temporary orders requiring health care providers to report certain information related to communicable diseases or conditions that may present a danger to the public's health;[76] to inspect medical and other records as necessary to prevent, control, or investigate certain diseases and health hazards;[77] to exercise a right of entry upon the premises of any place where entry is necessary to enforce tribal public health laws;[78] and to order the abatement of public health nuisances and imminent hazards.[79]

PHHS coordinates with NCDHHS, DPH, the CDC, and LHDs in Jackson, Swain, Cherokee, Graham, and Haywood counties on various public health activities. For example, provisions in the EBCI Code of Ordinances establish environmental health requirements for food handling and preparation, lodging establishments, and public pools that are enforced through collaboration between state, county, and tribal public health agencies.[80] Additionally, in 2020, NCDHHS and the Cherokee Indian Hospital Authority, the primary health system for the EBCI, partnered to establish the EBCI Tribal Option, a managed care program available to tribal Medicaid beneficiaries and the first of its kind in the United States.[81] These collaborations are important for promoting the health, safety, and well-being of those living on and around the Qualla Boundary.

Notes

1. Cabarrus and Person counties each operate CHSAs that include social services but not public health.
2. *Who We Are: Our Story*, Commissioned Corps of the U.S. Pub. Health Serv. (Feb. 3, 2025), https://perma.cc/97JP-9VGB.
3. *General Information*, N.C. Dep't of Health & Hum. Servs. (Jan. 27, 2025), https://perma.cc/87XT-7CDY.
4. E. Band of Cherokee Indians, *Public Health Programs*, Pub. Health & Hum. Servs. (Feb. 3, 2025), https://perma.cc/HX29-VJ7Y.
5. *About HHS*, Dep't of Health & Hum. Servs., https://www.hhs.gov/about/index.html (last accessed Dec. 3, 2024).
6. *Disease Control and Prevention*, NIH Nat'l Lib. of Med. (Feb. 3, 2025), https://perma.cc/4NBS-YDGA.
7. Cong. Rsch. Serv., CRS Rep. R44916, Public Health Service Agencies: Overview and Funding (FY2016–FY2018) 2 (n.d.), https://www.everycrsreport.com/files/20170816_R44916_a55864b368ab021aef7483e36c6f4e92733a85fa.pdf.
8. *Who We Are*, Dep't of Health & Hum. Servs. (Feb. 3, 2025), https://perma.cc/97JP-9VGB.
9. *Mission and Org Charts*, Ctrs. for Disease Control & Prevention (Feb. 3, 2025), https://perma.cc/ZH9U-Q3Q3.
10. 42 C.F.R. parts 70–71.
11. *Id., see also* 42 U.S.C. § 264.
12. Agency for Toxic Substances & Disease Registry, U.S. Dep't of Health & Hum. Servs., *About the Agency for Toxic Substances and Disease Registry* (Feb. 3, 2025), https://perma.cc/SML4-RU2P.
13. *Mission and Budget*, Agency for Healthcare Rsrch. & Quality (Feb. 3, 2025), https://perma.cc/4RWN-FTLJ.
14. *Mission and Goals*, Nat'l Insts. of Health (Feb. 3, 2025), https://perma.cc/7722-VRYY.
15. *About HRSA*, Health Res. & Servs. Admin. (Feb. 3, 2025), https://perma.cc/U5CS-CPAS; *Agency Overview*, Indian Health Serv. (Feb. 3, 2025), https://perma.cc/VV2P-JNAK; *Who We Are*, Substance Abuse & Mental Health Servs. Admin. (Feb. 3, 2025), https://perma.cc/FW4S-LXJZ.
16. *About FDA*, Food & Drug Admin. (Feb. 3, 2025), https://perma.cc/334F-2WSQ.
17. *Title X Service Grants*, Off. of Pop. Affs. (Feb. 3, 2025), https://perma.cc/7HL4-TEFH; *About Us: Who We Are*, Ctrs. for Medicare & Medicaid Servs. (Feb. 3, 2025), https://perma.cc/2ULW-D7QB.
18. *Lead Regulations*, Env't Prot. Agency (Feb. 3, 2025), https://perma.cc/CD36-BELJ; Food & Nutrition Serv., *WIC: USDA's Special Supplemental Nutrition Program for Women, Infants, and Children* (Feb. 3, 2025), https://perma.cc/BTX5-QMTC.
19. G.S. 143B, §§ 6, 9.
20. G.S. 130A, §§ 4, 5.
21. G.S. 130A, §§ 17–18.
22. G.S. 130A-19.
23. G.S. 130A-20.
24. G.S. 130A, §§ 3, 6.
25. G.S. 130A-141.1.
26. G.S. 130A, §§ 15(a), 144(b).
27. G.S. 130A-145.

28. G.S. 130A-29.
29. G.S. 130A-29(a)–(c).
30. G.S. 130A-29(d).
31. G.S. 130A-30.
32. G.S. 130A-33.
33. The statutory definition of *local health department* at G.S. 130A-2(5) includes county health departments, district health departments, and public health authorities. The definition does not mention consolidated human services agencies that include public health; however, G.S. 130A-43(a) states that such agencies "shall have the responsibility to carry out the duties of a local health department." Pursuant to S.L. 1997-502, § 12, a hospital authority may take on the responsibility of providing public health services to a county under G.S. 130A-34 and operate as a local health department. Therefore, consolidated human services agencies that include public health and hospital authorities that operate as local health departments are required to obtain and maintain accreditation by the NCLHDA Board.
34. G.S. 130A-34.4.
35. G.S. 130A-34.1.
36. Title 10A, Chapter 48A, Section .0205 of the North Carolina Administrative Code (hereinafter N.C.A.C.).
37. G.S. 130A-34.
38. G.S. 130A-2(5) defines *local health department* to include "a district health department or a public health authority or a county health department." The creation of consolidated human services agencies by boards of county commissioners is authorized under G.S. 153A-77(b). G.S. 130A-43 tasks consolidated human services agencies that include public health with carrying out the duties of a local health department. Pursuant to S.L. 1997-502, § 12, a hospital authority may take on the responsibility of providing public health services to a county under G.S. 130A-34.
39. G.S. 130A-1.1(a).
40. G.S. 130A-1.1(b).
41. Fátima Coronado, Denise Koo, & Kristine Gebbie, *The Public Health Workforce: Moving Forward in the 21st Century*, 47 Am. J. Preventive Med. S275–S277 (2014).
42. G.S. 130A-1.1. The list was last updated in 2020. *See* Ctrs. for Disease Control and Prevention (CDC), *Ten Essential Public Health Services*, https://www.cdc.gov/public-health-gateway/php/about/index.html. At the time of publication, G.S. 130A-1.1 includes an older version of the list.
43. G.S. 130A-9.
44. 10A N.C.A.C. 46, § .0201–.0216.
45. *Id.*
46. *Id.*
47. G.S. 130A-130.
48. G.S. 130A-144(e).
49. G.S. 130A-153(a).
50. 10A N.C.A.C. 41A, § .0202(9).
51. 10A N.C.A.C. 48B, § .0102.
52. *See* 10A N.C.A.C. 48B, § .0804, .1306.
53. 45 C.F.R. parts 160, 162, 164.
54. Civil Rights Act of 1964, 42 U.S.C. § 2000d to d-7; Exec. Order No. 13166, 65 Fed. Reg. 50121 (Aug. 11, 2000); Patient Protection and Affordable Care Act, 42 U.S.C. § 18116.
55. G.S. 130A-41(a).
56. G.S. 130A-41(c).
57. G.S. 130A-41(b).
58. G.S. 130A-94.

59. G.S. 153A-225(a).
60. G.S. 130A-41(b).
61. G.S. 130A-41(b)(7).
62. G.S. 130A-144(b).
63. G.S. 130A-145.
64. G.S. 130A-19.
65. G.S. 130A-20.
66. G.S. 130A-21.
67. 10A N.C.A.C. 46, § .0301.
68. 10A N.C.A.C. 46, § .0302.
69. G.S. 153A-77(e).
70. G.S. 153A-77(d). To date, the majority of counties that have created CHSAs have opted to remove employees from SHRA coverage in favor of making them subject solely to county personnel policies and procedures.
71. G.S. 130A-39.
72. EBCI, *Our Community*, Pub. Health & Hum. Servs. Div. (Feb. 3, 2025), https://perma.cc/YML5-QC4J.
73. The Cherokee Code of the Eastern Band of the Cherokee Nation, § 130-103 (Supp. No. 36, Update 1, Apr. 28, 2025), https://library.municode.com/tribes_and_tribal_nations/eastern_band_of_cherokee_indians/codes/code_of_ordinances (for Chapter 130, Public Health, see https://library.municode.com/tribes_and_tribal_nations/eastern_band_of_cherokee_indians/codes/code_of_ordinances?nodeId=THCHCO_CH130PUHE).
74. *Id.*, Chapter 130, § 130-201(a).
75. *Id.*, § 130-910.
76. *Id.*, § 130-906.
77. *Id.*, § 130-110.
78. *Id.*, § 130-200(a).
79. *Id.*, §§ 130-202(a), -203(a).
80. *Id.*, § 130-1.
81. N.C. Dep't of Health & Hum. Servs., *NCDHHS and Cherokee Indian Hospital Authority to Create First-in-Nation Indian Managed Care Entity* (Oct. 30, 2020), https://www.ncdhhs.gov/news/press-releases/2020/10/30/ncdhhs-and-cherokee-indian-hospital-authority-create-first-nation-indian-managed-care-entity.

Chapter 17

The Consolidated Human Services Board's Role in Accreditation

What Is Local Health Department Accreditation?

North Carolina law requires that every local health department (LHD) obtain and maintain accreditation as a condition of the LHD's eligibility to receive state and federal funds.[1] This requirement applies to a consolidated human services agency (CHSA) that includes public health. An LHD that has obtained accreditation must be reaccredited every four years.[2] Accreditation helps standardize and support equality in the public health services that are provided by LHDs to communities across the state.

The Accreditation Process

The accreditation process is managed by the North Carolina Local Health Department Accreditation (NCLHDA) Board. The NCLHDA Board is established within the North Carolina Institute for Public Health at the University of North Carolina at Chapel Hill and is composed of seventeen members who are appointed by the Secretary of the North Carolina Department of Health and Human Services (NCDHHS). The seventeen-person board must include four members recommended by the North Carolina Association of County Commissioners, four members of a local board of health (BOH) as recommended by the Association of North Carolina Boards of Health, three LHD directors, three NCDHHS Division of Public Health employees, and three at-large members.[3] Members serve staggered four-year terms.[4] The North Carolina Commission for Public Health is responsible for consulting with the NCLHDA Board and adopting administrative rules that establish accreditation standards.[5]

The accreditation process involves a self-assessment by the LHD using the Health Department Self-Assessment Instrument (HDSAI) and a site visit to the LHD's premises and facilities to assess whether the LHD has sufficiently met the accreditation requirements. After the self-assessment and site visit, the NCLHDA Board issues a decision on the LHD's accreditation status.[6] The NCLHDA Board has provided detailed guidance on the accreditation process and standards in its publication titled "HDSAI Interpretation Document."[7]

Achieving Accreditation or Reaccreditation

To be accredited, an LHD must satisfy a minimum number (but not necessarily all) of the accreditation requirements.[8] An LHD that has satisfied the accreditation standards is assigned the status of "accredited" (if it is the LHD's first time undergoing accreditation) or "reaccredited" (if the LHD has undergone accreditation before). An accredited or reaccredited status is in effect for four years, at which point the LHD must apply for reaccreditation.[9]

Failure to Meet the Accreditation Standards

What happens to an LHD that does *not* meet the accreditation standards? In these situations, the NCLHDA Board assigns the LHD the status of "conditionally accredited," which means that the LHD is granted short-term accreditation subject to any conditions identified in writing by the NCLHDA Board.[10] An LHD may operate as conditionally accredited for a period of up to two years.[11]

During that two-year period, the LHD may seek to demonstrate that the conditions set by the NCLHDA Board have been met and request to be granted accredited or reaccredited status.[12] If the NCLHDA Board determines that the conditions it set have been met, then it will change the LHD's status from conditionally accredited to accredited or reaccredited.[13] The LHD's status as accredited or reaccredited is in effect for four years from when the status of conditionally accredited was assigned.[14]

If after the two-year period of being conditionally accredited, the LHD has not satisfied the conditions identified by the NCLHDA Board, then the LHD is assigned the status of "unaccredited."[15] The NCLHDA Board must provide the LHD and the NCDHHS secretary with written notice of the LHD's unaccredited status.[16] State law requires an LHD to maintain accreditation to be eligible to receive state and federal public health funding from the NCDHHS, Division of Public Health; therefore, an LHD that is assigned unaccredited status is at risk of losing access to key funding streams.[17]

The Role of the Governing Board in Accreditation

At the time of this book's publication, the accreditation rules and HDSAI Interpretation Document assign various responsibilities to the LHD and local health director related to supporting and advising the board of health (BOH).[18] The BOH should work with the local health director and LHD staff to prepare for the accreditation process and determine how satisfaction of any requirements related to the BOH can be best documented and presented to the NCLHDA Board. For a CHSA that includes public health, the BOH is the consolidated human services (CHS) board. When the board of county commissioners has assumed the powers and duties of the BOH (or the CHS board, in the case of a CHSA), the board of commissioners is responsible for satisfying any accreditation requirements related to the BOH.

Anticipated Changes to the Accreditation Administrative Rules

In 2013, the North Carolina legislature established a process called Periodic Review and Expiration of Existing Rules (colloquially referred to as *periodic review* or *readoption*).[19] The periodic review process requires North Carolina rulemaking bodies, including the Commission for Public Health, to review and either repeal or readopt all of their rules in the North Carolina Administrative Code.[20] Periodic review occurs every ten years. The first round of periodic review began in 2014, and the second round began in 2024.[21]

Because LHD accreditation and the Commission for Public Health's adoption of accreditation standards in rule are both currently required by statute, it is unlikely that the rules governing accreditation will be repealed by the Commission for Public Health during periodic review—which means that they must instead be readopted. It is possible that changes will be made to the accreditation rules during the readoption process. LHDs and their governing boards that are preparing for the accreditation process should review the most current versions of the accreditation rules and the HDSAI Interpretation Document to ensure they understand the latest accreditation requirements.

Notes

1. Chapter 130A, Section 34.4 of the North Carolina General Statutes (hereinafter G.S.).
2. Title 10A, Chapter 48A, Section .0205 of the North Carolina Administrative Code (hereinafter N.C.A.C.).
3. G.S. 130A-34.1(a).
4. G.S. 130A-34.1(b).
5. G.S. 130A-34.1. At the time of this book's publication, the accreditation rules may be found at 10A N.C.A.C. 48B.
6. G.S. 130A-34.1(e)(1).
7. The HDSAI Interpretation Document is updated regularly and is available on the NCLHDA Board website, https://nclhdaccreditation.unc.edu/ (last visited Apr. 18, 2025).
8. 10A N.C.A.C. 48B, § .0103(a).
9. G.S. 130A-34.1(d)(1).
10. G.S. 130A-34.1(d)(2), (g)(2).
11. G.S. 130A-34.1(g)(2).
12. *Id.*
13. *Id.*
14. G.S. 130A-34.1(g)(2).
15. G.S. 130A-34.1(d)(3).
16. G.S. 130A-34.1(i).
17. G.S. 130A-34.4(a).
18. *E.g.*, 10A N.C.A.C. 48B, § .0601(2), (3), (4).
19. S.L. 2013-413.
20. G.S. 150B-21.3A(c).
21. *Id.*

Chapter 18

Setting Public Health Fees

Every local board of health (BOH)—including a consolidated human services (CHS) board for a consolidated human services agency (CHSA) that includes public health—is authorized to set certain fees that are charged by the local health department (LHD) for specific public health services. The BOH must base its fees on a plan proposed by the local health director (or the human services director, in the case of a CHSA), and any fees adopted by the BOH must also be approved by the board of county commissioners.[1] Fees that are set by the BOH and collected by the LHD must typically be used to support the LHD's public health programs and expended in accordance with the Local Government Budget and Fiscal Control Act.[2]

Environmental Health Services Fees

Generally, a BOH may not set (and the LHD may not charge) fees for activities carried out by an LHD employee acting as an agent of the state. This includes most (but not all) LHD environmental health programs, which are typically led by LHD employees who are authorized by law to enforce rules promulgated by the North Carolina Commission for Public Health under the supervision of the North Carolina Department of Health and Human Services (NCDHHS).[3]

However, there are four areas of environmental health services where a BOH may set (and the LHD may charge) "cost-related" fees: on-site wastewater treatment, public swimming pools, tattoo regulation, and inspection and permitting of drinking water wells.[4] North Carolina's public health laws do not define *cost-related*, but such fees should be based on a calculation of the actual cost incurred by the LHD for providing the service. The calculation could include variables such as staff time, the cost of materials, or other resources that are needed to provide the service.

Services That Must Be Provided at No Cost to Recipients

Various North Carolina public health laws require that an LHD provide specific health services at no cost to the person receiving them. As a result, the BOH cannot set a fee for these services that would be charged by the LHD to the service recipient. The services that must be provided free of charge to the recipient include

- testing and counseling for sickle cell syndrome,[5]
- examination for and treatment of tuberculosis,[6]
- examination for and treatment of certain sexually transmitted diseases,[7] and
- testing and counseling for HIV.[8]

In addition, immunizations that are required by law and supplied by the state must be provided at no cost to certain uninsured or underinsured patients.[9]

Other Limitations on Fees

While an LHD may charge fees for some of their clinical services, the BOH may have limited control over setting these and related fees. Fees for clinical services, for example, may reflect Medicaid reimbursement rates or sliding scales established by a state or federal program that provides funds for a particular service. Fees for other services may also be capped or limited by state and federal laws. For example, Title VI of the federal Civil Rights Act of 1964 prohibits recipients of federal financial assistance from charging their clients with limited English proficiency for interpretation services.[10] Similarly, North Carolina law and the federal HIPAA Privacy Rule limit the fees that may be charged for providing patients with copies of their own medical records.[11]

Notes

1. Chapter 130A, Section 39(g) of the North Carolina General Statutes (hereinafter G.S.); G.S. 153A-77(d)(1).
2. G.S. 130A-39(g).
3. G.S. 130A-4(b).
4. G.S. 130A-39(g).
5. G.S. 130A-130.
6. G.S. 130A-144(e).
7. *Id.*
8. Title 10A, Chapter 41A, Section .0202(9) of the North Carolina Administrative Code. This rule allows third-party payers (such as insurance) to be billed for HIV testing and counseling services only when the patient provides written consent.
9. G.S. 130A-153(a).
10. Civil Rights Act of 1964, 42 U.S.C. § 2001d to d-7; *see also* Executive Order 13166, 65 Fed. Reg. 52,762 (August 30, 2000).
11. G.S. 90-411; 45 C.F.R. § 164.524(c)(4).

Chapter 19

Local Public Health Rulemaking

What Are Rules?

At the state level, the North Carolina Commission for Public Health (CPH) is the primary rulemaking body responsible for promulgating public health rules.[1] CPH rules are regulations that carry the weight of law and apply statewide, in every county and municipality. At the local level, a local board of health (BOH)—which, in a county with a consolidated human services agency that includes public health, is the consolidated human services board—has the authority to adopt rules necessary to protect and promote the public health.[2] A local public health rule (also called a BOH rule) applies only throughout the county or counties that the BOH serves (referred to as the BOH's *jurisdiction*).[3]

Like CPH rules, BOH rules carry the weight of law. BOH rules can be enforced using various methods set forth in North Carolina's public health laws, such as a criminal charge (typically a misdemeanor), a civil action, or, in limited cases, the imposition of administrative penalties.[4] In a county where the board of county commissioners (BOCC) acts as the BOH, a violation of a local public health rule adopted by the BOCC that triggers a civil penalty will not also result in a misdemeanor charge unless the BOH rule specifically states that violation of the rule is a misdemeanor offense.[5]

BOH Rulemaking Authority

A BOH cannot adopt local public health rules addressing anything and everything the BOH sees fit to regulate. Instead, the BOH's rulemaking actions must fall within the scope of authority that has been granted to local boards of health by the state legislature.

The North Carolina General Assembly has authorized local boards of health to adopt rules as necessary to protect and promote the public's health.[6] The scope of this rulemaking authority was interpreted by the North Carolina Court of Appeals in a 1996 case, *City of Roanoke Rapids v. Peedin*.[7] The *Peedin* decision established a five-part test that a BOH rule must satisfy to be lawful and valid. To succeed under this test, a BOH rule must[8]

1. be related to the promotion or protection of health;
2. be reasonable in light of the health risk addressed;
3. not violate any law or constitutional provision;
4. not be discriminatory; and
5. not make any distinctions based on policy concerns traditionally reserved for legislative bodies.

Express Preemption: Statutory Limitations on BOH Rulemaking Authority

Several North Carolina laws impose additional limitations on BOH rulemaking authority. The state statute that gives a BOH its rulemaking authority imposes several limitations. First, the law prohibits a BOH from adopting rules related to the issuing of sanitation grades and operating permits for food and lodging facilities.[9] Additionally, the law provides that a BOH must obtain approval from the North Carolina Department of Health and Human Services (NCDHHS) before adopting local rules that govern on-site wastewater management. For the local on-site wastewater management rules to be approved, NCDHHS must find that the rules are at least as stringent as the state-level rules promulgated by CPH and that the local rules are necessary and sufficient to safeguard the public health.[10]

Another statute addresses local BOH rules that restrict smoking in public places.[11] A BOH may adopt a rule restricting or prohibiting smoking that is stricter than state law and that applies in local government buildings, on local government grounds, in local government vehicles, or in the enclosed areas of public places.[12] Local BOH rules may not, however, restrict smoking in private residences or vehicles, nor may they regulate certain other public places specified in the law. A BOH rule restricting smoking must also be approved by the BOCC for the county served by the BOH.[13]

Implied Preemption of a BOH Rule by State Law

If a BOH adopts a rule governing an issue that is already addressed in state law, then the local rule may be preempted (overridden) by that state law. This limitation is sometimes referred to as *implied preemption*, or preemption that may be implied even in the absence of a clear statutory limitation (such as the limitations discussed in the section above). In the 2002 case *Craig v. County of Chatham*, the North Carolina Supreme Court held that a BOH rule may be preempted by state law if the state has already provided "a complete and integrated regulatory scheme" in the area addressed by the local rule.[14] However, the North Carolina statute that gives

BOHs their rulemaking authority also specifically says that a BOH may adopt rules that are more stringent than state rules if the BOH determines that more stringent rules are necessary to protect the public health.[15]

What does this mean for BOH rulemaking? The court's decision in *Craig v. Chatham County* does not outright preclude a BOH from adopting a rule regulating an issue already addressed in state law and implementing more stringent standards; however, to do so, the BOH must be able to provide a rationale for why higher local standards are needed to protect the public health. One way to justify the need for such a rule is to demonstrate that conditions in the BOH's jurisdiction are different from the rest of the state in a manner or to a degree that warrants the creation of a local rule with more stringent standards.

BOH Rule Versus Local Ordinance

A BOCC and a city council both have ordinance-making authority, including the authority to adopt ordinances addressing certain public health issues within their jurisdictions.[16] There are important differences between a BOH rule and a local ordinance adopted by the BOCC or city council.

Territorial Jurisdiction

A major difference between BOH rules and local ordinances is their territorial jurisdiction. County ordinances apply only in the unincorporated areas of the county and not inside any municipalities (unless the municipalities consent to be governed by the county ordinance).[17] Similarly, municipal ordinances typically apply only within the municipality.[18] In contrast, a BOH rule applies throughout the board's territorial jurisdiction, which is all of the county or counties represented by the BOH, including any municipalities contained therein.[19]

Scope of Authority

Another key difference is that a BOH (including a BOCC acting as the BOH) is subject to certain limits on its local public health rulemaking authority that do not apply to a BOCC when adopting a county ordinance. These limitations were described briefly earlier in this chapter, but two are worth further elaboration here. First, a BOH may only adopt local public health rules that are related to the protection and promotion of health, whereas a BOCC is authorized to adopt ordinances that address a wider range of issues and concerns.[20] The second and perhaps more significant limitation is that a BOH must not "make distinctions based upon policy concerns traditionally reserved for legislative bodies" when engaging in local public health rulemaking.[21]

How do these differing scopes of authority play out on the ground? A BOCC may make distinctions based on policy concerns having nothing to do with public health when adopting county ordinances. For example, a BOCC may enact an ordinance imposing certain general requirements on businesses in the community but exempting small businesses for whom compliance with those requirements might pose economic hardship. In contrast, a BOH may not craft exceptions to a generally applicable local public health rule that are based on businesses' economic concerns and that lack a health-based rationale. When a BOCC serves as the BOH, it is important that the BOCC be aware of these differences in scope of authority for adopting local public health rules (done by the BOCC in its capacity as the BOH) and adopting county ordinances.

Enforcement

A final significant difference between BOH rules and local ordinances is in how they are enforced. BOH rules are enforced using the specific remedies set forth in North Carolina's public health laws, such as a criminal charge, a civil action, or (in limited circumstances) the imposition of administrative penalties by the local health director.[22] Ordinances may be enforced using similar methods, but a BOCC has broader authority than a local health director to impose penalties for local violations, as well as the option to make violation of an ordinance an infraction.[23]

BOH Rulemaking Process

Considerations Before Beginning the Rulemaking Process

Before a BOH begins the rulemaking process, it should consider the following:

- Why is this rule necessary? Are there state laws that already address this issue? Are there local BOH rules or local ordinances that already address this issue?
- Does the BOH have legal authority to adopt the rule?
- Is approval by another party required to adopt the rule?
    - Does the rule regulate on-site wastewater management and therefore require approval by NCDHHS?[24]
    - Does the rule regulate smoking and therefore require approval by the BOCC?[25]
- Who is affected by the rule? Should stakeholders be consulted on the language of the rule and if so, which stakeholders?
- What is the enforcement mechanism for the rule (e.g., a misdemeanor charge, an administrative penalty, etc.)? Does the enforcement mechanism allow local government to effectively respond to a violation of the rule and achieve the desired public health outcome?
- Once drafted, is the language of the rule clear and unambiguous?
    - Are important terms defined?
    - Does the rule specify an effective date (if different from the expected date of adoption, amendment, or repeal)?
    - Is the rule clear about how timeframes for any deadlines are counted (e.g., counting business versus calendar days)?

Once a BOH has drafted a rule, it must follow the rulemaking process set out in state law and described in the following sections.[26]

At Least Ten Days Before the Rulemaking Action

At least ten days before any BOH rule is adopted, amended, or repealed, notice of the BOH's intended rulemaking action must be published in a newspaper "having general circulation" in the area served by the BOH.[27] The notice must describe the subjects and issues addressed by the proposed rulemaking action, the proposed effective date of the rule, and a statement that copies of the proposed rule can be accessed at the local health department.[28] There is no requirement that the notice or a copy of the rule be posted on the BOH's or local health department's website, and posting on these websites cannot be done in lieu of publishing the required newspaper notice.

Additionally, and also at least ten days prior to the rulemaking action being taken by the BOH, a copy of the proposed rule must be made available in the county clerk's office.[29]

Meeting to Take the Rulemaking Action

The BOH may vote to adopt, amend, or repeal a local rule at a regular or special meeting of the BOH. The BOH meeting must be properly noticed in accordance with North Carolina's open meeting law (discussed further in Chapter 10), even if the BOH's only action item is to vote on the rule.

After Taking the Rulemaking Action

A BOH's adoption, amendment, or repeal of a rule is effective immediately unless the rule itself specifies a delayed effective date.[30] A copy of the rule must be filed with and maintained by the secretary to the BOH.[31] If the BOH adopted any materials by reference in its rule, then a copy of those referenced materials must be filed alongside a copy of the rule text.[32] Finally, the BOH should confirm with NCDHHS whether it is required by the Consolidated Agreement or another contract to provide a copy of any adopted, amended, or repealed rules to NCDHHS.

Notes

1. Chapter 130A, Section 29 of the North Carolina General Statutes (hereinafter G.S.).
2. G.S. 130A-39(a); G.S. 153A-77(c).
3. G.S. 130A-39(c).
4. *E.g.*, G.S. 130A, §§ 17, 18, 22(h), 22(h1), 25(a).
5. G.S. 153A-77(a).
6. G.S. 130A-39(a).
7. 124 N.C. App. 578 (1996).
8. *Id.* at 587.
9. G.S. 130A-39(b).
10. G.S. 130A, §§ 39(b), 335(c).
11. G.S. 130A-498.
12. G.S. 130A-498(a); *see also* G.S. 130A-492 (defining *public place* and *local government building, grounds,* and *vehicle*).
13. G.S. 130A-498.
14. Craig v. County of Chatham, 356 N.C. 40, 45 (2002).
15. G.S. 130A-39(b).
16. G.S. 153A-121(a); G.S. 160A-174(a).
17. G.S. 153A-122.
18. G.S. 160A-174(a).
19. G.S. 130A-39(c).
20. G.S. 130A-39(a); G.S. 153A-121(a).
21. City of Roanoke Rapids v. Peedin, 124 N.C. App. 578, 587 (1996).
22. *E.g.*, G.S. 130A, §§ 17, 18, 22(h), 22(h1), 25(a).
23. G.S. 153A-123(a).
24. G.S. 130A-39(b).
25. G.S. 130A-498(a).
26. *See* G.S. 130A-39(d)–(f).
27. G.S. 130A-39(d).
28. *Id.*
29. *Id.*
30. *Id.*
31. G.S. 130A-39(e).
32. G.S. 130A-39(f).

Chapter 20

Adjudications

What Is an Adjudication?

In certain circumstances, a person who is aggrieved by the enforcement of a local board of health (BOH) rule or imposition of administrative penalties by the local health director may appeal the enforcement action or penalty to the BOH (which, in the case of a county with a consolidated human services agency that includes public health, would be the consolidated human services board).[1] When the BOH hears evidence and makes a determination on whether the enforcement action or administrative penalty was appropriate, the BOH is conducting an "adjudication." A BOH adjudication may also be referred to as a *quasi-judicial* hearing because the BOH is acting somewhat ("quasi") like a court ("judicial") when it hears and decides the appeal.

The rules governing accreditation for local health departments (LHDs) require the BOH to "assure a fair and equitable adjudication process" by following the process set out in G.S. 130A-24(b)–(d).[2] The rules do not specify how the BOH must ensure such a process, but some boards have done so by adopting policies that reiterate a commitment to complying with the statutorily required process for adjudications.[3]

When May an Adjudication Be Sought?

Subject Matter Jurisdiction

A BOH's authority to conduct an adjudication is established in state statute.[4] Adjudications cannot be used to handle any and all public complaints—the law only authorizes a BOH to adjudicate appeals involving the enforcement of BOH rules (described in Chapter 19) or appeals concerning the imposition of administrative penalties by the local health director (this may be referred to as the BOH's area of *subject matter jurisdiction*).[5]

A BOH does not have subject matter jurisdiction to hear complaints regarding actions taken by local health department employees to enforce statewide rules promulgated by the North Carolina Commission for Public Health. Instead, those cases are heard by the North Carolina Office of Administrative Hearings.[6]

Aggrieved Persons

Only an "aggrieved person" may appeal enforcement of a BOH rule or imposition of an administrative penalty by the local health director to the BOH.[7] The term *aggrieved person* is not defined under North Carolina's public health laws. When considering the concept, the North Carolina Supreme Court has opined as follows:

> The expression "person aggrieved" has no technical meaning. What it means depends on the circumstances involved. It has been variously defined: "Adversely or injuriously affected; damnified, having a grievance, having suffered a loss or injury, or injured; also having cause for complaint. More specifically the word(s) may be employed meaning adversely affected in respect of legal rights, or suffering from an infringement or denial of legal rights."[8]

A person who qualifies as an aggrieved person and is therefore eligible to appeal an issue to the BOH for adjudication may be described as having *legal standing*. By contrast, a member of the public who hears about an enforcement action or administrative penalty and thinks it unfair—but who was not subject to or impacted by the action or penalty—would likely not have the legal standing necessary to appeal the enforcement action or administrative penalty to the BOH for adjudication.

Statute of Limitations

An aggrieved person has a limited window for appealing an enforcement action or administrative penalty by seeking a BOH adjudication. The statutory time limit for appealing a BOH adjudication is thirty days after the enforcement action at issue was taken or after the administrative penalty at issue was imposed.[9]

Exhaustion of Administrative Remedies

The BOH adjudication process includes a final step that allows a party to appeal a BOH decision to district court.[10] However, an aggrieved person seeking to appeal an enforcement action or administrative penalty cannot skip over the BOH adjudication process and go straight to district court. The North Carolina Supreme Court has ruled that "where the legislature has provided by statute an effective administrative remedy, that remedy is exclusive and its relief must be exhausted before recourse may be had to the courts."[11] This means that an aggrieved person seeking to appeal enforcement of a BOH rule or imposition of an administrative penalty by the local health director *must* exhaust their administrative remedies—that is, go through the full BOH adjudication process—before being permitted to bring the claim before a district court.

The Adjudication Process

The BOH adjudication process is set out in state law[12] and involves various deadlines and quick turnaround periods. A BOH should consult with legal counsel to ensure that the deadlines for the adjudication process are met and that all required components of the adjudication process are carried out correctly.

Written Notice of Appeal by the Aggrieved Person

To initiate an adjudication, the aggrieved person must provide written notice of the appeal to the local health director.[13] The written notice must be given to the local health director no later than thirty days after the enforcement action at issue was taken or after the administrative penalty at issue was imposed.[14] The written notice of appeal must include the following information: the name and address of the aggrieved person, a description of the challenged action (the enforcement action or administrative penalty at issue), and a statement of why the aggrieved person believes that the challenged action was improper.[15]

Transmission of the Notice of Appeal by the Local Health Director

Once the notice of appeal has been given to the local health director, the director has five working days (business days) to send the notice of appeal to the BOH. The director must also send the BOH any documents or other materials that informed the challenged action within the same five-day timeframe.[16]

Noticing the Adjudication Hearing

The BOH has fifteen days from when it receives the notice of appeal and any related documents or materials from the local health director to hold an adjudication hearing.[17] The BOH must also satisfy two notice requirements related to the hearing: (1) providing notice of the hearing to the aggrieved person and (2) noticing the hearing in accordance with North Carolina's open meetings law. The BOH must give the aggrieved person at least ten days' notice of the date, time, and place of the hearing.[18] The law does not require the BOH to give notice in writing, although written notice (as opposed to verbal notice given in person or over the phone) has the benefit of helping memorialize that the notice requirement was satisfied in a timely manner.

A BOH meets the statutory definition of a "public body" that is required to make its "official meetings" open to the public and to give advance notice of those meetings.[19] The adjudication hearing should therefore occur during a special or regular BOH meeting that is properly noticed in accordance with North Carolina's open meetings law. North Carolina's open meeting law is further discussed in Chapter 10.

During the Adjudication Hearing

During the hearing, the BOH may receive evidence, including oral testimony, from the aggrieved party and other experts or witnesses. The BOH should consult with legal counsel in advance of the hearing to discuss any best practices for the presentation of evidence during the hearing. Once the BOH has heard all evidence in the case, it may vote on whether to affirm, modify, or reverse the challenged action.

After the Adjudication Hearing

The board's decision to affirm, modify, or reverse the challenged action must be memorialized in a written decision that is based on the evidence presented at the hearing and issued by the BOH. The decision must include a brief statement of the reasons for the board's determination.[20] State law does not specify how quickly the BOH must issue its written decision. However, prompt action is recommended, as the board's decision is not final (and the aggrieved person's timeline for appealing to district court does not begin to run) until the written decision is issued.

Once the BOH has rendered its decision, the aggrieved person has a right to further appeal the matter to a district court with jurisdiction. The aggrieved person must file their appeal to district court within thirty days of the BOH decision. The district court's scope and standard of review for hearing the appeal is set forth in the North Carolina Administrative Procedure Act at G.S. 150B-51(c).[21]

Notes

1. Chapter 130A, Section 24(b) of the North Carolina General Statutes (hereinafter G.S.). Note that although this statute describes appeals "concerning the enforcement of rules adopted by the local board of health *and* concerning the imposition of administrative penalties by a local health director" (emphasis added), the North Carolina Court of Appeals has determined that the word "and" may be substituted for "or" in this provision. *See* Justice for Animals v. Robeson County, 164 N.C. App. 366 (2004) (quoted as saying: "Our review of the grammatical structure of the statutory provision [G.S. 130A-24(b)] reveals that the General Assembly must have intended to allow an appeal either to challenge the enforcement of rules or to challenge the imposition of administrative penalties. Plaintiffs' construction would render the portion relating to 'the enforcement of rules' meaningless since the imposition of administrative penalties will always involve the enforcement of rules").
2. Title 10A, Chapter 48B, Section .1302 of the North Carolina Administrative Code.
3. *See, e.g.*, Stokes Cnty. Health Dep't Meeting Minutes, July 15, 2019, at 11 (BOCC Adjudication Policy, 2015), https://cms9files.revize.com/stokescountync/administration/Minutes/2019/m071519_doh.pdf; Halifax Cnty. Bd. of Health Meeting Minutes, January 24, 2022, at 4, https://www.halifaxnc.com/DocumentCenter/View/2944/BOH-Minutes-Jan-24-2022-?bidId=.
4. G.S. 130A-24(b)–(d).
5. G.S. 130A-24(b). There are only two instances where a local health director may impose an administrative penalty: violation of public health smoking laws (state or local) or violation of local BOH (not Commission for Public Health) on-site wastewater rules. *See* G.S. 130A-22(h)–(h1).
6. G.S. 130A-24(a)–(a1).
7. G.S. 130A-24(b).
8. *In re* Assessment of Sales Tax, 259 N.C. 589, 595 (1963) (quoting 3 C.J.S. *Aggrieved* (n.d.)); *see also* Justice for Animals v. Robeson County, 164 N.C. App. 366 (2004), and N.C. Forestry Ass'n v. N.C. Dep't of Env't & Natural Res., 357 N.C. 640, 644 (2003).
9. G.S. 130A-24(b).
10. G.S. 130A-24(d).
11. Presnell v. Pell, 298 N.C. 715, 721 (1979).
12. G.S. 130A-24(b)–(d).
13. G.S. 130A-24(b).
14. *Id.*
15. *Id.*
16. *Id.*
17. G.S. 130A-24(c).
18. *Id.*
19. G.S. 143-318.9. *See* G.S. 143-318.10(b) for the definition of *public body* and G.S. 318.10(d) for the definition of *official meeting.*
20. G.S. 130A-24(c).
21. G.S. 130A-24(d).

Appendixes

Appendix A

Comparisons of Local Social Services Boards

Table A.1. Types of Local Governing Boards for Social Services

Board	Organization	Board Members Selected by[a]	Director Appointed by
County board of social services	County DSS	Appointment (3 or 5)	Board
BOCC as board of social services	County DSS	Election	BOCC
CHS board	CHSA	Appointment (up to 25)	County manager, with the advice and consent of the CHS board
BOCC as CHS board[b]	CHSA	Election	County manager, with the advice and consent of the BOCC
Regional board of social services	Regional DSS (multicounty)	Appointment (12–18)	Board

Note: BOCC = board of county commissioners; CHS = consolidated human services, CHSA = consolidated human services agency.

[a] Numbers in parentheses represent the number of members on each appointed board.

[b] An advisory committee for public health must be appointed if the CHSA includes public health. G.S. 153A-77(a). There is no corresponding requirement to appoint an advisory committee for social services, though the BOCC may choose to do so.

Table A.2. Selected Powers and Duties of Local Social Services Boards

	County Board of Social Services	CHS Board	Regional Board of Social Services
Appoint agency director	Yes	No, county manager appoints director with the advice and consent of the CHS board.	Yes
Help director to prepare and recommend the agency budget	Yes, along with director	Yes[a]	Yes, though BOCCs establish the amount or method for county funding of the department.[b]
Review certain confidential social services records	Yes	Yes	Yes
Consult with director about problems affecting the agency	Yes	Yes	Yes
Advise local officials	Yes	Yes, through the county manager.	Yes
Adopt local public health rules	No	Yes[c]	No
Adjudicate appeals related to local public rules or fines imposed by the local health director	No	Yes[c]	No
Impose fees for public health services	No	Yes[c] (subject to BOCC approval)	No
Develop dispute resolution procedures for contractors and clients	No	Yes	No
Enter into contracts for legal services without BOCC approval	No[d]	No[d]	Yes
Purchase liability insurance	No[e]	No[e]	Yes

Note: BOCC = board of county commissioners; CHS = consolidated human services.

[a] The CHS board plans and recommends the agency's budget (G.S. 153A-77(d)(7)) but is prohibited from transmitting or presenting the budget for local health programs (G.S. 130A-43(b)(2)) and does not approve the final budget.

[b] It is the BOCCs for each county in the region—not the regional board of social services—that must agree upon the amount or method in which each county will appropriate funds to the department for the administration of social services and public assistance programs, the county share of public assistance programs, and any recoupments following fiscal or program monitoring or audit findings (Title 10A, Chapter 67A, Section .0301 of the North Carolina Administrative Code).

[c] The CHS board has this authority only if the consolidated human services agency includes public health.

[d] If a BOCC has assumed the powers and duties of a social services board or CHS board, the BOCC has authority to contract with an attorney.

[e] If a BOCC has assumed the powers and duties of a social services board or CHS board, the BOCC has authority to purchase liability insurance.

Table A.3. Social Services Board Member Term Length and Term Limit

Board	Regular Term Length	Term Limit[a]	County Commissioner's Term on Board Contemporaneous with Term on BOCC?
County board of social services[b]	3 years	2 consecutive terms	No
CHS board[b]	4 years[c]	2 consecutive terms	Yes
Regional board of social services[b]	3 years[d]	3 consecutive terms	Yes
BOCC (assuming powers and duties of board of social services or CHS board)	Coincides with term as county commissioner	No limit	Yes

Note: BOCC = board of county commissioners; CHS = consolidated human services.

[a] The maximum number of consecutive terms that a board member may hold.

[b] Board members selected by appointment.

[c] When a CHS board is first formed, members may be appointed for less than a four-year term in order to establish a uniform staggered-term structure for the board. G.S. 153A-77(c).

[d] When a regional social services board is first formed, term lengths must be staggered: Two of the original members must serve one-year terms, another two original members must serve two-year terms, and the remainder of the original members serve regular three-year terms. G.S. 108A-15.8(d).

Table A.4. Appointment of Social Services Board Members

	Appointing Authority		
Board Type (No. of Members)	BOCC	SSC	Board Members Appointed by BOCC and SSC
County social services (3 or 5)	Appoints 1 member on a 3-member board or 2 members on a 5-member board	Appoints 1 member on a 3-member board or 2 members on a 5-member board	Appoint 1 member
CHS (up to 25)	Appoints all members from a slate of nominees presented by the CHS board[a]		
Regional social services (12–18)	BOCC of each county involved appoints 2 members[b]	Appoints 2 members	Appoint members to fill all remaining vacancies on the board

Note: BOCC = board of county commissioners; SSC = Social Services Commission; CHS = consolidated human services.

[a] When a CHS board is first formed, the BOCC must create a nominating committee composed of members of the current (preconsolidation) board of health and social services board, as well as the board responsible for managing mental health, developmental disabilities, and substance abuse services in the county. The nominating committee recommends members for the new CHS board and the BOCC must make appointments based upon those recommendations.

[b] If more than eight counties join the regional department, each BOCC appoints only one member.

Appendix B

Comparisons of Local Boards of Health

Table B.1. Types of Local Boards of Health

Board	Organization	Board Members Selected by[a]	Director Appointed by
County board of health	County health department	Appointment (11)	Board
BOCC as board of health[b]	County health department	Election	BOCC
CHS board	CHSA	Appointment (Up to 25)	County manager, with the advice and consent of the CHS board
BOCC as CHS board[b]	CHSA	Election	County manager, with the advice and consent of the BOCC
District board of health	District health department	Appointment (15–18)	Board
Public health authority board	Public health authority	Appointment (7–9 for a single county agency; 7–11 for a multi-county agency)[c]	Board[d]

Note: BOCC = board of county commissioners; CHS = consolidated human services, CHSA = consolidated human services agency.

a Numbers in parentheses represent the number of members on each appointed board.

b An advisory committee for public health must be appointed when the BOCC acts as the board of health (for a county health department or a CHSA including public health). G.S. 153A-77(a).

c A public health authority board that intends to pursue federally qualified health center (or look-alike) status may have no fewer than nine and no more than twenty-five members.

d In the case of a public health authority that serves multiple counties, the chair of the county board of commissioners of each county in the authority shall appoint one county commissioner, or the commissioner's express designee, to the authority board and these members shall jointly appoint the other members of the board.

Table B.2. Selected Powers and Duties of Local Boards of Health

Power or Duty	County Board of Health	District Board of Health	Public Health Authority Board	Consolidated Human Services Board
Adopt local public health rules	Yes	Yes	Yes	Yes
Create policy for the local health department	Yes	Yes	Yes	Yes
Adjudicate appeals related to local public health rules or fines imposed by the local health director	Yes	Yes	Yes	Yes
Appoint the local health director after consultation with the BOCC(s)	Yes	Yes	Yes	No
Set fees for certain services provided by the local health department, as permitted by law	Yes	Yes	Yes	Yes
Prepare and approve the local health department budget	No	No	Yes	No
Set salaries for local health department staff	No	Yes	Yes	No
Hire and fire local health department staff (other than the health director)	No	No	No	No
Sign contracts on behalf of the local health department	No	No	Yes	No
Hire its own legal counsel	No	Yes	Yes	No
Construct or otherwise acquire property on its own for use as public health facilities	No	No	Yes	No
Sell surplus buildings, land, and equipment on its own	No	No	Yes	No

Table B.3. Local Board of Health Member Term Length and Term Limit

Board	Regular Term Length	Term Limit[a]	County Commissioner's Term on Board Contemporaneous with Term on BOCC?
County board of health[b]	3 years[c]	3 consecutive terms	Yes
CHS board[b]	4 years[c]	2 consecutive terms	Yes
District board of health[b]	3 years[c]	3 consecutive terms	Yes
Public health authority board[b]	3 years[c]	No limit	Yes
BOCC (assuming powers and duties of a county board of health or CHS board)	Coincides with term as county commissioner	No limit	Yes

Note: BOCC = board of county commissioners; CHS = consolidated human services.

[a] The maximum number of consecutive terms that a board member may hold.

[b] Board members selected by appointment.

[c] Members may be appointed for less than a four-year term in order to establish a uniform staggered-term structure for the board. G.S. 130A-35(c), 153A-77(c), 130A- 37(c), 130A-45.1(d).

Appendix C

Selected Resources for Consolidated Human Services Board Members

For the most up-to-date resources that may be relevant to consolidated human services (CHS) boards, please visit the **North Carolina Human Services Hub** at humanservices.sog.unc.edu. Selected additional resources that may be useful to CHS boards are listed by topic below. All web addresses are current as of June 2025.

Consolidated Human Services Agencies

Kristi A. Nickodem, *Personnel Decisions for North Carolina's Consolidated Human Services Agencies,* Social Services Bulletin 49 (UNC School of Government, December 2021), https://www.sog.unc.edu/publications/bulletins/personnel-decisions-north-carolinas-consolidated-human-services-agencies.

Ethics

A. Fleming Bell, II, *Ethics, Conflicts, and Offices: A Guide for Local Officials,* 2nd ed. (UNC School of Government, 2010).

Kristina M. Wilson and Crista M. Cuccaro, "Ethics and Conflicts of Interest," in *County and Municipal Government in North Carolina,* 2024 ed., edited by Christopher B. McLaughlin (UNC School of Government, 2025).

Liability

Trey Allen, *Local Government Immunity to Lawsuits in North Carolina* (UNC School of Government, 2018).

Kristi A. Nickodem, "Civil Liability of the Local Government and Its Officials and Employees," in *County and Municipal Government in North Carolina,* 2024 ed., edited by Christopher B. McLaughlin (UNC School of Government, 2025).

Open Meetings

Trey Allen, *"Full and Accurate" Minutes: A Primer,* Local Government Law Bulletin No. 140 (UNC School of Government, January 2019), https://www.sog.unc.edu/publications/bulletins/full-and-accurate-minutes-primer.

Frayda S. Bluestein and David M. Lawrence, *Open Meetings and Local Governments in North Carolina: Some Questions and Answers,* 8th ed. (UNC School of Government, 2017).

Kristina M. Wilson, "Open Meetings and Other Legal Requirements for Local Government Boards," in *County and Municipal Government in North Carolina*, 2024 ed., edited by Christopher B. McLaughlin (UNC School of Government, 2025).

Public Records

Kristina M. Wilson, "Public Records," in *County and Municipal Government in North Carolina*, 2024 ed., edited by Christopher B. McLaughlin (UNC School of Government, 2025).

David M. Lawrence, *Public Records Law for North Carolina Local Governments,* 2nd ed. (UNC School of Government, 2009).

Records Retention

"Local Government Agencies," State Archives of North Carolina, North Carolina Department of Natural and Cultural Resources, https://archives.ncdcr.gov/government/local.

Rules of Procedure

Trey Allen and A. Fleming Bell, II, *Suggested Procedural Rules for Local Appointed Boards* (UNC School of Government, 2020).

Public Health

Association of North Carolina Boards of Health, https://www.ancbh.org/.

Jill D. Moore, *Local Boards of Health in North Carolina: Overview of Membership Requirements and Legal Authorities* (UNC School of Government, March 2018), https://www.sog.unc.edu/resources/microsites/north-carolina-public-health-law/boards-health-north-carolina.

——. *North Carolina Communicable Disease Law* (UNC School of Government, 2017).

Jill D. Moore and Kirsten E. Leloudis, "Public Health," in *County and Municipal Government,* 2024 ed., edited by Christopher B. McLaughlin (UNC School of Government, 2025).

Social Services

Kristi A. Nickodem, "Social Services," in *County and Municipal Government*, 2024 ed., edited by Christopher B. McLaughlin (UNC School of Government, 2025).

North Carolina Association of County Boards of Social Services, https://www.ncacbss.org.

Coates' Canons Selected Posts

Coates' Canons: NC Local Government Law (canons.sog.unc.edu) is a UNC School of Government blog featuring blog posts from School of Government faculty regarding legal issues affecting local governments and other public agencies in North Carolina. The list below is a small sampling of hundreds of posts that may be useful to CHS board members. Individuals can subscribe to the blog, search posts by keyword, and browse posts by blog topic categories.

Posts by Frayda Bluestein

"How to Approve Minutes and General Accounts of Closed Sessions," June 5, 2018, https://canons.sog.unc.edu/2018/06/how-to-approve-minutes-and-general-accounts-of-closed-sessions/.

"Retention Schedules for Local Governments: Five Things You Should Know," May 16, 2019, https://canons.sog.unc.edu/2019/05/retention-schedules-for-local-governments-five-things-you-should-know/.

"Setting Salaries and Closed Sessions," December 17, 2015, https://canons.sog.unc.edu/2015/12/setting-salaries-and-closed-sessions/.

"Quick-Reference Guide for Closed Sessions," March 13, 2014, https://canons.sog.unc.edu/2014/03/quick-reference-guide-for-closed-session-meetings/.

Post by Kirsten Leloudis

"S.L. 2024-34: Impacts for Local Health Directors," September 4, 2024, https://canons.sog.unc.edu/2024/09/s-l-2024-34-local-health-directors/.

Posts by Kristi Nickodem

"County Legal Authority to Fund Non-Mandated Social Services Programs," June 6, 2023, https://canons.sog.unc.edu/2023/06/county-legal-authority-to-fund-non-mandated-social-services-programs/.

"Health and Human Services Advisory Committees vs. Appointed Consolidated Human Services Boards—What's the Difference?," June 9, 2025, https://canons.sog.unc.edu/2025/06/health-and-human-services-advisory-committees-vs-appointed-consolidated-human-services-boards-whats-the-difference/.

"North Carolina's Changing Landscape of Public Health and Social Services Governance and Agency Structures: Where Are We Now?," March 4, 2022, https://canons.sog.unc.edu/2022/03/north-carolinas-changing-landscape-of-public-health-and-social-services-governance-and-agency-structures-where-are-we-now/.

"Who Is Required to Take an Oath of Office in the Human Services Field?," January 3, 2022, https://canons.sog.unc.edu/2022/01/who-is-required-to-take-an-oath-of-office-in-the-human-services-field/.

Posts by Aimee Wall

"Access to Confidential Client Records by Social Services Governing Boards," April 26, 2016, https://canons.sog.unc.edu/2016/04/access-confidential-records-social-services-governing-boards/.

"Boards of Social Services and Fraud Investigations," April 18, 2012, https://canons.sog.unc.edu/2012/04/boards-of-social-services-and-fraud-investigations/.

Posts by Kristina Wilson

"The Court of Appeals Addresses Emergency Meetings and Remote Quorum," August 13, 2024, https://canons.sog.unc.edu/2024/08/the-court-of-appeals-addresses-emergency-meetings-and-remote-quorum/.

"Closed Session Deep Dive: Privileged or Confidential Information," August 1, 2024, https://canons.sog.unc.edu/2024/08/closed-session-deep-dive-privileged-or-confidential-information/.

"Closed Session Deep Dive: Attorney-Client Privilege," May 7, 2024, https://canons.sog.unc.edu/2024/05/closed-session-deep-dive-attorney-client-privilege/.

"Closed Session Deep Dive: Personnel Matters," April 1, 2024, https://canons.sog.unc.edu/2024/04/closed-session-deep-dive-personnel-matters/.

"Remote Meetings Still Up in the Air: Part 1," May 27, 2025, https://canons.sog.unc.edu/2025/05/remote-meetings-still-up-in-the-air-part-1/.

"Remote Meetings Still Up in the Air: Part 2," June 4, 2025, https://canons.sog.unc.edu/2025/06/remote-meetings-still-up-in-the-air-part-2/.